Jasmuheen • In Resonance

»Every thing you think creates, through energy.
You have within you the most remarkable machines,
the entireness of consciousness.
You have the power that creates life,
and when that power is drawn up intentionally,
it will create reality.
All you have to do is give it the pattern you want.«

Ramtha

Jasmuheen

In Resonance

KOHA-Verlag

First published in May 1995 by the
SELF EMPOWERMENT ACADEMY
P.O. Box 737
Kenmore QLD 4069
Australia
Internet:http://www.selfempowermentacademy.com.au

KOHA-Verlag GmbH
Almstrasse 4
84424 Burgrain
Germany

e-mail: koha-verlag@t-online.de
Edited by Professor Dr. Guillaume De Meuter
Cover and book design by Karin Schnellbach

Printed by Wiener Verlag, Austria

Die Deutsche Bibliothek – CIP-Einheitsaufnahme

First Edition 1999

ISBN 3-929512-36-X

Contents

Page

Dedication

It is with much love and pleasure that I dedicate this book, firstly, to my delightful daughters, Anjie and Jesse, from whom I have learnt, and with whom I have shared, so much as we have travelled this path of life together.

Secondly, to the rest of my family who have always been loving and accepting of my often »off-beat« interests. To my beloved mother, Enid, who left her physical body in 1994, but is still with us in our hearts. To my wonderful father, Arent Ulrik, for his belief and encouragement that we could all be whatever we wished to be.

Thirdly, to my strong and beautiful friends for their warmth, nurturing support and complete unconditional love regardless of my preoccupations. So to Jeff, Michael, Tonia, Sam, Margaret and Tora (my sister and friend) – thank you. Special thanks to Michael for allowing me uninterrupted use of his computer for the first edition of this book and to Natalie for her patient editing service.

To Sananda, Arcturius, Kwan Yin, Paul the Venetian, Mother Mary, Kuthumi, St Germain – to all the Ascended Ones and beings of light for their love and inspiration and guidance – thank you. May this book, that you have all »overshadowed« – in one way or another – for the last eight years, open the hearts and minds of many. Since 1987 your wonderful energies have inspired me to keep detailed journals of my research and to write relevant paragraphs verbatim from things that simply interested me personally. Little did I know at the time that it would all be utilised some day. All this, plus direct telepathic communication of further information, has been drawn from you to form the Art of Resonance Education series which is the basis of this book.

I also dedicate this book to all who seek simplicity,
truth, purpose and joy in life.

Foreword

The book which followed »In Resonance« – apart from the »Inspirations« Trilogy of received teachings – was »Living on Light«. Thanks to my German publisher, KOHA Verlag, this fourth book has achieved what some would call a large degree of success by being well-received in various European countries. When I wrote »Living on Light«, I assumed that most people would have read »In Resonance«, and as a consequence, they would be well on the way to being self-tuned and self-responsible.

The book »Living on Light« was written for the warriors, those already tuned and well-connected to the voice of the Divine One within. The research on, and story of my personal experience with, living on light was offered to those whose joy-filled hearts clearly guided them that it was a valid step for them.

Maintaining the choice of being continually sustained by prana is only possible for those in various degrees of self-mastery and for those whose blueprint this is. Most of those who go through the process (see chapter 27) return to eating, but they do so for the pleasure, not for the nourishment, and so they are freer. Free from the limiting belief that if you don't eat you will die. While this belief may be true for an untuned instrument, it is not necessarily the case for someone on the journey of conscious self-mastery. Being able to live from light is a very small by-product of what I have now come to term – radiating the Supreme Splendour.

»In Resonance« is written as part of my personal service work which is to offer tools and well-researched information to inspire individuals to begin the process of self-tuning and self-responsibility. Having attained a degree of evident self-tuning, they may then be interested in looking at the validity of the pranic nourishment option.

As such, »In Resonance« introduces the reader to the basic idea that we are systems of energy and touches on what we, as systems of energy, may achieve. As Jesus said, »All I have done, you can do – and more.«

»In Resonance« focuses on bridging the worlds; the etheric and the physical, science and religion, East and West. Having bridged the worlds to create a personal working model of reality that honours all, and having accessed our personal blueprint from within the Divine Blueprint, we are then invited to demonstrate impeccable mastery.

As impeccable masters we are far more capable of being an effective global force to seriously and pragmatically create planetary transformation. This is supported by our work as M.A.P.S. Ambassadors in the social, educational, economic and political arenas where M.A.P.S. represents the »Movement of an Awakened Positive Society.« Each of us has her/his gift to bring to this planet, and every life lived has the potential to make a positive difference. Finding out what our gift to the planet is comes from self-refinement which, in turn, comes from the decision to be self-responsible. It is also part of the challenge or the joy, depending on our perspective, of our journey through life. Demonstrating this gift effectively is the art of being »In Resonance«.

So we offer the following information and quotations simply to inspire you to begin, or continue, your personal path of understanding. Life generously provides us with many wonderful experiences that allow us to continually alter our perception of reality. Many of the quotations that I have used throughout the book have given me personal inspiration or insights that helped form my own model. Regardless of whether we call the Divine, »God«, »Buddha«, »Allah« or »Supreme Intelligence«, we can all focus upon this creative force and invite it to express itself fully in each moment of our lives.

Brisbane, December 1998, Jasmuheen

Introduction

This book has been written from course notes utilised in the sharing of the Art of Resonance Series of workshops and seminars conducted by the Self Empowerment Academy (S.E.A). The underlying principles of S.E.A. are:

1. That we are all pure energy systems expressed in physical form. As energy systems, we are governed by the same laws that govern all energy and matter.

2. That we all have our own unique Divine Blueprint encoded on a cellular level. This blueprint holds not only the answers to our divine purpose and life destiny, but also to our part in the collective whole. Consequently, when we access this blueprint we feel completely in tune with the »bigger picture.« When – as preordained – we start to manifest true mastery of expression, our lives become abundant and purposeful on all levels.

S.E.A. has been founded to share practical self-help tools and techniques to allow you to access this blueprint, as well as to provide well-researched educational data and reference material to help awaken you to your higher purpose and self-mastery.

The motivation of S.E.A. is to help facilitate the dawning of the New Age, or Golden Age, by providing keys to be utilised for your individual self-discovery. All the great sages, avatars and masters say that salvation or enlightenment lies with the inner journey. This inner journey allows us to discover our uniqueness and is the common thread that binds us all.

Inspiration can be gained by working with others for a common goal. However, what is required to bring about the great changes that we seek within ourselves and upon this planet is to individually lift our level of vibration and resonance to the higher octaves of light. We will then be guided by the divine Source that sustains us and moves through our being. No one but us can bring about the changes required to create Heaven on Earth, and we can do so simply by changing our frequency.

- All lifeforms are systems of energy, transmitting signals and vibrations. Change your vibrations and you change your life. It is that simple.

This book is intended to reach all levels of society: to inspire you to begin your inner journey in search of peace and happiness; and to inspire those already consciously on the path to continue to explore all facets of this wondrous unfoldment of self-mastery. In all my years of research I have not found a handbook that begins with basic self-help tools and information and then progresses through to, what many feel, are more complex esoteric practices such as bi-location, telepathic communication etc. Hopefully this manual will fulfil these criteria.

Those wishing to find methods of de-stressing positively and naturally, or finding inner peace and relaxation, will find the first few chapters helpful. If intrigued, continue reading as the balance of the book leads into discussing what some may call miracles. These miracles, to me, are natural abilities revealed to us as we tune our frequencies and vibrate harmoniously within the higher octaves of light.

Numerous techniques and guided meditations are described throughout this book. They are to be utilised as required. It is recommended that you record the meditations that interest you onto a tape – adding, deleting or elaborating according to your inner guidance so as to gain maximum benefit for your own growth. You will find that your inner being also responds more powerfully to the sound of your own voice. Alternatively, S.E.A. has most of these meditations on tape for those interested. They have been professionally recorded. Please contact the Academy for further details.

Some of the information will be repeated for two reasons – the first being emphasis, as we learn through repetition, and the second being that all the information is interrelated and cannot be easily segregated and compartmentalised.

You may find as you read this book that statements are made that you may question. Hopefully, everything will be explained in satisfactory detail as the book progresses, or you can research what interests you from the reference material listed in the back. Concepts like reincarnation, telepathic communication, and being sustained by only light – due to my research background, understanding of universal law and experience – have become factual and commonplace, yet I realise that these things may seem far-fetched for some people. One of the greatest lessons we can learn at this time is discernment (see chapter 6), along with how we form our reality (see chapter 8). All I ask of readers and students alike is to keep an open mind.

There are basically three ways of learning. The first is where we attend classes and/or lectures with teachers who, we know or assume, have had particular training in their field. They then impart their knowledge to us, as in a university or school curriculum. We accept it as correct due to their qualifications, training or proven track record and credibility. If in doubt, we can access their reference sources or do our own research.

The second type of learning is where various hypotheses are rigorously tested under specific conditions allowing for minimal error, as in the world of science, and either accepted or discarded. This is the »I'll believe it when I see it« method. It is very »left brain«.

The third method is that of intuitive knowing that is accessed via meditation and contemplation where much that occurs cannot be »proved.« This is learnt by activating our sixth sense of *intuition* and our seventh sense of *knowing*. It is also learnt by consciously using the »right brain«: by following our »own star« and by listening to the Inner Teacher. What S.E.A. has to share falls into this category.

S.E.A.'s work is to bridge the world of religion and science, and also the worlds of the physical and the etheric. S.E.A. works with the universal life force energy which is the basis of all science and religion. Research of both Eastern and Western religions and philosophies will show common denominators and beliefs that simply carry different labels. As Jesus said, »Seek first the kingdom of Heaven within and all else will be revealed to you«.

Chapter 1

The Art of Resonance

Resonance is defined in the Oxford Dictionary as, »Responding to vibrations of a particular frequency especially by itself strongly vibrating«. When related to metaphysics it is associated with the universal Law of Resonance. This law basically states that like attracts like.

Our bodies are energy systems, and we all oscillate at our own unique vibrational frequency that reflects the sum total of everything that we have experienced through eons of time. We have what is termed a four-body system of »lower« bodies – termed »lower« due to their vibrational frequency or resonance – and we also have higher bodies or energy fields which resonate at a higher or finer frequency. Their resonance can be compared to the musical notes played on a piano or string instrument. It can be on key or off key.

Toxicity from negative thoughts, unresolved negative emotions, pollutants, dross, poor diets etc. affects the energy fields of the body. These, in turn, influence our vibrational frequency and determine whether we are »on key« or »off key«. Past life experiences and current life experiences are all held in cellular memory and are also reflected in our vibrational frequency. Dr. Deepak Chopra states in his book »Quantum Healing« that a cell is a memory that has built matter around itself, forming a specific pattern, and that the body is the place that the memory calls home.

Many individuals are now being motivated by a strong inner desire to really experience joy, balance, harmony and unconditional love in life. These experiences are automatically ours when we realign our physical, emotional, mental and spiritual bodies to higher, more refined frequencies. Realigning our frequency is like tuning a string on an instrument to its perfect pitch. The finer the frequencies we emit, the finer the life experiences we attract via the universal Law of Resonance.

For example, the physical body may resonate perfectly to the musical note of »C«, the energy field of the emotional body to »D«, the energy field of the mental body to »E«, and the spiritual body to »F«. When these energy fields are perfectly tuned to their »notes«, they play together harmoniously and life becomes magical. When they are out of tune the music is discordant, off key, and our life does not flow or feel harmonious.

Standards and expectations vary from individual to individual. Just as the precise tuning of an instrument is critical to a professional musician, a layman with an untrained ear cannot recognise the fine nuances and is, accordingly, less demanding. There are, then, personal frames of reference and we all set our own standards of acceptability. However, anyone who feels in the slightest that their life may be better, will benefit by realigning and tuning their energy fields to a finer resonance and finding the perfect pitch for them.

In their desire to improve the quality and/or length of their life, many individuals today are following inner guidance to cleanse themselves – not just on a physical level, but also on an emotional and mental level. They are eating less, preferably light food. Emotionally, they are also »processing« and letting go of emotional baggage – emotions of fear, hate, guilt, worry, anxiety, anger etc. – which, when unresolved, are stored in the various organs of the physical body. This storage of negative emotion creates blockages in our energy fields and eventually disease. On a mental level, they are recognising the limitations imposed in our lives by negative thinking and how energy follows thought to create our reality.

Thoughts, words and actions are energy forms and whatever we send out comes back to us according to karmic law and the the Law of Resonance. This is the nature of energy: anything that life presents to us is there because we have attracted it to us by our vibrational frequency.

Positive thoughts, words and actions coupled with the intention to always act for the highest good of all beings plus the highest good of ourselves, will change our resonance and consequently our experience of life.

How we can consciously go about realigning our vibrational frequency to be more in tune with the divine light beings that we are in essence, is covered in greater detail throughout the following chapters. Briefly, one of the most powerful ways to tune our energy fields to their »perfect« resonance is through meditation and spending daily time in the Great Silence within us. Apart from facilitating an effective energy realignment, meditation allows us to open to inner guidance – to learn to listen to the whispers of our Divine Self until the whispers become a strong clear voice. When acted upon, this guidance allows us to experience the joy and love and harmony that we seek in all aspects of our lives. Meditation aligns our spiritual, mental and emotional energy fields. This realignment is reflected in, and alters, our physical energy field or body.

Diet, eating lightly, drinking fresh pure water and engaging in gentle, stress-free exercise allows us to realign, rebuild and alter the energy field of the physical body daily and promote health, vitality and longevity; but none has the power of meditation when we maximise the intake of prana through specific breathing and allow the white light energy to heal and transform us.

We live in such a wondrous time – the dawning of a new age – and we have the capacity to create the reality that we desire simply by altering the energy signals we emit and by understanding the laws that govern all matter.

Chapter 2

The Uniqueness of Being

For eons of time, our beloved Planet Earth has experienced great suffering, chaos, war and devastation for the simple reason that many of the beings who live upon her have forgotten who they are in essence, beyond the mask of their personality and ego. This forgetfulness has meant that many have also ceased to honour, understand and accept individual uniqueness.

Our uniqueness comes simply because there are no two beings who have experienced exactly the same genetic encoding and environmental influences *plus* past life experiences. All three make up the sum total of who we are today. The third factor is important as it explains why identical twins, for example, who share the same genetic encoding and environmental influences may still react completely differently to given situations. The missing factor is that they have not been twins for all their lifetimes and so they each hold unique cellular memories.

Individually and collectively, humanity desires a change upon this planet at this current time. The desire of many is that we discover true unity, brotherhood and sisterhood. This desire is for a new world where we live in peace with respect for all races, creeds and cultures. Where we understand and connect with a higher will and a greater plan. This is the underlying motivating factor for many who are beginning, or continuing, their inner journey.

Many are no longer interested in being subjected to fear or limitations and ignorance, (the results of which abound around us on the physical plane) and have recognised that in order to change the planet, we have to clean up our own backyard. The masses are made up of individuals and to change the consciousness of the masses – the consciousness of the individual must alter. As we alter our consciousness and awareness, we will understand who we are, why we are here, and what part we are destined to play in creating this new age.

It is our planet and we alone will create the changes we seek by going within and tapping into our own *unique* Divine Blueprint. This blueprint not only holds the answers to our individual questions, but it also holds the higher plan that mankind is destined to evolve into *plus* our part in this joint venture. When we tap into this inner blueprint, we will understand that we all have unique roles to play and we will be able to relate to each other with unconditional love and acceptance of each others choices.

Life upon this planet can be likened to a huge theatrical production that keeps the audience and participants mesmerised by its complexity. Not only does the script cover a depth of experiences from the humorous and light to the suspenseful and dramatic, but the production itself is quite amazing. Some time ago while I was in deep meditation, there unravelled a vision related to the above, or the »play of life« – and I »saw« exactly that. There were actors, support crew, critics and even an audience. They were, however, out of sync. The actors were interfering with the duties of the sound crew, the musicians meddling with the work of the lighting crew, and so on. The participants were simply not concentrating on their own roles. As the vision continued, so did the inner commentary from Lord Sananda who said that while all was unfolding perfectly, if we wish to enhance this collective play of life, we can – *as humanity is intuitively driven by an inner knowing of the potential perfection of all that can be made manifest on all planes.*

Firstly, he said, we may wish to focus on finding our role in this play of life. We would find this to be easier if we stopped focusing on what everyone else was doing. We could then redirect our energy and attention to open up to our inner guidance and develop our discernment. This would allow us to *enjoy the training* and recognise our role. *Joy is Spirit expressing itself in life*, so the level of joy we feel is always a good indicator of when we are in alignment with Spirit and our destined path.

Secondly, having recognised our predetermined role and that we are part of a whole, it would be of benefit to »learn our lines« and allow our natural talents, and/or studied abilities to manifest and evolve to perfection.

Thirdly, we should understand that we have been attending the school of life for eons of time, and have been trained, developed skills, and acquired a vast repertoire of knowledge (often held in cellular memory) that we can utilise to play our role effectively. This should be done in harmony and alignment with all other players in the knowledge that these players have also undergone their own training for their part in this play. So the third suggestion is that we *trust* that and *honour the choices of others,* as they, too, have been trained to play their role in harmony with ours.

Sananda shared that only then will this »play of life« flow harmoniously – tuned to divine expression and be given »rave reviews«. Only then will the Golden Age be anchored and abundance on all levels of life be a reality for humanity *collectively.*

When we do the above, our personal reality and state of awareness is altered accordingly, especially as the vibrational frequency of the planet, and its inhabitants, is tuned to the higher octaves of light and the light quotient within our beings is increased.

This is a state of awareness where the energy field of the heart is fully open, where we can recognise the uniqueness of all and connect with the master in all, where the play becomes magical. It is a state of awareness where a being lets go of the »I«, moving beyond separateness and limitation, seeking only to serve the greater plan for the good of the whole, not just the individual. This discussion is pursued in the chapter on destiny and service.

As we understand the laws of energy and how we create our reality by our thoughts (see chapters 8 and 9), we know that, while we may not always be able to change the immediate circumstances, *we can always change our attitude and consequently our experience of life.*

Lessons for a harmonious life:
- Discernment – knowing the next step for us.
- Acceptance of individual uniqueness – learning to dance our dance without treading on each other's toes. You may choose to dance a waltz, another the samba.
- Uniqueness of being – find the dance you wish to dance. Learn the steps. Share the floor space!

Chapter 3

The Body as an Energy System

Energy – according to the Oxford Dictionary, is the »ability of matter or radiation to do work«. According to Stephen Hawking in »A Brief History of Time«, the term »conservation of energy« is the law of science that states that energy (or its equivalent in mass) can neither be created or destroyed – but it can and does, change form.

Dr. Deepak Chopra in his book »Ageless Body, Timeless Mind«, states that every atom is more than 99.9% empty space and the subatomic particles moving at great speed through this space are bundles of vibrating energy which carry information and unique codings.

In order to build life from lifeless matter, energy and information have to be exchanged through the RNA and DNA to create cellular structure. The flow of this intelligence is what sustains us and is what Dr. Chopra calls the universal field. He states that the physical world is just a mirror of deeper intelligence organising matter and energy, and it also resides in us. We are part of all; so we need to take care of all lovingly. Even though we are unique in our individuality, we are bound together by a common thread of pure energy that sustains each cell, our being, and all life as a whole.

Religions call this energy God and consider it to be omnipresent, omnipotent and omniscient. Quantum physics calls this energy the »grand unification energy« and also considers it to be everywhere, all powerful and all knowing. »New Agers« call this energy by other labels – the All That Is, Divine Intelligence etc. They are all just labels describing the same force or power.

Our body's composition is of atoms and cells which hold this energy and information. Thoughts, words and actions are also energy. Energy expands, contracts and changes form, so that what we send out comes back to us. This is covered in more detail in future chapters. In religious terms it is, »As you sow, so shall you reap«. In energy terms all is governed by the universal Law of Resonance and the Law of Attraction, where like attracts like.

As mentioned in chapter 1, human beings have four »lower« bodies of energy which resonate at different frequencies.
1. The physical (the only one visible or appearing solid to our physical eyes),
2. the emotional,
3. the mental and
4. the spiritual.

We also have higher energy bodies – termed higher because they resonate at higher frequency pitches. Barbara Ann Brennan's book »Hands Of Light« covers these bodies and energy fields in great detail and is recommended reading for those interested.

When we bring these bodies of energy into perfect alignment with each other, we achieve higher »knowing« and experience a more fulfilling purpose to our existence as everything just *clicks into place*. This state of enlightenment, so keenly sought by Eastern esoteric students, is achieved by fine-tuning the four lower bodies, not only in perfect resonance with each other, but to a pitch that allows the higher energy bodies of the I AM Presence, inner God or Christ consciousness (all labels describing our more refined Self) to fully express its power and magic within the physical body.

So in summary: We are energy systems, we transmit and emit signals. If we send random signals, we get random or haphazard life experiences. If we control our signals, we can then gain a large measure of control over our life. Taken one step further, if we tune our bodies and realign our frequencies (the energy signals we transmit) to a purer, more harmonious pitch, we can then control the quality and quantity of our life and life experiences.

On reincarnation: Having established scientifically that energy cannot be created or destroyed but can change form, and having understood that human beings are systems of energy, I would like to make the logical statement that reincarnation simply allows for the indestructibility of energy, and while matter such as our physical bodies can decay and die, the energy within – that sustains the body – simply changes form and moves on. Anyone interested in exploring the concept of reincarnation may care to research the Edgar Cayce material, known to be the most widely documented of all case studies on this topic.

There is a universal law called the Law of Evolution and Rebirth that states that humankind goes »through a slow process of development carried on with unwavering persistence through repeated embodiment in forms, of increasing efficiency, whereby all are in time, brought to a height of spiritual splendour in recognition of Source and true identity. This law is also known as the Law of Periodicity« – quote from »Vision of Ramala«.

From my detailed research and personal experience, reincarnation is a basic occurrence within linear time and will be referred to sporadically throughout the rest of the book. A simple understanding is as follows ... life in embodiment is a school, a process of growth and learning. When we »die«, we drop the energy field of the physical body but for a while retain the energy fields of the emotional, mental and spiritual bodies. These are integrated into one conscious energy field and we are then literally on holiday.

Holiday is a time of reflection, where we look at the past school term, see what we learnt, how well we have or have not passed our tests. Tests not passed must be re-sat next term, and so we then plan for the next school term and select the »curriculum« and subjects we wish to study.

This learning and testing is to do with our growth as beings and lessons generally and deals with intangible things like empathy, love, compassion, service etc. School time is also a period of learning about relationships and life in a dense, material plane generally. Why sparks of the Divine (us) have chosen to be in the school of life on Planet Earth is another story.*

When we have learnt all there is for us to learn at this school and have passed all our exams, we move on to another learning institution, thus breaking the cycle of reincarnation on this plane of Earth.

Our energy fields continue to change form, just as energy itself does, according to the universal Law of Change and Transmutation which states that the only constant thing is the changing form of, and the indestructible nature of, energy. This has been referred to as the immortality of the »soul«. Physical immortality is also possible and allows us to continue in the same physical form to not only complete this learning, but stay and improve the curriculum, if we desire. This is covered in the chapter on immortality.

* Covered in Jasmuheen´s book »Our Camelot - the Game of Divine Alchemy«

Chapter 4

Visualisation

The physical world around us is solid and real to us because we have spent our lives developing our senses to experience it as such. Imagine if you had spent the last 20 to 60 years, or the term of your life, experiencing the »inner realms« every day with those same senses and with the same consistency that you have applied them to the physical world? How real would those inner realms be to you then?

Just as we have explorers and researchers in the outer world, we also now have many people who have begun to explore the inner realms in search of the elusive key to happiness, love and abundance.

Throughout history, some individuals have been motivated by higher mind, to seek answers to the riddle of human existence. But now many more are seriously beginning the inner journey commonly reserved for mystics, sages, avatars and the mystery schools of days gone by.

Since the dawn of history, humanity has been in search of higher wisdom and knowledge. The problems plaguing modern society can be said to be a direct result of a lack of higher wisdom and of feeling separate from the Creative Force. When we begin to experience and understand higher knowing by going within and merging our awareness with the energy that sustains us, lack of purpose and unhappiness are replaced by joy from self-discovery and by feelings of fulfilment.

By learning how to open up to – and by listening to – inner guidance, we find ourselves on the right path, fulfilling our destiny. Unhappiness, disease and stress are indicators that something is wrong with our lives. These indicators are not there by accident; they serve to advise us that our current actions and/or the path we are on is not the right one for us, and they prompt us to correct our attitudes and conduct.

Creative visualisation allows us to explore the inner realms by activating our higher mind and working with Divine Intelligence to create a reality in another dimension. When experienced regularly, this »reality« then filters through and changes our day to day reality on this plane. In her book, »Ye Are Gods«, Annalee Skarin writes, »The imagination is a God-given gift. It is the power of the mind to »image in« to the spiritual realm the seeds of desire« (using the power of visualisation). All our waking reality is created by thought. Everything which exists on the physical plane is the product of thought and the will of man and the thought and will of the Creative Power.

Modern research has shown that the body cannot tell the difference between a strong visualisation experience and an actual event, and treats the two as if they were the same. This idea opens up a whole realm which was previously unexplored and allows us to understand that the body truly is the servant of the mind. The physical and emotional bodies serves the mental body which, in turn, uses the the spiritual body as a conduit for all bodies to connect into the higher heaven world. Higher mind is our Higher Self (soul) and connects us to Divine Intelligence. Divine Intelligence manifests fully in our I AM Presence.

The knowledge of the power of creative visualisation allows us to understand how we can »program« away – or create – disease and illness. There is nothing we cannot achieve without the right »mind set« but first we must have clarity and vision to create a new reality. Vision comes through meditation, contemplation and opening up to higher mind using visualisation techniques.

Grace Cooke, in »The Jewel in the Lotus«, states that the real meaning of spiritual imagination is the creation in the higher mind of a language which expresses pure beauty, pure goodness and pure love. She goes on to say that man can express his soul in worlds remote from this with his imagination and vision. She says that people's fear of the unknown, or of being deceived, causes them to create a barrier between themselves and the real world of Spirit and that real imagination is the doorway into the etheric world and higher realms.

Esoteric studies show that the four-fifths of the brain man is known not to use – the cerebrum – houses our higher mind and is the database for higher consciousness. The more we tune to, and use, the higher mind through techniques such as visualisation, the easier it becomes to create the reality we desire and access our Divine Blueprint. Details and techniques to activate the cerebrum and other brain centres are covered in the chapter on telepathic communication.

The difference between higher mind and lower mind is that while lower mind is concerned with everyday issues of survival on this physical plane, higher mind prompts us to evolve further and ask questions like, »Is there a greater purpose to life?«, »Is there a life after death?«, »Is there a higher power, a grander scheme?« – and many more!

By using the ritual of visualisation and the white light energy, we bring into operation a superconscious mind and, when used in meditation, this mind creates a real world which is inspirational or tranquil, depending on the images accessed. If practised regularly, this experience then spills into our everyday waking reality.

Many people ask how to tell the difference between true imagination and mere fantasy. »True imagination comes as a result of the reaction on the brain of higher vibrations which have been set in motion by your sincere aspiration and prayer. You can think all kinds of unworthy and foolish thoughts with your lower mind but when you have touched that power and golden light ... you are suffused with that God power, and that affects not only your higher mind but your brain, so that you are able to create, by the power of God, the form described to you (in guided meditation and visualisation) to help you break through into the world of Spirit« – Grace Cooke in »The Jewel in the Lotus.« (This text is wonderfully informative for those beginning meditation and creative visualisation).

For over 19 years, I avoided using techniques of creative visualisation. During my practice of meditation I had become addicted to the feelings of joy and love that I experienced through breath and light work. These tuned me to what I knew as »Holy Name«, the energy that drives the breath, and the light which I activated through the physical technique of turning the physical eyes inward and upward to focus on the brow chakra. I knew through experience that this form of meditation in some subtle, yet powerful, way changed me as I became calmer, more centred and focussed, and more able to act, rather than react, to the stimulus of life's experiences.

Then experiences I enjoyed led me to consciously begin working with the brotherhoods of light. (Discussed in the chapter 32 on the universal brotherhoods). Suddenly, I understood the purpose of my previous training, and I developed the committed desire to become the clearest channel that I could be for Divine Intelligence. Utilising creative visualisation allowed me to consciously activate higher mind, cleanse and realign my energy fields in a profound and consistent manner, and speed up the apprenticeship of mastery of self.

Specific visualisation techniques are described in this book to increase the light quotient in our bodies, to release negative programming and emotional baggage that no longer serves us, and much more.

At the end of chapter 7 is creative visualisation exercise 1. This combines visualisation with white light energy and breath work and is a great technique to de-stress and connect with the inner calm.

Creative visualisation allows us to fully activate our inner senses. We all have these senses activated to varying degrees. Some of us are naturally clairvoyant in that it is easy for us to »see« in guided meditation using visualisation techniques. Some don't seem to see anything but have a strong sense of feeling or clairsentience. Some seem to be naturally clairaudient and hear easily when in these inner realms.

The challenge is to develop all the senses so that, when we use creative visualisation techniques and go within, our senses of sight, taste, smell, touch and hearing are fully alive and our experiences of these things can be sustained at will.

Exercises to develop these senses via creative visualisation are at the end of chapter 13, called »Creating the Inner Sanctuary«. Throughout the next chapters are approximately 17 guided meditation exercises that use visualisation techniques, and there are many other profound visualisation exercises and guided meditation tapes now available.

It has been suggested that initially we should use tapes for only 40% of the time when meditating. When we have become proficient at visualisation this should substantially be reduced as our being has its own focus, agenda and vision to tap into to lead us on our inner journey. Always taking external instruction can inhibit the Inner Teacher.

Visualisation is like an artist being given a blank canvas. Our imagination – the paint brush and paints – is just a tool, a means to an end. What we focus on grows. Imagination and visualisation are seeds we sow today to create the reality of tomorrow.

Chapter 5

White Light Energy

White light is the visual aspect of the energy that sustains the human body and flows through the universe. This energy can also be experienced by all our physical senses when we turn these senses inward in meditation. So not only can we »see« this energy as white light, we can also hear it as inner harmonies.

We can touch or feel the light rays and sound waves of this energy as it brings with it an experience of love or well-being. We can also taste this energy as the pineal gland secretes a nectar, or fluid, referred to by the ancient yogis as the fountain of youth, or *amrita*.

The white light energy is the visual aspect of our divine essence and is the most healing and transformational energy in the universe. So if we seek transformation and healing, we should invoke this light in meditation and use specific breathing techniques and visualisation.

Yogananda in »Autobiography of a Yogi« states that when we focus calmly on the brow chakra – our seat of »inner vision« – and then shift our attention to a particular spot between the medulla oblongata and the hypothalamus, the energy current from the two eyes goes first to the point in the forehead and then to the medulla and the pure white light energy then appears in the third eye, or brow chakra, reflected there by the medulla.

Shortly after I was 17, I learnt a specific technique from my guru to experience this inner light, and I had my first powerful experience. I was lying on the back seat of my parents« car, practising the technique I had been taught under a blanket to shield out the outer light. A few minutes after holding my concentration on this brow centre, my whole head exploded with pure white light inside. My eyes were closed and outside light was screened off by the blanket. I was overwhelmed by the intensity of this light. It was like staring at a 1000 watt light bulb at close range then clos-

31

ing your eyes with the image firmly planted in your mind. Except that this light came from within and also brought with it a feeling of overwhelming unconditional love that flooded through my entire being, allowing me to feel completely connected to everything!

I felt an expanded state of awareness, as though I was vast and limitless and *very loved*. It was an introduction to the inner realms that allowed me to drastically move beyond feeling I was my body or personality and to really experience my divinity. Excited at this revelation, I jumped up joyously exclaiming, »I can see light! I can see light!«. My wonderful parents quietly said, »That's nice dear,« shared a look of concern and kept driving.

This was the beginning of many such awe-inspiring experiences that have continued consistently since the early 1970s, allowing me to understand my own uniqueness, enjoy my own divinity and recognise the same in others. So there are techniques we can utilise to experience this white light – motivated by our sincere intention to seek to experience the limitless nature of our being.

Practical techniques will be covered in conjunction with breathing techniques in the chapter called, »The Breath Of Life«. Through my personal experience and inner guidance, I have found that it is easier to achieve this when we have *tuned our frequency* via breath work. Also, the combination of experience of the vibration that sustains us *plus* its visual aspect as light is most powerful, as the two together trigger feelings of unconditional love and joy within us that can be likened to being *wrapped in the arms of the Divine!*

Working with vibration and white light energy is the basis for all healing and transformational work and, coupled with creative visualisation, allows us to powerfully tap into – and then create according to – our divine, limitless nature.

In the book »Mahatma I and II« (based on the teachings of Janet McClure) , Brian Grattan writes, »All is energy. All is God. The essence of God is love.« He goes on to state that the purest form of energy in all the universes is the Mahatma energy, which is golden white light, and that the Mahatma energy embodies consciousness through all the dimensions back to the Source. He calls this energy the energy of the future which will »bring forth the higher qualities and values of life as well as the spiritual good of mankind.«

Grattan states that the Mahatma energy aligns us to a finer, more spiritual life where the highest ideals of humanity can be realised. He goes on to say that the use of this energy will free mankind from the confines of the third dimension and allow the spiritualisation of matter to occur on this plane of existence.

Chapter 6

Self-Mastery and Discernment

Since we all have this Divine Blueprint encoded within us, (which has all the answers to all our questions – plus our life purpose), many of us reach a point in our life where we *consciously* begin our inner journey of self-discovery. This discovery is prompted by the superconscious mind or Higher Self which guides us to acknowledge, tap into and work with this blueprint. It is often only after lifetimes or years of seeking true fulfilment from external realms, and not finding the keys to complete abundance sought by the soul, that we consciously begin to look within.

In meditation and spending time in the Great Silence within, we learn to listen to our inner guidance which develops a most important aspect that we all require at this time, which is *discernment*. Discernment allows us to use our discrimination to evaluate the mass of information now available through books, articles, channelling etc. It allows us to only absorb into ourselves that which is »right«* for us.

In order to know what is right for us, we need to know ourselves. We have to decide if we wish to be preoccupied with the »self« which identifies with the lower mind and focuses on survival issues, or if we would like to be clearly instructed by higher mind, which has the greater picture, so that we can discover the purpose of our existence on this planet.

As we are all unique, we must choose from the vast array of self-help techniques and information now being made available. There is a smorgasbord of healing modalities available that we can

---

* To me there is no »right« or »wrong« for all is here to teach us, to inspire us so that we may continue our path of unfoldment. Events are neutral in nature. It is we who assign a value judgement - of good or bad, right or wrong - to the event according to our perception. More on this in future chapters.

choose from to heal ourselves e.g. not everyone responds to homeopathy in the same way, not everyone chooses to put their health care solely in the hands of our orthodox medical practitioners, not everyone seeks alternative healing methods. However, we can learn to experiment, to develop our discernment, and use what we feel works for us.

Discernment, going within, and being aware of what is right for us, will allow our journey of self-discovery to flow more easily, with less distraction. This discernment comes naturally to us as we tune more to the inner realms and our own higher guidance.

The more we go within, the easier it becomes to discern between guidance of the higher mind and the desires and guidance of the lower mind. We can always recognise correct guidance by the *results* that this guidance, when followed, brings.

When we have tapped into our blueprint, discovered our role and learnt our lines, we are too busy BEing the best we can be to even think of the path or choice of another. We are also guided by a knowing that all is unfolding quite perfectly and we can just love and honour each other's choices.

Many individuals make the statement that they don't »relate« to certain people, nor to their ideas, attitudes or even to their energy, and consequently they adopt one of the following attitudes. They may feel that if they don't »relate« to someone or some group, then the person, or people, concerned must be wrong. They know that they are sincere or »right« so therefore the other(s) must be »missing the point, off track or just plain wrong«.

A second possibility is that they may adopt the attitude that as they don't resonate with the energy of the person, group or idea etc. then they should separate themselves from it, go their own way and relate to only those they »tune to«. Or they may decide to form their own groups with people with whom they resonate more harmoniously. This attitude gives rise to the »live and let live« principle of acceptance.

The third attitude they may choose to adopt is the recognition, and acceptance, of differences, taken one step further. This involves the desire for unity, unconditional love and acceptance of each other's choices. It involves playing our unique roles in complete harmony, without judgement. Here they fully understand that all are learning, unfolding and progressing perfectly in accordance with a greater plan.

Chapter 7

The Breath of Life

It has been said that if we were to change nothing – not our eating, exercise or thinking patterns and habits – except our breathing pattern, we could radically alter our life span. Leonard Orr, the author of »Physical Immortality« and founder of rebirthing, states that if we reduce the number of breaths that we breathe per minute from say 15 to five, we will triple our lifespan.

When this is suggested to some they say, »I couldn't imagine living to 200 or so.« My reply is that they may imagine doing so if they found joy and purpose in life. (More on immortality and physical death later.) Suffice it to say that when we find our life purpose and destiny, we usually do not want to drop the physical body due to ignorance and disease, and then have to prepare a new vehicle to continue in. To begin again in a new body, to have to go through nappies, school, puberty and adolescence and to reawaken cellular memory is, to me, poor time management. We have been created with the most perfect life-sustaining, self-healing vehicle to carry consciousness. It is capable of sustaining us until *we are ready* to drop it or take it up into light.)

An old story in meditation circles to explain what sustains us, goes as follows: If a person were to die, even in hospital where life-saving equipment is available, and oxygen was pumped into his lungs, his »spark of life« would not necessarily return. It is not oxygen that keeps us alive. Oxygen is like petrol to a car and helps keep the vehicle running. That »spark« that sustains us is our divine essence. When that energy leaves the physical body, all symptoms of physical life disappear.

It is said that joy is that »spark« expressing itself in life (which is why the level of joy felt in life is a good indicator that we are in tune with Spirit and higher purpose). As this spark is a form of energy that permeates our being, it can be experienced by turning our awareness within. This energy can be measured as sound waves and light rays and can also be felt as a vibration.

Leonard Orr says: »Connecting the inhale to the exhale in a relaxed rhythm brings about an awareness of a direct mental perception of spirit, an emotional feeling of spirit and a physical sensation of the actual life energy, which is almighty God flowing throughout the flesh ... when the inhale is connected to the exhale, and the inner breath is merged with the outer breath, this merging of pure life energy with air sends vibrations through the nervous system and circulatory system cleaning the body, the human aura and nourishing and balancing the human mind and body.«

There are many breathing techniques available to choose from. Again, we can use our discernment, be open and try different techniques until we find one that will allow us to experience the energy that sustains us.

Apart from aiding in maintaining and restoring health and vitality and increasing longevity, the main benefit of seeking to experience the »breath of life« (the energy that sustains us) is that, due to its very pure and perfect nature, when we contact and experience it, we are given a range of experiences from deep inner peace, total complete relaxation and better sleep, to the overwhelming feelings of joy and bliss of nirvana or samadhi.

This energy is completely subtle and silent in its power as it goes about creating and sustaining life.

1. Consequently, the *first step* to contact this energy and »feel« its vibration and presence in our being, is with our breath – to keep our breathing *connected* where each inhale flows naturally into each exhale with no pause. The Buddhists call this »breath chasing«. The rebirthers call it rhythmical breathing.

2. The *second step* is to breathe finely. Short coarse breathing is what the body does when we are experiencing anger, fear or frustration. Fine breathing is like a leaf or a feather dancing in the wind – subtle, flowing. In the book »Mindfulness

with Breathing«, the Buddhists suggest that we hold a candle in front of our nose and allow our inhale and exhale to flow so finely and so rhythmically through the nostrils, that the flame will not even flicker. Coarse breathing will extinguish the flame.

The force that pervades all life is subtle, yet powerful, and must be charmed, not forced. If one is doing emotional release from the body via visualisation and breath techniques (such as rebirthing), coarse breathing is a very successful tool. But to contact the energy that sustains us we need to tune ourselves to its rhythm as it moves throughout our body.

It is also recommended to breathe through the nostrils as trying to sustain a period of deep, connected, fine breathing through the mouth dries out the throat and mouth and leads to discomfort and interruption in practice. Nostril breathing simply prevents this and also allows for a regulated flow of energy. If doing release work you may breathe in through the nostrils and breathe out with force, intent and will, through the mouth. Also try breathing through one nostril at a time (deep, fine and connectedly) as this will »switch« on the energy flows quickly through both sides of the body.

3. *The third step* in this first technique is for breathing to be deep or long. The Buddhists say that correct breathing keeps the body calm – calm breath, calm body. They say that long breathing i.e. taking less breaths per minute, cools and calms our bodies and allows the body to relax. Deep breathing where the abdomen contracts and the chest expands on the inhale and the chest contracts and the abdomen expands on the exhale, is what restores health and vitality.

Rhythmical, connected, fine breaths which are long, slow and deep allow us to connect to, and experience, the vibrational aspect of the energy that drives the breath. This energy that drives our breath is our divine essence. Connecting with this essence allows us to experience and enjoy the characteristics of its nature – love, joy, bliss etc.

When we breathe deeply, we maximise the intake of both oxygen and prana. Disease cannot exist in a highly oxygenated environment. This explains why regular, sustained exercise is recommended for good health. The more deeply and slowly we breathe, the more oxygen we ingest and also the more prana – both of which have beneficial affects on our health. Prana is the universal life force energy and revitalises, heals and transforms cellular structure and promotes longevity.

The technique of breathing deeply, finely and connected is like the technique of freestyle or breaststroke we would use to swim to the current in a river. There comes a point where we feel as though we are »*being breathed*« and no effort or technique is required once the rhythm has been tapped into – like the effortlessness we experience when we reach the current in a river and allow it to carry us downstream.

When using this technique we are looking to create a wave motion of *even* exhale and inhale to carry us into the experience of the vibrational frequency of life. We could, for instance, count to seven on the inhale, and then to seven on the exhale. Counting is a simple method to keep the mind focussed initially and also to ensure that the inhale and exhale are kept as even as possible.

This breathing technique is a way of *tuning ourselves*, and when practised regularly each day will promote feelings of peace

---

* Tuning our being is similar to the care we give to a motor vehicle or musical instrument. In order to gain optimum performance we need to keep the instrument »tuned«. We can treat the vehicle badly so that it deteriorates and performs like an old jalopy - and becomes prone to disease, decay and death - or can we control its performance so that it performs like a new Porsche. Breath work is a form of tuning, as is visualisation, diet, exercise, meditation etc. We can partake of top quality nourishment, regular exercise, intelligent company or training to stimulate the mental body and seek emotionally-satisfying experiences, but what do we do to soothe the soul and tune the spirit? This is covered in detail in the chapter on meditation and integral applications.

and tranquillity. If we feel anger, we can breathe deeply, finely and connectedly and feel this anger dissolve as we calm the body and mind. This technique can also be used while in traffic or any stressful situation to re-tune ourselves to a more relaxed state.

If we can begin each day using breath work to set the tone of the day, we will find the day unfolding in a more flowing manner. We can also spend five or ten minutes before sleep each night to re-tune ourselves for deeper, more peaceful sleep. So, we become *conscious breathers* – practise in the shower, in traffic, take five minutes in the bathroom at work and breathe to relieve stress build-up. We can control our emotions and stress levels through breath work.

Regular breath work also acts a preventative measure against stress as we deal with the release of tension daily and prevent cumulative build up and potential disease. (A breathing technique to consciously raise our vibrational frequency is discussed in the chapter on vibrational frequencies.)

Creative Visualisation 1
Breath and Light
Utilising White Light Energy With Breath Techniques

· Make sure you will not be disturbed – take the phone off the hook.
· Get comfortable and close your eyes. Establish your breathing pattern using deep, fine and connected breaths – inhale slowly to the count of seven, exhale to the count of seven. Make sure there are no pauses between the inhale and the exhale. First practise breathing that is rhythmical. Do five minutes of keeping each breath connected – where each inhale flows gently into each exhale, and each exhale flows gently into each inhale.
· Then when a rhythmical pattern is established with an even number of inhales and exhales, find a depth of breathing that you can sustain. Count to seven in, then to seven out, then to ten in, and to ten out. Breathe in and out as deeply as you can in a manner that you can sustain for at least five minutes. If you get dizzy, nauseous or short of breath or the breath becomes uneven, drop back your count from say ten to nine. Practise until you find your rhythm and count. Remember, you need to exercise and stretch your lung capacity so you may only be able to sustain a count of seven initially, but with practice this will become ten, 15 or even 20. The deeper you breathe, the healthier you will be. Breathe deeply from the abdomen, not shallow lung breathing.
· Next breathe finely – so fine, slow, deep and connected that it feels like a gentle river of energy flowing through your being. Practise holding a candle flame in front of you – your breath in and out should be so fine that it does not flicker.
· When your breath is connected, deep and fine, you may feel heat or tingling through your body as you are retuned electromagnetically to a different vibration level.
· Next visualise a cylinder of pure, white, golden light energy coming from the purest energy source and encircling you.

Imagine it has no beginning or end as it touches the ground around you, anchoring itself and engulfing you.

- See this cylinder filled with the most intense, pulsating, electrically vibrant energy. Know it to be healing and transforming – living, liquid light energy.
- Breathe this light into your body. Feel it fill your lungs and imagine it filling all your cells with its healing force.
- On the inhale, feel this light being absorbed through the pores of your skin. Feel as though every part of your being is sucking this light into itself like a giant vacuum cleaner. Feel yourself expand your lungs and your entire being as you inhale.
- On the exhale, imagine your cells are saturated with light and that you are releasing this light from your cells, out through the pores of your skin. Visualise that each cell's light is being switched on like a light bulb, then flooding out into the organs, through your body and out through the pores of your skin.
- Visualise, as this light pours out, that it comes from a never-ending energy source within, and that as it flows, it dissolves in its pathway any discordant energy (toxins, dross, pollutants, disease, negative emotions) held within the cellular structure.
- Also allow yourself to release stress from the body as you exhale. You have surrounded yourself with this powerful light energy. Know that whatever is released will automatically be dissolved and/or transformed by its power, because light is the visual aspect of the Creative Force.
- Feel yourself expand and become vaster, limitless, as this light is inhaled and fills every cell. When you exhale, feel the light dissolve negative vibrations as it floods each cell and then moves beyond the boundary of the physical form.
- Visualise yourself seated in a large circular bubble or balloon. See this bubble filled with light energy. As you breathe in, draw light energy to the centre of your being. As you exhale, radiate the light and fill the bubble which encases you with it. Make this bubble as large as you wish. See it attracting only light and positive, healing energies into its centre. Or visualise pure light energy flowing in through the top of this bubble, see

it flow into you and surrounding you. You feel safe, relaxed, healed and free. This bubble is an electromagnetic shield of light energy that encases you always. If you visualise it every day and fill it with light, its field will become stronger and it will shield you from negative energy. It will allow you to be revitalised and strengthened by the light within any time you require it.

· Let us practise ... breathe deeply, finely, connected. Breathe in the light from the energy around you. Feel it fill your cells, absorbed by the pores of your skin. Breathe slowly, feeling your body relax. Breathe in light. Exhale tension from your neck, feel it flowing gently from your body. Breathe in light. Feel it flood your cells. Exhale and breathe out tension from your shoulders. Slowly go through all of your body, breathing in light, releasing tension, keeping your breathing connected, deep and fine. Feel the light flow into you like a river, gently washing away all negativity and stress and tension.

Ten minutes of the above meditation each morning and night will:
1. Provide deep and lasting relaxation.
2. Promote better sleep.
3. Improve health and vitality.
4. Realign the body's energy systems to their natural state of resonance.
5. Heal cellular structure.
6. Repair tears in the electromagnetic field.
7. Create an electromagnetic force field of light around the body.

Chapter 8

The Nature of Reality

There is only one reality. This is the experience of the All That Is – the experience of a state of being when we have merged our awareness with the pure energy or God Force that permeates and creates all. It is a state of letting go of the »I« and of feelings of separation and limitation. It is a state of BEing vast, multidimensional – a state of simply BEing All That Is.

With this awareness comes a recognition of all as being an illusion; and yet we can also understand the purpose of the illusion. Just as we have created our beliefs of separation, we then need to create pathways to simply lead us beyond these veils of illusion or separateness. We have accepted the incongruous idea of God as being external to ourselves and yet simultaneously believing this God to be everywhere, in everything. As more choose to connect and merge with the God within, pathways through this illusion are created for our remembrance of, and conscious reconnection with, the source of all creation.

The formation of ideas about a Higher Self, spiritual hierarchies, dimensions, vibrations and angelic realms simply allows us an inspirational pathway to tread so that we can discard one more »veil of illusion« and separation. *Spirit and reason go hand in hand, with reason being birthed in Spirit.* In order to cross the bridge from limitation to limitlessness and truly embrace the inherent vastness of our nature, we may make use of reason to lead us to Spirit, a state beyond our intellectual capacity. So the ideas of illusion that we create to strip away our accumulated densities can be seen as important, as the way is then made clear for all beings to make this transition when/if they desire it.

It is all very well for us to realise that we are lost and must go home, but if we are surrounded by dense forest, how do we find our way? However, if there are trails left through the forest by others who have begun their return journey, it makes it easier for us. Using our discernment and inner guidance, we can choose the trail we wish to follow or be motivated to create our own simply by *knowing* that others have gone before us.

Day to day reality on this plane of existence is different for us all because we are unique and no two beings have the same physiological, psychological or emotional make-up. Our »reality« is largely created by our thought processes. Firstly, from the perception we have, i.e. how we »see« something. This is always based on previous experience, or belief systems, either held in conscious memory, or subconscious and cellular memory (including past life experiences). Secondly, from the attitude that we choose to adopt from our perception of a given set of circumstances. This attitude gives rise to further thoughts which, in turn, will trigger an emotional response, word or action. This thought, word or action then creates *our* reality by the nature of the energy transmissions sent out as per the laws of energy, where like attracts like. So we are what we think and life mirrors what we think back to us.

The emphasis must be on the word *our*. Over the past 20 or so years in my research of metaphysics and meditation experiences, I have met many people to whom my experiences are invalid or not real, simply because it is not part of their world of experiences. I have also met many who relate completely to these same experiences and understandings. I have learnt that we cannot set our standards according to those of another and we must be true to our own »inner calling« – even if this »inner calling« may appear to others to be unconventional or crazy.

Great dreams and visions have powerful creative capacity but often flow against the tide of conventionality. Change only comes from someone *daring to be different!* If we were all prepared to unquestioningly accept the views and values of our forebears, humanity would not evolve. Humanity has an in-built mechanism and drive to keep improving. We learn by our mistakes. We take risks. Not everyone was motivated to explore the South Pole or to discover if the Earth really was flat. History has been forged by those prepared to »rock the boat« and swim against the tide of conventional thinking.

People tend to condemn, fear or dismiss that which they do not understand. The saying that »ignorance breeds fear« can be quite relevant in society. For example, the fear of other cultural or religious practices – if we *know* that we are »right«, then many logically feel that if someone else's choice or understanding differs from their own, then they must be wrong. Perhaps we should say »right for me« with the emphasis being on *for me* (meaning according to what I know to be true) – for what others may experience to be right is based on their exposure, choices, conditioning and a multitude of other valid factors. The Ascended Ones say that *everything is valid, everything is here to teach and inspire us.*

Combining an open mind, research and practical experience simply allows us to choose more wisely *for ourselves.* Lord Sananda, one of the Ascended Masters, says in his discourse on true love in the book »Inspirations«, that we need to see the Planet Earth as a gigantic library. There are many sections of the library dealing with science, religion, art, music etc. Many of us come simply to study, learn or browse through either one or more sections of this library. Some may spend a whole lifetime studying science or religion. Some may spend a lifetime skipping from one section to another, spending whatever amount of time required to familiarise themselves with the information or experience required to move on. Some, having studied all the relevant sections necessary to evolve further, come and ask who built the library and why, and so *consciously* begin their inner journey. Still others, having understood who built the library and why, have chosen to see if the system can be improved for the collective use of the whole. So their life here is spent in service to the greater plan and humanity as a consequence.

Many beings feel they have no control over situations when their emotional response and reaction seems instantaneous. This may often leave them with a feeling of powerlessness and, again, this is covered in future chapters. We are, however, actually built to think before we feel; consequently the nature of our reality is determined by our attitude and thoughts. We have the power to change and control our thinking so that our reality, *in each new moment*, is as we wish it to be rather than feeling victimised by life.

I say »each new moment« because the emotional body does not recognise time. Cellular memory holds old emotional patterns – fears, hurts and sorrows that span into other lifetimes and experiences. These can create blockages or unexplained emotional responses that are seemingly unwarranted or unjustified in the current situation. For example, a child on the beach may fear going into the water. At two years of age, this fear seems irrational as it may have no current life experience of being dumped by waves. However, if that child drowned at sea in a previous life, the emotional body would remember and hold this fear which could surface under certain circumstances. In the child's present life, this fear can be eliminated. The mother may, for instance, hold the child in her arms and enter the surf gradually, each time going deeper and deeper until the child realises that, at this point in time, there is nothing to fear. This re-sets its emotional memory pattern and dissolves the fear.

A common example of how we create reality is illustrated in the way we choose to see a litre container holding half a litre of fluid. Those who are positively inclined will see it as half full, those with negative inclinations will see it as half empty. Both views are valid. However, the person who views it as half full will be pleased to have something to drink and will experience gratitude; whereas the individual who views it as half empty may experience disappointment. *All life's events are emotionally neutral – we are the ones who assign an emotional reaction to them.*

If our car breaks down it is simply a car that has broken down – no more, no less. One person may experience anger, frustration and annoyance at being late. Another may phone for help, then sit and enjoy the view or choose to take the time to read another chapter of a book or whatever, knowing that help will come, and accepting the situation. The lesson may be to take the car for repairs sooner or make sure the tank is full of petrol – retrospection serves to teach us, but will not change that moment as it is unfolding.

Those who respond in anger carry that negative energy with them and may possibly infect others with it. They may blame this external event for their anger rather than accept responsibility for *their reaction to the event.*

When we are aware that in any given moment we can choose an experience to be positive or negative according to our *perception* of the event, we can then consciously choose to view things positively. Choosing this perception creates a reality which is then more beneficial to all concerned. This is not a fatalistic attitude to life, it is one of *empowerment where we take full responsibility for every experience we have* by understanding how our attitude and thoughts really do create our reality.

Individuals who choose to see the cup as half full tend to enjoy and appreciate what they have in life generally. *The universe responds to our expectations.* (»The Celestine Prophecy« by James Redfield covers this idea beautifully.)

A few years ago I had the experience of being literally stripped bare – of income, assets and loved ones. On top of all this, I was told that I had cancer. I felt that the weight of it all had the potential to »swallow me up« in negativity. I realised that as I had no power to change the physical actuality of events, I could only change my attitude towards what was happening. So began a journey of thought control where every day I found reasons to be thankful. My children were healthy and happy. We had a roof over our head (at least temporarily), warm beds and some food in the fridge. Each day I found something else to appreciate – a sunset, a flower, the love of friends, the experience of joy and love in the stillness within, and so on. My reality became quite wonderful and my learning from these experiences very powerful and indelibly printed in my awareness. By changing my thinking pattern alone, I literally created a life that I could cherish and enjoy.

Yogananda, in his booklet »Scientific Healing Affirmations«, says that as the world we know operates under the Law of Duality, man in his mental aspect experiences duality and contrasts in life. Life and death, health and disease, happiness and unhappiness. He says that when man tunes to *soul consciousness*, that higher state of awareness inherent in all, all duality disappears and he knows only the eternal and blissful spirit. He says that in the divine mind (higher mind) our unchangeable perception of bliss is ever-present.

So, to sum up, we can say that the nature of our reality is governed by the way we *perceive* life. This is influenced by our previous experiences. Our perception, however, can be changed by changing our level of awareness through the practice of meditation and also through being aware of the power of our thoughts. Being aware of our inherent ability to fashion reality by thought alone is the first step to mind mastery and the creation of life as we truly wish it to be.

Chapter 9

Mind Mastery and The Power of Thought

All creation is birthed in thought. But thought is energy. If we think positively then that positive attitude will be reflected back to us through positive life experiences – unless we have certain learning experiences to achieve first. However, it is always our choice whether we experience this learning as painful or not. All events trigger an experience or an emotion according to our perception of the event. We live in a plane of duality so every life event has two facets. We can govern our emotional response by how we choose to view, or think about, the event.

Dr. Deepak Chopra reminds us that, »there is no objective world to the observer« and that »perception is a learned phenomena«. Perception is governed by environmental influences, genetic encoding and previous life experiences – all of which are held in cellular memory. These memories can be accessed through meditation, hypnosis and/or past life regression and can, and do, influence our current life experiences.

Chris Griscom of The Light Institute of Galisteo and successful past life regressionist says in her book »Time is an Illusion«, that, »Attitude and understanding do not control the emotional body! To the contrary, it is the emotional body that determines our existence on all levels of consciousness on this planet, and yet it has remained behind in its own conscious development. The reason for this is that emotionality on energetic levels belongs to the astral dimension, which is outside time-influenced reality. Unaware that »time passes«, the emotional body continually revisits or reassembles emotional components of its own design. Since we ourselves have become so identified with our mental body, we practise the illusion that we are influencing and directing the emotional body with our conscious will.« And, »Since the consciousness of any of our bodies is not dependent on the actual material vehicle, our »sticky« imprints from the emotional body just revisit themselves through each incarnation. The »old« emotional body brings into the »new« physical body all those experiences, reactions, and perceptions of reality that it gained in other bodies«.

Consequently, I feel that while *we can control, or deal positively with, the emotional body through our choice of perception in »each new moment«,* we *also* need to look at past issues *and* resolve them. This will allow us to release the energy of the past. These cellular memories or patterns are often the basis for current life blockages. When these energy blocks were created by past unresolved emotions, it was as a direct result of our point of perception and mental understanding of the event occurring *at that time.* As we have grown and evolved, so has our awareness which allows us to retrospectively view life from a different, more informed perspective.

At this point I would like to share a personal story that relates to how cellular memory, from a past life experience, can affect our current life. Some time ago I was given clear guidance while in meditation to undergo past life regression in particular relation to my last life. I had experienced dreams and visions of an Indian incarnation quite vividly in the past. As a child, I had always become extremely emotional when viewing classic cowboy and Indian movies, and I always sided with the Indians. I had also felt in my travels to the USA a profound negative reaction to the white populace there that was both unjustified and unexplainable.

Under hypnosis, I again had vivid visions of my previous incarnation. I was a large, relatively unattractive, male Apache Indian. I »saw« our tribe breaking camp due both to seasonal influences and threat of attack. I then »saw« much chaos and bloodshed and found myself in the midst of it all. I bent down and picked up my two year old son who had had the left side of his face blown off. As I held his limp body in my arms I experienced rage, hurt, anger and intense sorrow (to the alarm of the hypnotist who wasn't expecting such a strong reaction). There was much more that is not relevant to this story.

I knew instinctively that my son then was my youngest daughter today, with whom I had been having no end of behavioural problems virtually since her birth. No matter what approach I took, I could not bridge the gap between us. The moment we shared this experience and she remembered (which is a story in itself) she also *knew* that my rejection of her energy at conception was due to my feeling that I could not stand the pain of maybe losing her again. In that instant of remembrance for us, all changed dramatically and our relationship has been generally wonderful since. (She had been classified as having a behavioural problem of attention seeking which, regardless of the amount of love and attention received, did not abate. I had reacted very negatively over her conception to the point of seeking the possibility of an abortion. For the foetus this laid the groundwork for feeling intensely rejected. So we both held deep cellular memory; she from conception and me from our last life together. Understanding, tapping into and clearing that cellular memory, created profound and lasting changes.

We are aware, then, of the fact that thoughts emit and transmit »unseen« energy fields which operate via biofeedback loops. These fields thus rebound and are received by their original transmission source. Consequently, everything that comes to us in life, everything that stands before us, we have attracted to ourselves by the nature of the energies we have emitted.

We – our physical, emotional, mental and spiritual bodies – are energy fields in motion, all resonating and vibrating at specific frequencies and transmitting energy waves. In simplistic terms, the human body can be seen as the computer hardware, the mind the disk operating system, the thoughts as software programs, and our lives as the »print-out« of the three. The physical body reacts to the emotional body, which reacts to the mental body which, when in alignment, serves Spirit and Divine Intelligence. So our mental programming affects not only our emotional well-being but also our health.

Our thinking processes are habitual and learned but may appear automatic and beyond our control. In his audio tape of the book »Unconditional Life«, Dr. Chopra says, »We are prisoners of our thoughts. Through memory and habit we literally become bundles of conditioned responses and nerves, constantly being triggered by people and circumstances into predictable outcomes of biochemical response in our bodies. And so the conditioned mind leaves little room for anything new. Emotions seem beyond our control. We erect and build a prison, and the tragedy is that we cannot even see the walls of this prison. The lack of meaning we currently endure can only become worse if we remain within this prison«.

We are taught our thinking processes by those we have associated with in our formative years where we often learn to:

- Over generalise.
- Think only in terms of black and white.
- Draw conclusions without evidence.
- Assume the worst in a situation or blow things out of proportion.
- Take everything personally.
- Always focus on our failures or our problems.

When one understands that:

- Thoughts are energy (that can also trigger emotions).
- Universal laws govern this energy.
- We have the power to create our personal reality.
- We can then be forever free from limited thinking and the belief that life »just happens to us«.

Then we become apprentices in mind mastery. We realise that we need to be disciplined and vigilant with each and every thought. We also need to question the basis of our beliefs, habitual thinking patterns and reactions. If our lives are abundant on all levels, then we have mastered the mind and its ability to create. If we still feel limitation and lack, then we need to scrutinise our thoughtforms carefully. *A positive thought followed by a negative thought will neutralise the energy field* or vice versa. So if we catch a negative thought, we must follow it with positive ones, and watch our reality change.

In the short term, mind mastery and being responsible for every thought, word and action requires far more energy and application than victim mentality where we blame the world and others for our sorrows and circumstances. In the long run, once we have graduated, through discipline and discernment, from apprenticeship to mastery, the benefits are abundant and the quality of our life improves dramatically. (Using meditation as a tool to develop mind mastery via deprogramming and reprogramming is covered in chapter 14.)

Chapter 10

The Power of Emotion

Research by many alternative therapists plus some medical practitioners, including Dr. Chopra, has shown that emotional disease is a significant factor in the creation of disease. Our inability to cope with stress, often due to feelings of uncertainty or lack of control, is also very damaging to the physical body and can lead to a nervous breakdown.

Even though it may appear that our emotional reactions are automatic, the nerve pathways that carry the information to the brain take approximately three seconds to relay this information before the emotional responses, and our mind's experience of them, are triggered. In these three seconds the rest of the brain has already received the information via faster nerve pathways, so even though we are unaware of this process, we are *built to think before we feel.* We are not »victims« of our emotions.

When we »spontaneously« have an emotional reaction, because our buttons are being pushed, we need to learn to deal with these emotions effectively so as not to create energy blockages and, eventually, disease. As we have discussed, events are emotionless. We assign an emotion to them according to our *perception.* Strong emotions that are unresolved are stored in the body and create blockages as they impede the flow of energy through the body's energy systems.

If we wish to increase both the quality of life, if we desire to experience more joy, happiness and harmony in our life, we must firstly decide to accept nothing less. By deciding to focus on, and accept, positive feelings in our lives, we learn to bring our attitude into line with positive thinking and always look to see the silver lining in every cloud. Both positivity and negativity exist; we choose to focus on the positive aspects of life and, as a result of the laws of energy, *what we focus on grows.*

By understanding that *all experiences are here to teach and inspire us.* By understanding how *we* assign an emotional response to an event via our perception of it, we gain more control over the quality of our experiences. Even if a situation initially appears negative, we can choose to see it and accept it as positive. We can, and will, learn from it so it can be embraced for its teaching power.

Storing negative emotions in the physical body serves no purpose. If we were to dam a free-flowing river by building a wall, the plant life beyond the dam wall would atrophy and die due to lack of water. So it is with our bodies. Emotions must flow freely for the body to be healthy. They must be accepted and not denied. They need to be dealt with in a positive manner via honouring, acceptance and release without overindulgence. The computer hardware of the body stores negative emotions in databases called our organs i.e. the liver stores anger, the lungs store sadness etc. simply because we have not learnt how to effectively deal with these emotions.

In his book »Ageless Body, Timeless Mind«, Dr. Deepak Chopra states that emotional pain in the present is experienced as hurt, in the past it is remembered as anger, in the future it is perceived as anxiety. Unexpressed anger redirected against yourself and held within is called guilt and the depletion of energy that occurs when anger is directed inwards is called depression. If, as he says in »Quantum Healing«, cells are just memories clothed in matter, then it is extremely important that we begin to look at and access cellular memory with a view to releasing energy blockages as we cleanse our cells of negativity and toxicity.

We can learn to deal with our emotions on a two-fold level. Firstly, we can release negative emotions from past experiences stored in the cells and organs of the body. Secondly, we can learn to deal more effectively with negative emotions as they confront us in an effective manner. By regular meditation we can take this one step further. We can learn detachment. We can act and not react. We can constantly experience life from that deep place within and see things in perspective.

1. Releasing negative emotions held in cellular memory
   a) This can be achieved by using creative visualisation techniques such as the simple one described at the end of this chapter.
   b) A large selection of healing modalities are also available to aid the physical body to effect this release quickly and effectively: for example, kinesiology, homeopathy and body harmony. Aid in the realigning and cleansing of the cellular structure and energy fields of the body can be achieved through a number of alternative therapies which can achieve in hours what may otherwise take years of meditation.
   c) We can also *ask* that our emotional body be cleansed and released of all negative beliefs and patterns of limitation while we sleep at night. Simply tune into your Higher Self and ask for this to be done. Do not doubt. You can ask for awareness of this being done via your dreams or you can specifically request that it be done without conscious memory.

I feel that all emotional release work can be a gentle and free-flowing experience and not traumatic unless one requires it to be. I do not support the saying »no pain, no gain«, and feel that all can be achieved gently and lovingly if that is our intention and desire.

2. Learn to deal with negative emotions and hurt effectively
   a) Dissipate negative emotions through breathing to regain a calm mind, body and emotions. Establish a deep, fine, rhythmical pattern and continue until you feel settled.
   b) Tuning our being is similar to the care we give to a motor vehicle or musical instrument. In order to gain optimum performance we need to keep the instrument »tuned«. We can treat the vehicle badly so that it deteriorates and performs like an old jalopy – and becomes prone to disease, decay and death – or can we control its performance so that it performs like a new Porsche. Breath work is a form of tuning, as is visualisation, diet, exercise, meditation etc. We can partake of top quality nourishment, regular exercise,

intelligent company or training to stimulate the mental body and seek emotionally-satisfying experiences, but what do we do to soothe the soul and tune the spirit? This is covered in detail in the chapter on meditation and integral applications.

Express your feelings in a non-attacking, non-threatening manner to the person who triggered the hurt and then deal with the issues that allow your buttons to be pushed. Remember, the external situation is only a mirror. If you held no issue within, you would not react. A good indicator for the success of the release work conducted is when you cease to react strongly to a situation that in the past was guaranteed to make you react.

c) Take responsibility for how you think and feel. Feelings always follow thought and perception. If you don't like how you are feeling, change what you are thinking.

d) Approve of yourself and don't seek approval from others. Set your standards of what is acceptable to you. We all have different standards of what we wish to experience and accept in life.

e) Top up your own energy by accessing your inner reservoir in meditation. By merging with the divine essence within we learn to love, honour and accept others and become our own well of happiness. Don't depend on others to make you feel good.

f) Remember the most important person is you. If you are happy, you can positively deal with others and share more effectively.

g) Be in touch with your physical and emotional responses – do not deny how you feel. Burying something »under the carpet« or holding emotional dis-ease within, e.g. »swallowing our tongue« for the sake of peace or to not »create waves«, will lead to disease, peptic ulcers, cancer, heart problems etc.

h) Resolve why you feel hurt and let it go.

i) Learn to live in each moment.

j) Be willing to change – the only constant thing in the universe is change.

k) Don't poison your body with harmful food, thoughts or emotions.

l) Release judgement. Choose to have only positive thoughts and assessments about others, and also about yourself.

m) Replace fear motivation with love motivation.

One of the most powerful tools in healing the emotional body, and consequently the physical body, is *forgiveness* – forgiving both ourselves and others.

For years I practised meditation, exercised regularly and followed a relatively pure diet. All this kept the cancer tumour in my liver relatively small. However, it was a direct result of unresolved anger. Although I had done much »personal growth«, rebirthing and used other tools to heal myself, I had not been able, or perhaps willing, to forgive until the diagnosis and »life threatening« situation forced me to. Orthodox medicine can save lives if cancers are detected early enough and removed. We must, however, also look at why the cancer was created in the first place and remove the cause, not just the symptom.

3. Meditation as a preventive tool

This is covered in detail in the chapter on meditation and its benefits. The major benefit of meditation is in dealing with the emotions and the detachment we can achieve so that we no longer feel we are »at the mercy of others«. It allows us to be responsible for our own happiness in a dependable, guaranteed manner and also to readily identify problem ownership.

Chris Griscom in »Time is an Illusion« states that apart from past life regression work, meditation and changing the frequency of our energy fields to higher octaves is the most powerful way to release the old, negative patterning held in the emotional body and cellular memory.

Mastering the emotional and the mental body does require discipline. After years of thinking we are powerless to our thoughts and subsequent feelings simply because society teaches us adopt this attitude, we now can be aware and learn to discipline our thinking. An Indian guru once said that you cannot expect a wild horse that has roamed the plains since birth (like our undisciplined minds) to come into a corral simply because we whistle.

Television has created expectations of instant results which makes spending time in inner silence and disciplining and stilling the mind quite difficult for many. TV soap operas reinforce victim mentality, game shows reinforce greed and news casts reinforce fear and negativity. All are powerful emotions that are reinforced subliminally in our day to day lives. However, television is also a powerful communication device and we can control, via selective viewing, this device in a manner that can be used to our advantage. We have the power to choose our perception, our thoughts, our reality and our emotional experience.

4. Set the standards

I call the following technique and exercise »positive memory association«. It is designed to achieve two things. Firstly, to set a minimum standard of what is acceptable to you regarding your emotional experience. Secondly, to be used as a tool to tune your day when you get »out of the wrong side of the bed«. The technique is simple but powerful in its effectiveness.

Positive Memory Association

a) Sit in contemplation – breathe deeply, finely and connected until you feel a sense of inner peace. This will allow you to access memory more quickly.

b) Go back in time, search through your memory database. Find a time when you experienced your life to be just great, happy and fulfilling.

c) Recapture the details, the time, the place, who you were with, what made it so special. In particular, *pay attention to how you felt.*

d) When you have accessed the feeling of this event, decide to accept no less. The exact form the memory takes is not relevant. What is important is how you can use this memory to trigger feelings of joy and harmony.

The majority of people I have done this exercise with report that the most common feelings remembered were ones of joy, contentedness and being carefree. They also report that these are the same experiences they miss most in their current lifestyle and their adult world of »responsibility«.

The fact is that we have had these experiences in the past and, while we may not be able to recreate the same circumstances, we can *set the standard for ourselves of what we wish to accept on an emotional level.*

Simply by beginning each day by accessing a positive memory from your personal data base of memories, we can set the tone for each day. We can decide to accept no less and then evoke the feeling by reliving the memory. This will allow the day to begin on a positive note.

If the universe responds to our expectations and if we always expect the best for ourselves while vigilantly counteracting negative thoughts by being persistently positive, we will find our life changing quite magically – guaranteed!

Dreaming and Guidance

The dream state can be used most effectively for receiving guidance, emotional and mental body clearing and/or healing and training. If ever I am unsure over an issue or decision, I will always meditate before going to sleep and ask the higher mind, my I AM Presence, or the master I may be currently working with, to give me a *clear answer* via the dream state plus *total clarity in recall* and *easy understanding of the symbolism* of the dream. This technique never fails! I always wake up immediately after receiving the dream with its answer or instruction, and can interpret it and any symbolism it may contain.

However, it is very important that we spend time in meditation and contemplation prior to sleep so that the subconscious mind can bring to the conscious mind any unresolved issues from the day's events so that those issues do not preoccupy our dream state. Dream interpretation is an excellent way of gaining self-knowledge and there are many wonderful books on the subject for those interested.

We can go beyond the subconscious mind and its need to communicate issues to the conscious mind for attention and resolution via dreaming, when we pay attention to ourselves via meditation and contemplation at the end of each day. This leaves the dream time free to explore other realms and dimensions of reality. Personally, I find my night time »activities« are now divided. The earlier part of the evening is spent in training, while the latter part is spent working through issues of a more personal nature via dream instruction. One state is where one actually leaves the physical body to work in the etheric realms, the other is the interaction between the subconscious, the conscious mind and the superconscious mind.

Affirmation to program to remember dreams: »I ask my I AM Presence to allow me *full memory and easy conscious recall* of dreams, instructions, preparation and teachings that I receive during the sleep of my physical body.«

Creative Visualisation 2
Cleansing and Realigning the Emotional Body Meditation

This meditation is designed to a) release emotional baggage that is held in cellular memory from unresolved past issues, and b) allow us to effectively deal with negative emotions on a day to day basis. (Refer to the meditation for creating the inner sanctuary before you do this.)

· Get comfortable where you won't be disturbed.
· Tune yourself with breath and light work.
· When relaxed, visualise yourself to be standing on a mountain. In front of you see steps leading downwards.
· As you step down, begin to count. Between each breath take one full inhale and one connected exhale.
· Let yourself relax deeper and deeper as you count. With each step down you feel lighter and freer, knowing that you are about to enter a »special, safe place«.
· Breathe in and out ... 9 ... breathe in and out ... 8 ... breathe in and out ... 7 ... 6 ... 5 ... 4 ... 3 ... 2 ... 1 ... 0 ...
· As you reach the ground you feel deeply relaxed. Take a few deep connected breaths – look around you, open up all your inner senses.
· You »see« (visualise or imagine) that you are in a most beautiful sanctuary – a place that is yours alone, where you feel completely safe, at peace, nurtured and loved. This is your internal »cubbyhouse« like the one children have to enact their games and »fantasies«.
· Let your mind wander. See the trees, the flower beds. See yourself picking a flower. Hold it to your nose and smell its fragrance (allow your sense of smell to be activated).
· Listen to the birds singing and the wind rustling in the trees.
· Feel the sun on your skin and the wind in your hair.
· Pause for a moment. Allow higher mind to create this inner sanctuary. Remember this is your place. You can create it to be whatever you wish – there are no limitations to your vision

here.

- Take a few deep, fine, connected breaths. Allow yourself to bathe in the beauty of this place. If you could have a place of physical perfection what would it be? A beach, a rainforest, a valley or a mountain top?
- See before you now a pathway lined with flowers. Intrigued, you begin to follow it. The ground feels soft beneath your feet and as you continue to breathe in the cool, fresh air you feel lighter and lighter, energised and freer.
- You notice you are wearing long flowing robes. Your feet are bare and you feel as though you are gliding through a forest.
- You come to a clearing, a beautiful leafy glade, and in its centre is a large, clear, sparkling rock pool that is fed by a beautiful, cascading waterfall at its far end.
- The sunlight dances on the surface of the crystal clear water. The air feels regenerating, alive, energised with oxygen and prana.
- Scoop water from the pool and bring it to your lips to »taste« and refresh your thirst.
- The plant life is lush and tropical and abundant and lines the perimeter of the pool.
- You notice a large flat rock jutting out over the water and you sit yourself gently down upon it.
- Breathing here is easy – the oxygen and prana flows naturally into you, filling your lungs with their healing power and as you exhale you give yourself permission to release all the cares and worries of your world.
- You sit in a glorious beam of healing light energy that streams out from the clear blue sky above you. It surrounds you and seems to penetrate all the pores of your skin.
- You feel as though you want to surrender to its healing power, to allow it to transform you, re-energise and realign you to its purity.
- As you breathe in its golden white light energy, you feel it fill your lungs and then flow into your cells and organs. It feels as though all the pores on your skin are also absorbing this light

into themselves – as you exhale you do so through your mouth, sighing gently as you begin to release the emotional baggage that has been stored in your cells and organs for eons of time.

· Breathe in the light.

· Exhale and affirm »I NOW release all ————-« (allow your being to release what it feels – the first thought that comes into your head is what you should be releasing – e.g. anger, fear, jealousy, sorrow etc.)

· Allow your vocal release to be louder, sighing or groaning.

· Feel all negative vibrations flow out of your being and be dissolved by the light around you.

· Breathe in the light and affirm »I AM healthy, I AM vibrant«.

· Exhale deeply and affirm »I NOW release all ————«.

· Continue this until you feel you have released all of the energy of that negative emotion from your being, then ask yourself what else you need to release.

· Alternatively, simply release **all** harmful vibrations with the affirmation »I NOW release all dross, all toxicity, all pollutants, all stress and all negative emotions stored in my cellular memory and everything that no longer positively serves me at this point in my life!«

· As you release it from your cells, visualise an intense beam of light coming in through the top of your head and cleansing all the energy pathways, all the cells and organs, dissolving all the »garbage« and filling your being with healing light energy. It is like a gigantic inner spring clean!

· Continue to affirm as you inhale the light energy from the beam that surrounds you »I AM light, I AM love, I AM free, I AM a glorious radiant being!« etc. Affirm whatever feels right to you.

· Alternatively, visualise that you are holding a knapsack or container on your lap. Visualise your hands filling with the released emotions etc. and then dumping it all into the knapsack in a strong, forceful motion. When the knapsack is full, seal it shut and then »see« yourself offer it up to the light, and see it dissolve in love and light. Feel as though you have been deeply cleansed.

- As you breathe in the light and prana, feel yourself becoming stronger, healthier, free from all disease, from all discomfort. Feel yourself becoming transformed and willing to accept only love and joy and laughter in your life from this moment on.
- Cast your memory back to the best time in your life (positive memory association) and decide to accept only the best for yourself emotionally from this point on.
- Affirm »In joy, in safety, in harmony I step into the unknown, I willingly embrace all that is for my highest good«.
- The above technique may be used to release anger, frustration or stress that you may have accumulated during that day or week.
- When you have completed this, or feel you have done enough, visualise the top of your head opening like a lid on a jar of honey and healing, loving, liquid light pouring in and filling your entire being with its beautiful energy.
- Then see it close up and continue to breathe deeply. Feel calm, fresh and energised.
- Be grateful for the use of this tool. Ask your Higher Self to allow you to deal positively with all future emotions and situations and to recognise that all occurs for us to learn or be inspired by.
- Now visualise yourself slipping into this beautiful rock pool. Feel its waters energise you, soothe you and restore you as you swim gracefully and joyously.
- Swim to the waterfall. Stand under it and allow it to cascade gently over you. It recharges and energises you. Then allow yourself to be dried by a whispering breeze and the rays of the sun as they gently caress your skin.
- When centred and relaxed, feel your arms, your legs and the cushions or chair on which you are seated.
- Bring back the feelings of peace and tranquillity from the time in your sacred place, by the rock pool. Know that you can go there any time you desire. Savour your feelings.
- Take five deep breaths.
- Bring your attention back to the room and open your eyes.

conscious mind should be impressive enough to permeate the subconscious, which in turn automatically influences the conscious mind. Strong conscious affirmations thus react on the mind and body through the medium of the subconsciousness. Still stronger affirmations react not only on the subconscious but also on the superconscious mind – the magic storehouse of miraculous powers.«

He also states that people »who use affirmations without comprehending the truth upon which they are based – man's inseverable unity with God – get poor results and complain that thoughts have no healing power.« So we must understand the power of mind, of thoughts as energy, and the laws that govern energy. We will then no longer doubt the power of thought and the ability of affirmations to heal and transform our lives. *We are creators and the only limitation is that which we wish to place upon ourselves.*

If we wish to compartmentalise our life and use the aforementioned understanding and affirmations to create positive change, we may do so. Affirmations can be used to create health, wealth, happiness and even immortality (to be an immortalist, one must let go of the belief that we need to die or that death is inevitable!). Affirmations can also be used to create wonderful relationships. It is important, however, that we are completely clear about what we wish to create so that the wording can be precise and powerful.

Personally, I prefer affirmations that cover all aspects in one single swoop! Something that covers everything in one hit. For example: »I AM healthy. I AM happy. I AM successful in all that I do. My life is abundantly joyous and prosperous and I AM in perfect harmony and synchronistic alignment with Divine Will, fulfilling my true purpose and destiny.«

Relevant affirmations must be tailor-made to suit your desires and I could fill a book on the range of affirmations alone. There are many wonderful books available on affirmations to cover all aspects of life, ranging from Shakti Gawain's »Reflections in the Light« to Stuart Wilde's book on abundance.

Chapter 11

The Power of Affirmation

Affirmation is defined in the Oxford dictionary as »a solemn declaration by person«. To affirm, then, is to assert strongly, state as a fact, make a formal declaration.

Before we begin, I must state that affirmations alone do not work! You must exercise mind mastery via thought control and reinforce this with any relevant supporting action that you consider necessary e.g. meditation, if you wish the desired event to concretise. Making a positive affirmation, and then allowing thoughts of doubt or disbelief, will be counteractive and achieve nothing.

Successful results with affirmations come from:
· Intensity of intention.
· Continuity and repetition.
· Faith and devotion.
· Absence of doubt.
· Acceptance that results will be forthcoming.

We know that self-talk and thoughts control emotions and that unresolved negative emotions held within create dis-ease. Conversely, we can retrain self-talk via affirmations and create ease.

In Yogananda's booklet »Healing With Affirmations«, he says that strong conscious affirmations react on the mind and body through the medium of the subconscious. He explains that »while attempting healing, one often concentrates more on the gripping power of the disease than on the possibility of the cure, thus permitting the illness to be a mental as well as physical habit.« ... »The subconscious idea/habit of the disease or health exerts a strong influence. Stubborn mental or physical diseases always have a deep root in the subconscious. Illness may be cured by pulling out its hidden roots. That is why all affirmations of the

Note: When creating affirmations, avoid using negatives for the subconscious mind picks up certain words. If you say »I never get sick«, the mind still picks up the word »sick«, so it is preferable to say »I always enjoy perfect health«. Also, always use the present tense: »I AM« and not »I will« – »I will« is a state of eventuality. We need it to occur NOW, not tomorrow. »I AM« is a powerful statement and pays direct homage to the God within.

There is a universal law called the Creative Law of Divine Affirmation which states that thoughts, words and action affirm what you believe yourself or your reality to be. *As you think, so shall you be.*

Affirmation is covered by the Law of Mind. Jesus said, »As you believe, so shall you receive.« The mental law operates in the realm of the mind which is the realm of belief. Belief sets thought in motion.

The *spiritual law* works through the medium of the Law of Mind. This law is perfection everywhere now and states that the absolute, complete goodness of God is available to everyone, everywhere, anytime. It is also called First Cause as it is the only true cause and the only truth.

Body is servant to mind; mind is servant to spirit. Both these facts have been forgotten by mankind and so many live in a state of fear and disease, limitation and death.

Inner harmony is achieved through the balance and daily application of contemplation (prayer, attunement), meditation (for self-realisation) and affirmation. As Ann and Peter Meyer point out in »Being a Christ«, »Meditation is a subjective state of the receiving of Spirit. Treatment (affirmation) is the objective activity of directing the spiritual law.«

At the end of the chapter on vibrational frequencies, I have looked more closely at the power that the spoken word and sound – as in toning and mantras – has on the energy fields of our being.

Affirmations

The following are some interesting affirmations:

· »I am highly pleasing to myself in the presence of my parents, my lover, my children, my friends and everyone. They are all highly pleasing to themselves in my presence«.

· »I am love, I am free, I am forgiven. I am that I am«.

· »In joy, in safety, in harmony, I step into the unknown«.

· »It is my intention that I am successful. It is my intention that I am safe in all the things that I do. It is my intention that I receive love and give love in all that I do. It is my intention that I have a great time and am provided for with prosperity according to all my needs and desires.«

· »As much as I am able this day, I will go within, ask and listen. I am going to trust and risk by doing what I feel to be true. Thus I will follow the response and inner guidance rather than habitual patterns.« (S. Wilde)

· »Money comes to me readily and easily and I have more than enough for all my needs and desires.«

· »I have a right to be happy, to be free, to have everything that I desire, to experience joy, ecstasy and unconditional love in all of my life.«

· »I am free from past limitations. I create my own reality«.

· »Infinite wisdom guides me, Divine Love prospers me, success is with me«.

· »Love and light is what I am. Acceptance is the key to my happiness«.

· »I am a radiant and divine being«.

· And many more!

Programming vs Affirmations

In chapter 9, we began the discussion on the necessity of mind mastery as all is created by thought. Working with affirmation is very different to conscious programming as the following section on mind power will cover.

The main difference is that we can often utilise powerful affirmations yet their power can be diffused by what we term, the

»internal saboteur«. This saboteur is cellular memory from other timeframes and is based on an experience that may not be in alignment for the fulfilment of our current affirmations.

For example, we may program that, »I accept and give thanks for all the abundance of financial wealth that is mine« and yet be constantly »just scraping by« financially. This may be because we have a deeply held belief on a cellular level that we cannot be spiritual and also enjoy financial abundance. This belief may have come from previous lifetimes spent as monks or nuns where poverty and chastity were common vows. It may have come from subliminal programs from childhood where we were told that »you can only make money if you are prepared to work hard« and now we love our work so much that it just doesn't feel like »hard« work or even work.

Thus we have two conflicting patterns running simultaneously: one in this now moment to be abundant financially, and another held in cellular memory that says it's either not OK or not possible to be abundant. Thus the positive energy force and the negative energy force cancel each other out and nothing is manifested.

Programming is about setting in place specific commands: from higher mind to lower mind, from higher mental body to emotional body, and from mental body to physical body so that we can manifest all that we desire.

Manifesting all we desire is guaranteed provided we:
· Are in alignment with Divine Will and the Divine Blueprint.
· Are in tune with the *timing* of the unfoldment of this Divine Plan.
· Have eliminated our internal sabotage patterns.

Does this sound simple? Actually it is. And the next section will provide very powerful programs to do just that!

72

Mind Power – Beyond Motivational Psychology

After the completion of the first draft of this book, my inner guidance was to stop reading. Perhaps it was because the project had been so intensely focussed. For over six months I had written and woven together the researched material gathered from well over 40 texts. My intention was to present a manual of easy to utilise self-help tools that honoured the heart and the intellect by providing well-researched data from many sources.

More important than the need to »take a break« from research and reading, was the understanding of the importance of allowing what had been absorbed intellectually to settle into a *cellular knowing*. This can only be achieved through putting what one has learnt into practice – by living it. I also intuitively knew that I held within me all the knowledge needed to be the limitless being I was seeking to manifest.

As I witness others make this journey, a pattern appears that seems to utilise all our inner »knowing«. The soul stirs, we begin to awaken. We thirst for knowledge. We honour the intellect by researching, and we find the common threads of truth that emerge through all the teachings of the ancient schools and Earth's religions. We combine the knowledge of quantum physics. We discover the universal laws and recognise that they govern all energy and matter and are in fact the foundation of all science and religion. We understand that these laws are the laws of creation, and when we work with them, the results are magical. We practise, we play, we create consciously.

Knowing we create reality via our vision, we diligently monitor our thought processes and delete everything except limitless thinking. We refine and re-program ourselves. We witness the laws of energy respond and manifest our new paradigm in our day to day reality. Meditation brings the gift of detachment. We become both the witness and the creator, experiencing and living within our own creation. *We have realised that the impact of BEing and living what we intellectually understand, empowers our reality further.* For a beam of energy of thought is less powerful than the deep cellular knowing that emanates out of every cell, every fibre, of our being, altering the energy patterns around us. The whole body sends out a frequency – a resonance – that makes a statement to a responding, fluid universe. It is said that the universe literally rearranges itself to accommodate our model of reality. This is the Law of Resonance at play.

Through conscious creation, via tuning and programming, we find Universal Mind speaks to us. We are free from suffering for our divinity as we consciously program for joy, grace, ease and more. Awakened and empowered via intention, programming and *playing by the rules of the divine game* we create a bridge between the worlds, between paradigms, and experience the Oneness in all.

We witness the beat of the lightworkers and of »mainstream« society. Many are seeking to have fun, to make money, and also to »do good«. Many simply wish to create a model that allows them to live their life to their highest maximum potential physically, emotionally, mentally and spiritually in a way that honours all. These are *positive paradigms for a new age.*

Positive paradigms can be created by specific, intentional programming. Programming is repetitive instruction. As the physical and emotional bodies are governed by the mental bodies – higher and lower mind – in each »now« moment, effective programming frees us and also directs us through life. It allows the journey of survival to be simplified so we can thrive harmoniously. The following is a program that many have found most powerful: *»Dear Mother/Father Creator God, I ask that each and every moment of each day unfold in complete and perfect synchronistic alignment with Divine Will«.* This guarantees successful fulfilment of all aligned dreams and visions and stops us constantly wondering if we are »meant« to be doing something. It also allows us to know that if something doesn't manifest, it is not in alignment with Divine Timing. So we can let it go.

»I ask that all my sharing in each moment be for the highest good of others and the highest good of myself.« Why would we want our sharing to be anything other than the highest? This also gives our relationships permission to be all that they can be, free of our expectations.

»I ask that the energy fields of my physical, emotional, mental and spiritual bodies be brought into perfect alignment so that my Divine Self may consciously be made fully manifest on the physical plane, and all planes of existence, in a manner that brings me great joy, ease, grace, pleasure and abundance.« The most powerful transmuting and creative force in the universe is that of our Divine Self (our I AM or monad). Commanding it to align us means that the alignment will be done powerfully and in a manner that is also joyous because we won't need to suffer for our divinity any more or be bound to a cycle of constant processing. This program also eliminates the internal saboteur.

Many of us experience life as less than perfect due to cellular memory and due to what we choose to focus on in each »now« moment. Since cells, to use the metaphor of Dr. Deepak Chopra, are just memories clothed in matter, if we have had 1000 embodiments at an average of 30 years each, then we hold 30000 years of cellular information based on memory. So to delve into cellular memory without specific programming can keep us busy for eons. Whatever we focus upon grows and becomes our reality. Therefore, if we seek to know our true selves – to experience limitlessness – then the most logical approach would be to focus on our limitless Divine Self.

I term the above a »baseline« program and it is designed to achieve what we wish to create. Programs can be long-term or short-term. The latter are used to achieve a specific result. However, after re-programming, we also need to be vigilant with our thoughts – choosing only to accept thinking that is aligned with limitlessness.

A specific maintenance program for those already tuned and which is designed to keep us primed during busy times where we cannot always implement our »normal« or desired routine runs as follows (we call it programming for limitlessness): *»All my bodies are tuned, toned, fit and healthy. They vibrate, and also express themselves, in perfected and synchronistic harmony to the beat of the Mother/Father Creator God. This is truth whether I eat, sleep, exercise or meditate.«* This program overrides the »self-talk tape«

that we continually run about the above habits and any guilt or limiting thoughts we may have about e.g. our eating, sleeping, exercising, meditation *or other* habits. If you are already programming, insert your own agendas. The above program simply overrides beliefs that we are only in our power if we do certain things like »eat right« or meditate etc.

One of the challenges in manifestation – after aligning our will with the »bigger picture« (Divine Will) – is *timing*. No doubt many have also found that just because you are in alignment doesn't mean things will manifest when you expect them to. There are often other pieces (and people) of the puzzle yet to be revealed, created, manoeuvred into position etc. I have been using the following program with great success as it allows for a guaranteed perfect, step by step, aligned unfoldment. It also allows everything to unfold fluidly, in Divine Time: »*I ask that my next perfect piece/step in the Divine Blueprint clearly reveal itself to me and bring to me now both the resources and the perfect players that share in the creation and implementation of this blueprint so that it can be physically made manifest NOW*«. As many are now aware, we are now undergoing a »group initiation« where we are learning to work harmoniously together on this physical plane. This program also calls forth the right people (those who share in the manifestation of our piece of the blueprint) for us to be working with to make our visions manifest now.

For those who work with, or who understand, simultaneous time patterns, the following program allows us to re-access our past and future gifts to empower ourselves in the fulfilment of our pre-agreed piece of the »bigger plan«: »*I instruct my I AM Presence to bring to my conscious awareness all talents, gifts and information from all past, present and future lives that are relevant and that will empower me further in the fulfilment of my piece of the Divine Blueprint upon this physical plane NOW.*«

Those who are interested in eventually being sustained purely from light, may begin the conversion process which will gently allow the body to be nourished from the etheric realms (prana) rather than from the atmospheric realms (food): »*I command the full attention and presence of my body consciousness. I command that from this now moment you absorb all the vitamins, nutrients and nourishment required to maintain peak physical health – from the pranic forces!«*

Increasing Consciousness with Programming

By Eltrayan

The human brain consists of 100 billion neurones, each of which forms networks with groups of up to 50,000 other neurones. Human consciousness involves the firing of a network system of neurones. Not all the neurones in the network fire each time, but when they do, they fire at 40 cycles per second, on the beat.

The neural networks are created by life's experiences. Consequently, the environment influences the brain. Neural maps – such as vision, speech, etc. – are imprinted in childhood. The basic maps must be created by certain stages of development or they do not form at all. Young brains are very elastic, but by the age of ten, the brain has been hard-wired to a large extent.

The process of refinement of our brain's neural connections is constant and the changes can be both destructive and constructive. A very effective procedure for the deliberate shaping of these neural maps, to create the life model that you desire, is termed »programming«.

Programming is the repetition of a specific request until a neural map has been formed, which then provides the construction of the reality of what was desired. The period of time necessary to succeed varies, but instant results should not be expected. The practice should be continued until intuition guides you that it is no longer necessary. *The greatest care must be taken with both the content of the request and the choice of words, since the result will literally mirror the statement that you make.* The form of the words used may be a humble request, or an instruction or command. The request may be directed to whatever higher power you recognise. If in doubt, addressing the Spiritual Hierarchy is advised. To assist in remembering to program each day, the repetition may be done when regular daily tasks are undertaken, for instance, when showering.

Programming is an extremely powerful tool. It has been used with success under various titles in the past, but it has rarely been pursued with the vigour and focus of concentration required to be very effective.

One beneficial program is for the release and elimination of negative and harmful memories from your physical, emotional, mental, and spiritual bodies. Traditionally, this would have been applied only to your present and past lives. *A significant recent insight is to include future lives.* As you are a multidimensional being, future events feed into your present condition. This simple addition to programming has provided remarkable results and is highly recommended.

To appreciate why future lives should be incorporated into your programming, consider that wizards or seers are said to live backwards in time. This is a difficult concept to grasp and requires an outline of how an increase in consciousness involves an alteration of time perception.

Time is simply another aspect of activity, motion, or dynamics, in the guise of a symbol. It denotes the amount of activity of a definite unit, using space as a background. This makes possible the correlating of events and the bringing of order into the universe. There can be no time without motion, nor motion without time, and neither without thought.

If human existence is considered as consisting of seven dimensions, then sequential time, as we normally understand it, exists up to the third level of the fourth dimension.

As a consequence of new planetary alignments in our galaxy which took place in 1987 – referred to as the Harmonic Convergence – the anchoring of higher rays were made possible by our planet's, and humanity's, access to the central sun of the galaxy, rather than being limited to the sun of our solar system. In early 1991, the Earth's and humanity's fourth dimensional circuitry was completed. Humanity is thus on the lowest level of the fourth dimension, which is the last dimension of physicality.

Beyond the third level of the fourth dimension, the rate of speed of consciousness makes the concept of an »eternal now« comprehensible. When this is understood, the clearing of problems from future lives is thus logical and helps enhance our progress.

The failure to release the negative and harmful memories of future lives is a major reason why certain unwanted conditions resist action which would be reasonably expected to resolve them. Any habit alterations sought – overeating, smoking, any of the variety of current addictions – should have this programming included to assist in their successful resolution.

Suggested programming statement: *»With the power of the intent of my Self, I humbly ask the Spiritual Hierarchy* to release and eliminate any negative and harmful memories from past, present and future lives from my physical, emotional, mental and spiritual bodies«.*

Be aware that once you are aligned with Divine Time and Divine Will and have no conflicting internal energies running, anything you envisage can be made manifest. Manifesting is easy, having a clear vision as to what you wish to make manifest requires a little more skill and forethought!

---

* You may wish to insert your own spiritual connection here.

Chapter 12

Understanding Stress and Stressors

Stress is an interactive process with forces that are applied to you and the effect of these forces. The result of *distress* is often felt as fatigue, anxiety, tension, and unpleasant feelings caused by an ongoing situation of either over-arousal or under-arousal and, if continued, can even result in death. In Western society signs of distress are often overeating, over-drinking, smoking and abuse of illegal or prescription drugs. *Eustress* generates positive emotions, excitement and even zest. Eustress is stress of a manageable level for short periods of time that gives spark and motivation.

In order to deal with distress effectively, we need to identify the main problem areas of stress in our lives and then apply self-help techniques that both deal with current stress effectively and also aid in the prevention of future stress.

In their book »Stress and You«, Dr. Bob Montgomery and Lynette Evans discuss a five factor stress model which covers the main causes of stress in society today. The five factor stress model is:

1. Stressors (the source of stress): The main stress we experience comes from feelings of uncertainty or lack of control (according to European research) and degrees of these feelings produce eustress or distress. Example – being uncertain about our job future, relationships or finances can cause distress. Too much certainty about one's job, relationships etc. can cause boredom and under-arousal and can also result in distress. Individuals in this position often counterbalance under-arousal (boredom) with over-arousal through risky sports etc. which also adds to distress. Individuals often increase distress through their imagination, i.e. over-reacting to a situation, imagining the worst, negative thinking, imagining future problems (anxiety), dwelling on past »mistakes« (self retribution and/or guilt). This leads to factor number two.

2. Thoughts – the effect of thinking and self-talk: Has an enormous effect on the level of either eustress or distress in our lives. This has been well-covered previously. To reiterate – we are governed by universal laws that relate to the nature of energy. Matter is energy and we are composed of matter – molecules closely bound by energy that gives the appearance of being solid. Thoughts are energy on a very subtle but powerful, unseen level. We cannot see thought energy but we can see its results. No action or event happens without thought from the human mind or Divine Intelligence. Our self-talk and thinking creates our beliefs, expectations and attitudes. Stressors from thinking often occur because:

a) We may see or interpret a situation as negative, unpleasant or harmful.

b) We may think we can or can't cope with the situation.

c) We may expect our inability to cope to have serious negative consequences.

Unrealistic or exaggerated thinking plays a major role in how a person handles stress. Regarding the ability to cope, I would like to point out at this point that we are never placed in a situation that we cannot cope with. In esoteric understanding, life on Earth can be likened to a school, a place of learning. We are trained through our experiences of life, learn a lesson and are then tested to see if we can move on to the next lesson and how well we have learnt the previous lesson. These lessons have usually to do with intangible things like trust, faith, empathy, compassion, humility, tolerance etc. which, having been learnt, allow us to be more in alignment with our perfect nature.

So if we undergo great stress through the loss of a job, or loved one, this is a lesson prechosen and designed to give great learning and consequent testing as to how well the lesson has been learnt. This is why if we choose to avoid a situation – e.g. we have four children and find the stress of parenthood and responsibility too trying and leave – we will attract to ourselves similar circumstances in this or another life as the lesson must be learnt, the test undergone, and then we can move on.

Readdressal of energy in the cosmic energy pool (karma) also comes into play, so a situation may not be a simple as it appears. The point is that because of our beliefs in limitation and underestimation of our innate abilities, we often feel overwhelmed in times of trial. But the knowledge that no test is given to us that we have not been well-prepared for can be quite comforting. Suicide rates would see a marked decrease if this were well understood. In simple terms, if we weren't ready, we would not be sitting the exam! Just because we lack confidence in our ability to perform and pass doesn't mean we don't have the knowledge or training to do so! Back to the five factor stress model ...

3. Physiological response and change: Often called the general adaptation syndrome (GAS) – this response of the body to stress can be categorised as follows: firstly the *alarm reaction* – increase in blood pressure, heart rate and blood flow to, and tension in, the voluntary muscles resulting in the fight or flight syndrome e.g. an over-demanding boss or undemanding job that we feel we can't leave due to financial commitments etc. When we can't behave aggressively to vent frustration, then we require a constructive, well-thought out mental response to relieve the physical and emotional symptoms of distress. If this is unresolved, it will lead to the second phase called the *resistance stage,* where the body tries to maintain the higher rate of running activated in the alarm reaction stage and burns up energy trying. Repeated or prolonged exposure releases hormonal chemicals such as cortisol and adrenaline, which weaken the immune system and increase the risk of blood clots and hardening of the arteries. Cholesterol is a hormone released under stress.

Modern stressors create physiological change and, when prolonged and repeated, physical damage. Stress in survival used to trigger the alarm reaction and was quickly dealt with as the danger passed. With industrialisation, urbanisation, automation and technological innovation, stressors are now generally more long-term as people experience uncertainty and lack of control. Physical disease is triggered as a consequence of stress (mental stress, stress on the body through inadequate diet, lack – or excess

– of exercise, emotional stress from unresolved negative emotions etc.). Psychosomatic illnesses are no longer separated from other illnesses as the negative effects on the body are identical. The next GAS stage is the *exhaustion stage* where the body's resources are so depleted that collapse – i.e. a nervous breakdown – is imminent.

4. Feelings and emotional response to a stressor: This includes eustress – happiness, excitement, joy, exhilaration – and distress – unhappiness, depression, fear, anxiety etc. As covered in discussions on the power of emotion, most people believe feelings are triggered by events beyond their control. Yet it is not the event that brings an emotional response, but how we think about it. We are not victims of automatic emotional responses. Feelings are a learned response to a particular situation. Previous experiences and repeated exposure fashion »automatic« responses. Changes in heart rate, blood pressure etc. are controlled by the nervous system which functions autonomously, so these responses are classified as automatic. We are, however, built to think before we feel.

We seek recourse to short-term solutions, like overindulging in food and drink, to suppress unpleasant feelings. But these »solutions« are, in the long term, damaging to our health and do not address the basic problem – our conditioned and learned responses to a problem. These conditioned responses again come from past lives, our childhood and previous experiences, and are held in cellular memory.

5. Behavioural choices: Basically, individuals choose fight or flight, aggression or escape. Active aggression provides no long-term resolution and is generally ineffective. A constructive strategy is one which leads to a win-win situation, where all the parties needs are considered and met. The win-win scenario is effective as it creates both short and long-term resolution and avoids repeated confrontation with the same issue. Passive aggression – sulking, withdrawal, being silent – is equally ineffective for long-term resolution of behavioural tensions.

»The Celestine Prophecy« by James Redfield, covers the roles we often adopt as a response to our parents« character (victim, interrogator, intimidator or aloof or a combination of these) in interesting detail and analyses the need we have to be free of the limitations of conditioned and habitual behavioural patterns. To be free we have to be willing to understand and then change. Sometimes we have to face up to short-term bad feelings for the sake of working out long-term genuine solutions.

The five factors outlined above interact and influence each other. Life is not static because we are energy systems and in constant dynamic flux. The only constant thing in life is change! To grow and evolve we have to learn to be flexible, especially if we would like to improve the quality of life.

Chapter 13

Practical Techniques to De-stress

This chapter will recommend practical tools for positive change that, when practised regularly, will:

a) Improve health, vitality and feelings of general well-being.

b) Improve the ability to cope in stressful situations.

c) Promote peace and tranquillity in life.

d) Promote better problem-solving skills.

e) Release, and effectively deal with, negative emotions in a more constructive manner.

f) Open us further to inner guidance.

g) Prevent negative reactions and the effects of future stress.

Yoga relaxes the mind and body, as does meditation and creative visualisation, but we need to become conscious of our thinking and conditioned emotional responses. We have, as previously mentioned, four lower bodies – the physical, emotional, mental and spiritual. We also have a pure energy force that sustains us and which is expressed through the energy fields of these bodies. Feeling complete, fulfilled and whole as human beings occurs when the energy fields of these bodies are balanced and operating in harmony with each other to their full potential.

Before we compartmentalise ourselves and look at solutions to achieve not just points a) to g) above, but to also unify the energy fields of our bodies, I suggest the following exercise: *Examine and break all habits.* Do this for a day, a week or however long it takes. Stop all habitual behaviour, good or bad. When you have looked at and honestly examined each habit, asked yourself why you do it. Is it because parents, society, peers expect it or taught you to act or feel in this manner? How many behaviour patterns have you adopted because your parents did them and their parents before them? Have you stopped and thought if those choices (given the current state of affairs on a personal and social level and taking personally accumulated knowledge into consideration) are still valid to you? Then decide that you will discard that habit or continue with it for no other reason than because it is your choice and it feels good to you.

I will use the eating of meat as an example because it is one of the most densifying substances that we can ingest on our vibrational frequency. (It has been my personal experience that the finer tuned our vibrational frequency, the finer and better quality our life experiences).

Many of us eat meat simply because it has been fed to us from birth. If we had to go and slaughter, skin and gut an animal to prepare for food, many of us would seriously consider other well-known alternatives as a protein source. These comments are made not in judgement, but as a reference for how we often continue choices that may not be in our best interest simply because we have not stopped to question other alternatives. Many choices are simply habitual.

If we wish to improve the quality of our lives, we should stop all our habits, and after an in-depth analysis, accept only those that we find to be the most positive for us. This would be a great start.

We have looked at the effect of emotions, thoughts and words, and chapters 14 and 15 will cover in depth the benefits of meditation and how to cleanse the energy fields of our bodies for a more powerful experience of meditation. These chapters and the chapter on vibrational frequencies, plus the creative visualisations recommended, will also aid in achieving points a) to g) above.

The breath technique and white light visualisation (creative visualisation 1) at the end of chapter 7 will also give positive long-term results for points a), b) and c) but will need to be practised daily to be used as a preventive measure for future distress.

In my experience, lack of self-knowledge, through lack of solitude and contemplation, as well as feelings of lack of self-worth are major contributing factors to stress in society today. Many people – this is especially true of women in our society – are well-conditioned to cater to the needs of lovers, children, family and friends, yet spend very little quality time in their own company without external distraction.

I would like to recommend that every night before bed we »tune« ourselves via breath work and then have a good talk to ourselves. This is taking the time to honour ourselves by listening and giving ourselves undivided attention as we do to lovers and children or anyone we care about. When we routinely take time to listen to others, especially if they seem disturbed, it allows us to keep communication open and free-flowing. This technique of self-acknowledgement, self-talk and listening promotes both better sleep and better health as we become more in touch with what we really think and feel, and it also aids in the promotion of inner guidance.

As a society we are conditioned to think that talking to yourself is a sign of dementia and is to be discouraged, and yet if we stopped really talking, listening and giving our undivided attention to our loved ones what would happen to our relationships? Surely *our relationship with ourselves is just as important.* We should follow the advice of Socrates and strive to know ourselves – not just the superficial likes and dislikes of lower mind, but the true being that resides within, beyond the persona, beyond the mask.

To elaborate further on the idea that how we think or perceive something determines how we feel, I have listed six steps to feeling better by thinking clearer. (I feel that all life situations are here to serve, teach and inspire us. The term »bad« refers to feelings that we are having and would rather not have, and I use this term without judgement).

1. When you have strong or prolonged bad feelings, don't deny them: Accept that these feelings are natural, but know that if they are left unresolved they will create dis-ease. These emotions need to be dealt with quickly and effectively so that energy blockages in the electromagnetic fields of the body do not occur. By learning to identify the nature and intensity of the feeling we can then decide on how best to resolve it.

2. Accept that you can cope with bad feelings: We have had bad feelings in the past. They are now in the past, just as the current ones soon will be. Feelings pass. If we can't change a situation that is triggering the feeling, we *can always* change your attitude. For example, a person who has had an accident could react along these lines: »Poor me. Why did it have to happen to me? What have I done to deserve this? It's not fair etc.«, and have feelings of self-pity, depression, general negativity, sadness, anger, frustration etc. Or, the person could think: »Thank God I'm alive. Life is wonderful. I'm so glad that no one was killed. My wounds will heal. Every day I'm getting stronger and better«, and have feelings of relief, appreciation, joy at being alive, joy at being given another chance, patience, determination to get better etc.

Thoughts are energy. Just as negativity perpetuates negativity and illness, when the mind expects the body to heal, it does. Denying or ignoring negative feelings perpetuates them. Accepting their validity and then choosing to deal with the feelings – and thoughts that gave rise to the feelings – in a constructive manner will improve the situation and allow the feelings to dissipate naturally. As we choose positive thoughts, mental relaxation occurs automatically, and as we change our self-talk, our feelings automatically respond in line with, and in response to, our thinking.

3. Reward yourself through self-praise and congratulations: We should Indulge in positive self-talk about how well we've coped or handled a situation. If we slip up, we should just accept it and resolve to do better the next time. We are apprentices in mind mastery and occasional errors and misjudgements are acceptable to anyone in training. Events are only errors when we refuse to learn from them. We learn then move onto the next lesson, we only keep on making »the same mistake« when we haven't learnt our lesson.

Rewarding ourselves builds self-esteem and reinforces the conviction that we can cope and do well. *Seek approval of ourselves, not others* – breaking habits and quiet contemplation allow us to set standards that are right for us rather than what others expect. If we take small steps, set realistic goals and give ourselves lots of self-praise and encouragement, one day we will feel the limitlessness of our own being, that we can do anything when our intention is for the highest good – not just of others, but also ourselves.

4. Identify self-talk: When we feel bad, we should become conscious about what we are thinking – a lot of thinking is habitual and without basis and can be a preset response that makes us feel we are not thinking anything. Remember, all feelings are based in a thought or perception. By writing down what we are thinking when we are feeling »bad«, we will become aware of how thoughts influence intensity of feeling.

5. Test self-talk: Many thought patterns are self-defeating (as are words and actions) and habitual and need to be broken. Nagging is like a broken record played over and over. Self-flagellation and negative talk are the same and reinforce limitation, fears and self-doubt. Retrospective regret and phrases like »If only«, »I should have«, »I could have«, »Why didn't I?,« etc. are unproductive. Passing judgement through retrospective reflection is very disempowering. When we are completely honest with ourselves, we will usually find that given who we were at the time, or given the information or knowledge we possessed, we did our best or what we felt to be our best. Very rarely do individuals set out to inflict pain or discord upon each other unless they themselves are suffering on some level.

Developing a strong connection to inner guidance keeps us on the »right« track and minimises self-retribution as we tune to the flow of the bigger picture and manage to be in the right place at the right time. This is really just hooking up with the universal Law of Grace (synchronicity). We can learn to be in a point of centredness and clarity, doing the best we can given all the facets of a situation. This gives freedom from self-recrimination. How much of our thinking and self-talk is a carryover from childhood? How much is still valid for the person we are today? We can create new habits, new thinking patterns, based on who we now are and what is really working and relevant in our life now. So we need to:

6. Teach ourselves to think rationally: Who determines if thinking is reasonable – society or us? Do we live to please society, or ourselves, or can we do both by honouring both? If our lives are abundant on all levels, then we have succeeded in mind mastery and graduated from our apprenticeship. If we feel any lack or discord, then perhaps we can examine our thought processes and how they serve us or disempower us. We reap what we sow. In order, then, to fulfil points a) to g) at the beginning of this chapter, we need to take full responsibility for all our thoughts, words and actions.

7. *Learn to think in an unlimited manner:* Indulge in our imagination! Energy follows thought and thought then creates. What sort of reality do we wish to create? If we have not allowed our imagination and thinking free reign, we will not have vision. Without vision we will not know what to change or evolve into. Dreams and vision allow humanity to keep evolving into the remembrance of perfection.

In the book »Creating Money – Keys to Abundance« by Sanaya Roman and Duane Packer, the authors explain, »Since your thoughts create your reality, you can create an even better life for yourself by learning to think in bigger and unlimited ways. Unlimited thinking increases creativity, expands your possibilities, draws opportunities to you and allows you to have more. Unlimited thinking lets you experience in advance the feelings you will have when you have received the abundance you want, and these feelings are the vehicle that brings abundance to you. Use these visions to open your mind to greater possibilities.«

Also from the same book: »To unfold your potential you will want to imagine having your dreams come true, for your dreams and fantasies are showing you your potential. Your dreams are there for a reason; they are guiding you to your higher path here on Earth. Enlarge your vision of what is possible for you to do. Dare to dream and think big.« A further excerpt of interest from the same text: »Your imagination is greater in its scope than you might think. It is the closest link to your soul. It is not bound by your past programs, beliefs and fears. Imagination was given to you so you could transcend your physical world. It gives you the ability to step outside of your personal limits and unleash your greatest potential. Your imagination can travel into any dimension or world. It can create unlimited future pathways for you and help you look at the possible outcomes of various choices.«

So we need to learn to think in terms of possibilities not impossibilities, to go beyond the boundaries of what we think we can have. If you can't believe something, then it won't be possible. You cannot create a thing if you cannot picture having it. So give yourself permission to dream, to fantasise, to imagine how you would like your life to be and what you can do to create it. Hold this vision in your mind, empower it with desire then you will recognise the opportunities as they present themselves to you. If you have no vision, you will not recognise opportunities. Energetically, it is simply opening up your antenna to receive transmission signals from other stations.

Creative Visualisation 3
Creating the Inner Sanctuary

This visualisation exercise is designed to create inner peace and tranquillity so that we can de-stress positively and naturally. It works with the breath, white light and also our visualisation capacity.

Creating this special sanctuary and spending daily time there will circumvent the need for a holiday from our hectic lives and is a powerful, quick de-stress technique when we utilise it. Spending ten minutes every day in this sanctuary will act as a preventive tool for the accumulation of stress and its negative effects. When we have practised and can easily access this place, and its inherent feelings of peace and calm, we can simply instruct ourselves to be there at any time.

In traffic, at work, whenever we begin to feel the body tense up, we can simply close our eyes, imagine ourselves to be there, take a swim in the »healing pool« or a shower in the magical, healing waterfall and feel the stress flow out of us. As we perfect this technique it can serve as a »pick me up« and is very powerful when used regularly.

Remember, the mind cannot tell the difference between an actual event and a powerful visualisation! Consequently, the benefits of being in this imaginary inner sanctuary will be as great as if we actually were there.

Every day that we access it, we can build on it, making it more beautiful, more powerful. We may wish to add halls of learning and wisdom for us to access higher learning and to meet guides etc. Remember the imagination is vast and limitless, and if utilised correctly today, will create a powerful tomorrow.

Deep breathing and counting down slowly is a form of self-hypnosis that allows us to tune our brain waves from beta to alpha to theta – the state of deep relaxation just prior to sleep.
· When beginning to create this place, give yourself practice time and get comfortable where you won't be disturbed.

- Tune yourself with the breath and light work.
- When relaxed, imagine yourself to be standing on a mountain, and now in front of you, see steps leading downwards.
- As you step down, begin to also count backwards (ten to zero), and between each count take one full inhale and one connected exhale.
- Let yourself relax deeper and deeper as you count, with each step down you feel lighter and freer, knowing that you are about to enter a special, safe place.
- 10 ... breathe in and out ... 9 ... breathe in and out ... 8 ... breathe in and out ... 7 ... 6 ... 5 ....4 ... 3 ... 2 ... 1 ... 0 ...
- As you reach the ground you feel deeply relaxed. Take a few deep, fine, connected breaths.
- Look around you, open up and utilise all your inner senses.
- You see that you are in a most beautiful sanctuary, a place that is yours alone, where you feel completely safe, at peace, nurtured and loved. This is your internal »cubbyhouse« like the one children have to enact their games and »fantasies«
- Let your mind wander: »See« the trees and the flower beds. »See« yourself picking a flower and holding it to your nose. »Smell« its fragrance (allow your sense of smell to be activated).
- Listen to birds singing or the wind rustling in the trees.
- You scoop water from a running stream and bring it to your lips to »taste« and refresh your thirst.
- You »feel« the sun on your skin, the wind in your hair.
- Pause for a moment, allow higher mind to create this inner sanctuary. Remember this is your place. You can create it to be whatever you wish – there are no limitations to your vision here.
- Take a few deep, fine, connected breaths. Allow yourself to bathe in the beauty of this place. If you could have a place of physical perfection how would it be? A beach, a rainforest, valleys and streams or a mountain top? Recall a time where you felt free, at peace, somewhere safe in nature – build on this memory.

- Perhaps you wish to create a magnificent dome or pyramid of light over this sanctuary – or a high wall of crystal or a vine-covered wall so you can feel safer.
- Perhaps the sky in this inner world is always tinged with the colours of dusk, of sunset.
- Perhaps you have wonderful beings who impart great wisdom or love or healing to you here.
- Again, this is your place. Create it according to the desires and dictates of your own heart and inner vision.
- Keep your breathing fine, deep and connected as you use your imagination to create. Create so that you *feel* intense joy, beauty, safety, peace, so that you feel that this place is just for you and you can let go of all the cares of your day to day life here. Here there is no responsibility except for you to feel wonderful – no kids, no mortgage, no bills, no pressure – just freedom, love and acceptance. This is a place where you can go to assess your life and learn to recreate it the way you wish it to be.

Many people who create this inner sanctuary report that, after practice, they can access it immediately by thinking »my place.« This triggers them to be there and if they feel stressed, they can release any stress virtually immediately by realigning themselves in the energy field of this inner sanctuary – like a shower on a hot day, it refreshes them instantaneously. They know that they are safe here and respond immediately to the memory association.

Chapter 14

Meditation – Integral Applications

Grace Cooke in »The Jewel In the Lotus« writes, »What we are working for and achieving in meditation is the spiritualisation of matter rather than the materialisation of spirit. In meditation every individual soul can reach the source of Truth and experience the reality of spirit for him/herself. With the development of man's intellect in this Aquarian Age, any material proof can easily be destroyed by the critical mind; but a conviction based on experience deep in the heart can never be shaken.«

Meditation is an ancient practice used for thousands of years to relax the physical body, calm the emotions, still the mind and open us up to the spiritual realms and higher understanding. Many are aware at this time of a need for something more in life, beyond material comfort or financial success. Once we have satisfied the needs of the »lower mind« for survival, we then begin to answer the inner call of the higher mind, seeking answers to questions concerning the purpose of existence.

Meditation and spending time daily within the Great Silence is the most powerful way we can tune to the God within and also to access our Divine Blueprint. As discussed previously, this blueprint holds not only the true purpose of life and information regarding our destiny but also the Greater Plan for all humanity at this time – the »script« of the play one could say.

As human beings, we are aware of the five physical senses that we use to explore the external world: our senses of sight, smell, taste, touch and hearing. Through these senses we have very powerful and real experiences because we utilise them for long periods every day. Similarly, we can activate our »inner« senses which are subtle counterparts to the five outer senses plus our sixth sense of *intuition* and our seventh sense of *knowing*. Meditation or contemplation with these inner senses allows us to fully tune to the inner realms, but takes practice. Many people expect to immediately have the same depth of experience on the inner planes as they do the outer, forgetting that they have had years of practice developing their senses to experience the latter.

The inner senses have been called the »super senses« and come into play when we have the following experiences:

- Clairaudience – higher and lower* telepathic communication.
- Clairvoyance – higher and lower* divine vision and realisation.
- Imagination, intuition, discernment, discrimination.
- Response to vibrations such as psychometry or tuning to another's energy fields.
- Being able to manipulate or clean and realign energy fields.
- Healing abilities using energy fields.

Simplistically, our lives may be likened to a TV channel. We all know that being tuned to receive a particular channel doesn't mean that other channels don't exist. Meditation and accessing the inner realms is simply learning how to access other channels. It allows us to move beyond our limited thinking. It's as if a whole community have only watched one channel because they thought that was all there was. Then some discover other channels, either accidentally (e.g. out of body and near death experiences) or through consciously changing their frequency. When first we begin to retune the TV to pick up the other stations, there is often initially some static or the picture may fade in and out. With persistence and perseverance this »inner« channel or alternate selection becomes clear and easy to tune to or access.

The key to switching to the other channels is a sincere heart and the desire to know. A clear picture comes with discipline and dedication.

The wonderful thing about changing channels is that once you can easily access them, you realise that not only can you decide

---

*»Higher« and »lower« here refer to vibrational frequencies. The purer the channel, the purer the communication, as like attracts like. Many people bring forth messages from the fourth dimensional astral plane (lower) and others concentrate on information from the fifth dimensional frequencies and above (higher).

what to screen, you can also create the programs themselves, and so it goes on. Better still, is that you can flick back and forth across channels at will, and if a program you have created on one channel would benefit all the viewers of another channel, you can bridge across stations and allow everyone to benefit (assuming certain pre-agreed rules are adhered to, which are universal laws). The more you create programs which accord with the Divine Blueprint, the more viewers of the other channels can benefit, if they choose.

Accessing the Divine Blueprint channel is also like accessing the video library of programs where each video in the library has the name of the viewing individual. When you wish to, you will find the library and your video and view it. *This is called finding our destined role in life.* It is held within your cellular memory. This »video« inspires you, instructs you, and allows you to »learn your lines« and bring that knowledge back to your day to day life and inspire others to go find their own video.

When your senses are fine-tuned, you will be able to access the universal records and higher wisdom quite readily. Telepathic communication, the ability to heal, bi-location etc. are then perfectly natural experiences.

There are many valuable meditation techniques that, when regularly practised, will achieve deep and lasting change. In essence, meditation is pure and perfect concentration on a pure and perfect point. It is the merging of our complete being with the God within – a state of BEingness and perfection.

Dr. Deepak Chopra says that »the only consistent, reliable way to break the spell of maya (worldly illusion) is to transcend to that level of awareness from which thoughts emerge«. He goes on to say that he relies on »meditation as the effective and reliable means to consistently go and transcend to that level from where all reality comes – to go to the background of non-change from where all change emerges«. He defines meditation as the art of turning the mind to its own source, to the field of silence. When the mind is left to its own devices, it spontaneously wants to go there. He then goes onto explain that our mind has many layers, from the conscious and subconscious to more abstract layers behind the fully verbalised thoughts, desires and concepts. Beyond that is pure consciousness or awareness – the energy that sustains us.

Daily meditation keeps us clean, free from attachments and negativity, tuned to a different frequency than that of our limited beliefs. It allows us access to our multidimensional nature and to fine-tune and control the signals we emit and consequently control our life experiences, creating reality as we desire it to be.

Meditation is essential to build a bridge from the physical world to the spiritual realms so that we can gain clear access to highest wisdom and true knowledge. It is then important for us to allow this wisdom and knowledge to manifest in our daily lives. This bridge has been referred to as the »rainbow bridge« or the »antakarana«. The antakarana is a filament of light that is created life after life and is energised and strengthened by spiritual vibrations. This bridge is built through meditation, spiritual work and endeavour, motivated purely by our desire for higher knowing. It allows us to bring the finer energies of the spiritual realms back to the physical plane, thus transforming reality as we know it.

If we were issued with an invitation to meet the creator of the universe, and *knew* it to be legitimate, how reverently would we approach this meeting? I like to approach meditation with the same respect and reverence. To me, each time I go within I am seeking to contact and merge with my God essence. Consequently, I recommend that you prepare for this occasion as follows:

· *Create a special place* where you can be undisturbed. You may like to have special cushions or a meditation blanket or rug used just for this purpose. Make the environment special, perhaps with incense and candles, both of which aid in changing the vibrational frequency of the room. Perhaps you could play very soft music suited to meditation or relaxation. Wear comfortable clothing. Make sure that the room temperature is agreeable.

· *Meditate regularly* every day, if possible at the same time morning and night, for at least half an hour to gain lasting benefit. One piano lesson per week or five minutes practice per day does not a concert pianist make, nor a master of anything. As with anything, the more effort or attention applied, the better the result.

- *Use breathing techniques and white light* as the basis for all meditation / contemplation work.

- *Use a specific hand position (mudra)* to symbolise your intention to meditate. Sit in a comfortable position that allows your attention to remain focussed within rather than be distracted by physical discomfort. Sitting in your special place, setting the scene, using mudras etc. signals to your inner being that you are about to begin meditation, just as showering, brushing your teeth, getting into your pyjamas etc. signals to the body you are going to go to bed.

- *Take the phone off the hook.* Put the answering machine on. Put a »do not disturb« sign on the door. Train the other members of the household to *respect your meditation time* and honour your desire for external quiet. Buy the TV watchers headphones and ask them to wear them for the time you wish to meditate so that you may be free of the distraction of noise. Lord Buddha said that you should be so connected to the internal realms that you could sit beside a road with a thousand bullocks passing by and not even notice or be disturbed. However, in the initial stages, less distraction is better.

- *Have a pen and notebook ready* in case you have a great inspiration and wish to recall it later: Jotting down a point will allow you to move on without fear of forgetting. This is especially relevant in times of contemplation/programming.

- *Meditate when you are wide awake and not sleepy.* Morning meditations are often preferable as night can see us sleepy. If possible, indulge in meditation without the constraint of time for one morning every week, when you do not have to rush off anywhere. This will allow the journey to be much deeper and/or will allow time for reprogramming or accessing inner vision. Imagine finally having accessed your true life purpose, the vision is unfolding in all its glory, guidance is flowing and suddenly the alarm clock rings! Your 15 or 30 minutes is up and you have to go to work!

The Seven Basic Applications

What we classify as meditation, can be compartmentalised into seven basic applications, all of which will increase and promote inner peace and tranquillity. They are of equal importance, and can be listed as follows:

1. Tuning.
2. Increasing or opening up to inner guidance.
3. De-programming and re-programming.
4. Accessing our inner vision and Divine Blueprint.
5. Dream control and guidance.
6. Accessing cellular memory.
7. Experiencing unconditional love, joy and bliss.

1. The first aspect or »use« of meditation can be for tuning:

Realigning our frequency and controlling the signals we, as energy systems, transmit. Working with breath techniques, sonic waves and white light energy allows us to:

a) De-stress naturally and easily.

b) Increase or create feelings of deep inner peace and tranquillity.

a) Increase the quotient of light into our energy fields.

b) Cleanse all cellular structure of dross, pollutants, negative emotions or memory.

c) Heal cellular structure (adding techniques of creative visualisation also allow us to realign and cleanse our emotional body and eliminate negative emotional baggage).

d) Regenerate cells, creating vibrant radiant health.

e) Create an electromagnetic shield of protection around our being.

f) By working with our chakras, we can also bi-locate and communicate telepathically.

The most recommended tuning technique is the one discussed previously where specific breathing and white light energies are combined. If you have unlimited time each day for meditation then all applications – one to seven – can be practised as desired. If however you have only 15 to 30 minutes in the morning, the tuning techniques and maybe a different creative visualisation to achieve points a) to e) each day is probably the best strategy. Leave bi-location to when you have no time constraints.

2. The second use of meditation is for opening us up to our inner guidance:

The best way to open up to inner guidance is through being silent, tuning ourselves by breath, mantras and white light, and *asking*. Since we have free will, *no guidance will be given unless it is requested.* This is universal law. As Jesus said, »Ask and you shall receive!«. Once we have stilled our minds by tuning, we can then ask for guidance and must learn to *listen.* It has been an aspect of Western society for people to always seek answers outside of themselves – to look to parents, peers, churches or governments to dictate how we should live our lives. However, if we accept the premise that no one knows us like we do, and that we hold in cellular memory all the answers to all our questions, then perhaps we should go within and open up to these answers. If life is not currently fulfilling our every expectation, then exploration of the inner realms will be most beneficial!

I have always held the vision of a lost child (the ego/personality in physical form) caught in the wonderment of the world (life on Earth) who one day wishes to go home (reunification with the divine being within) but can't remember the way. The parent (the I Am Presence or monad) has been watching, knowing that the child needed to explore and knowing that it could not offer assistance until the child acknowledged being lost and *asked* for help. When the child does this, it is a great joy for the parent, who with other loved ones (guides and/or guardian angels etc.) prepares a wondrous welcome home party and gives as much attention and aid as is accepted by the child until it is safely home again (fully awakened to the Oneness of creation).

Under the heading of inner guidance also comes *prayer*, and/or begging, as we often seem to do in our more desperate times!

Seeking inner guidance is learning to ask, being still, and listening for inner guidance from our Higher Self, I Am Presence or monad. Guidance from guides and telepathic communication employ the same techniques and are covered in detail on the chapter on telepathic communication.

3. The third aspect of meditation is being able to de-program and re-program:

This is a most valuable part of our meditation/contemplation time as it allows us to *play and erase inner tapes* and allow us to create the reality we desire. This is the time for using affirmations, mind mastery, de-programming and freeing ourselves from negative or limited belief systems and reprogramming the new reality we wish to create as we access our inner vision and destiny. Having understood the power of our thoughts, plus spending time in contemplation where we assess all habitual patterns of thought and action, will allow us time to rewrite and input new programs to our conscious and subconscious memory databases. All we need to do is find a quiet place where we will not be interrupted, take the phone off the hook, tune ourselves and sit and think – look at all aspects of our lives, assess them one by one. Have pen and paper handy, make a list.

We can start with the *physical* body. Let us, as detached as we can be, honestly look at our physical being. What can we change? How would we like it to be? Are our dietary habits positive and life-sustaining? Is our dietary intake merely habitual? Are there better choices we can make that are less harmful to us, to the planet, to animal life? Remember that, unless we are masters of transmutation, meat keeps our vibration very dense and it is possible for humanity to exist on light and prana alone as covered in detail in my »Pranic Nourishment« book.

For those wishing to change dietary habits, allow the change to be gradual and loving, without denial. First eliminate red meat. Then, as guided, stop eating white meat, and then aim to simply eat light, live food. Eventually you may find yourself being given inner guidance to allow only light or prana to nourish your physical body. However, this will not be possible unless you believe it to be. Seek inner guidance as to what you can do to free up the flow of energy within. It has been said that disease, death and decay are caused by stopping the flow of light at some point in the four lower bodies of man.

Next we look at the *emotional* body – the quality of our human relationships. Are they habitual? Are they positive or negative? Can they be improved? What lessons have we learnt, or do we still need to learn? Do we need to, or want to, heal and forgive? When you begin this exercise, your parent (the I AM Presence) will joyously volunteer all knowledge and inspiration required as reassessment and clearing on these levels makes the journey home easier. Many techniques are available to clear our emotional body and allow us to heal ourselves and our emotional relationships with others. Refer to the chapter on the power of our emotions plus the practical creative visualisation for healing relationships.

Then we can honestly *examine our self-talk and belief systems.* For example, politically, do we vote through choice and full knowledge, or do we vote as our parents do and as their parents did before them? Are we satisfied with life as we *perceive* it to be? We can change our perception and attitude and consequent reality.

This programming/contemplation time can be done each evening before sleep. We can then program that our dreams be clear and guide us according to what we wish to achieve from this contemplation and time of self analysis. How can we truly know ourselves if we never take time to be still and communicate with the real inner self? We are called human beings not human doings, but the majority of humanity is too busy doing to BE and know. This is what inspired John Lennon to say that life is what happens to you when you are busy making other plans. BEing allows for great KNOWing.

4. The fourth aspect is being able to access our inner vision and Divine Blueprint:

From my research, meditation experience and communication with the Ascended Ones, I have come to understand that we hold within ourselves our own unique Divine Blueprint. This blueprint holds not just our destined purpose and role at this time but also the Greater or Celestial Plan – the pre-laid destiny of humanity collectively. Consequently, we are attracted to each other like radar (according to the vibrations and signals we emit) so we can fulfil our roles in unison and harmony. Finding the »key« and accessing our roles is only done through the inner journey of self-knowledge. Everything we find ourselves attracted to and everything we undertake in life is part of our training and preparation for this role.

Our guidepost is joy. When we feel joy, we are on track. When we lose the joy, or it ceases, it is time to begin a new facet of training and maybe apply our energies elsewhere in the physical world. Joy is the one true sign that we are on our path, *for joy is Spirit expressing itself in our life.* When we have developed clear inner guidance, our lives blossom and manifest the full glory of who we are and our purpose. As we refine our being even further and become detached from the emotional body, our intention and motivation is for service alone – to work for the good of the whole and not just the individual. This is a natural part of our journey to Oneness and is covered in detail in the chapter on service.

5. The fifth use of meditation is to clear the slate for dreaming:

In the chapter on the power of emotion, I briefly mentioned the dream state and how we can cleanse our emotional body while we sleep. If we spend time in contemplation prior to sleep, talking to ourselves about our day or our life generally, the subconscious mind will have no need to bring to our attention – via dreams – all unresolved issues that we need to deal with. These will have been dealt with earlier and leaves the mind a clear slate so our dreaming can take a different form. While for many, our conscious awareness is limited to our day to day reality on this plane of existence, for others there is little separation between waking and dreaming while the physical body enjoys the sleep state.

When we are asleep the conscious mind is out of the way. We can then automatically tune to higher channels with absolute ease. There are dimensions within dimensions, and many other realms of existence to be explored during our dream time. In his book »The Complete Ascension Manual«, Dr. Joshua David Stone says that there are three main stages on the spiritual path. The first he calls the Hall of Ignorance where people identify only with the material world and where the five senses are always oriented outward. The second is the Hall of Learning where people go as they feel more restless and begin the search for the greater self. The third is the Hall of Wisdom which is where we gain identification with the spiritual self, expansion of consciousness and realisation. This learning occurs in the »dream« state usually between 10 p.m. and 5 a.m.

I have enjoyed countless experiences, vivid and detailed, of receiving in-depth training on various matters while in the dream state. Programming for full recall is advantageous when you wish for confirmation of this teaching. However, I am advised that all learning, knowledge and instruction is held on a cellular level and is revealed when needed. Many people are now recalling such experiences and are also finding themselves in situations where they open their mouth and share all this information, that someone just happens to require, and yet they didn't know they knew it!

6. A sixth use of meditation is to access cellular memory and inner knowledge of past training:

This is a flow-on from the above as all we need to fulfil our destined role is held within. We are the teacher, the trainer, the guide, the master, and all we need to do is reawaken and remember! Tuning ourselves, cleansing our beings of unwanted baggage (physical, emotional, mental and even spiritual limitations of belief), and asking for recall are like the polishing required for a rough diamond to reveal its true beauty. Spending quality time within the great silence of our inner being will allow this information to flow in as we ask and listen. This is why many people only have to spend short periods of learning or investigation before they feel they know it, as they have had intense training in other lives or other realms, and just need to reawaken their awareness of this knowledge.

I have also used the programming prior to sleep technique to access cellular memory and prior training with great success. For example, in relation to crystals ... one day I had been having some healing work with crystals used by a friend of mine. She had been guided to use a specific green crystalline wand which I found of great interest. For years I had collected crystals and books on crystals but had neither read the books or consciously utilised the crystals. No doubt until this point I had not been ready. I asked my friend about this green wand, which she handed to me. As she held one end and I held the other, I not only saw a bright and detailed »vision« of a past life she and I had shared, but I also knew that I had a vast amount of information about crystals and their power »stored« in me.

That night, prior to sleep, I tuned myself and asked my I AM God Self to reawaken all the knowledge I held within on crystals. So that night I woke intermittently – four times in all – and each time found I was being instructed and also felt »information« was flowing through my body. It was like information being retrieved from a computer file or database to the screen for viewing.

The topic was crystals, and at one point I recall asking how I would remember it all. Each time I woke I tried to recall consciously as much information as I could. I was advised, then and in all subsequent use of this technique for information retrieval, that all had been reawakened, was held in cellular memory closer to conscious recall, and would »flow out« as a situation required. I was told to trust that when the time was right, all would flow easily – and it has.

Many individuals share with me the experience of having information flow out of them at certain times that they felt they never really knew they possessed. This experience has happened to me so regularly with a various range of topics that it has become a simple way of accessing data held in cellular or subconscious memory.

Sometimes it is like you have to discover something on this plane which will consciously trigger a »knowing« which you can then desire to reawaken. Without the experience to act as a trigger, it may remain hidden.

Similarly, the night after I had been initiated into the healing modality of Reiki, I spent the whole night (while my physical body slept) on another »realm« using light energy and healing the electromagnetic grid lines through the bodies of many people. I remember they seemed to be lined up for miles and now and then I would stop for a physical body »bathroom break«. (A »trick« I was using then to ensure recall was to drink two or three glasses of water upon retiring so that the body would wake through discomfort. I would then record the information. As I have learned to trust and program better, full recall has become easier.) My body would rise and get out of bed, my consciousness half there and half in the »other realm.« I knew I was in both places and the healing continued all night.

A week or so previously I had completed the first degree of Reiki training and was aware that this was different. I asked what type of healing we (the other light beings who were with me and myself) were doing, and was told that it was different to Reiki as we were healing magnetically. Two weeks later, while being trained on the physical plane in the Kwan Yin method of Magnified Healing, I realised that these were exactly the same techniques I had been using during my sleep when healing in the »other realms«.

So where does one reality begin and another end? Can they overlap? The purpose of my mentioning the second story is that we often receive training in the schools of learning or the halls of wisdom while in the sleep state. This training is held in cellular memory to be utilised in our awakened state on the physical plane when we need it.

The practice of meditation makes us aware of our multidimensional nature. In other words, we not only have starring roles in the soap operas or news events on the channel of everyday reality, but we also simultaneously have starring roles on higher channels.

Until we begin to tune into the possibility, and then the reality, that these other channels exist, we will not be aware of the limitlessness and vastness of our multi-faceted nature. Being unaware of something does not mean it does not exist. These possibilities are discussed in the chapter on universal brotherhoods.

7. A seventh way to utilise meditation, is to experience unconditional love, joy and bliss:

One moment of feeling completely loved is powerful enough to create a lifetime addiction. The Siddhas call this state samadhi, a state of pure BEingness. This is a state we are led into after being showered with unconditional love and bliss. It is also a state of merging with the All That Is. It takes us beyond the senses, beyond meditation, and also beyond mental recollection. The only awareness to be had is the »lost time syndrome« – we disappear somewhere in deep meditation and afterwards recall intense feelings of love and bliss. We feel realigned, expanded and deeply peaceful.

One of the most predominant teachings I first gained in meditation was the deep realisation that I AM love, that I AM joy and that my pure, natural state of being is bliss. And that all emotions are within me and only »triggered« by external events. Until that time I felt that someone, or something else, was responsible for making me feel a certain way. Part of becoming self-empowered is realising that all is within us and that what is around us only serves as triggers, if we let them affect us. Meditation allows us to act rather than react as regular practice gives us the gift of detachment.

When we first have the experience of sitting in silence – away from distractions, with our eyes shut and with no external stimuli – and then begin to feel waves of love released from our inner being, it is an experience that is both overwhelming and awe inspiring. To feel completely safe, loved, honoured, accepted; to also feel so special as if the most benevolent, compassionate power has swept you into its arms and is cradling you like a little child. To then simultaneously feel all-powerful, humble, vast, unlimited. That experience becomes addictive for it empowers you to be in the world, but not of it, as you realise your real nurturing and emotional sustenance comes from within. As the Indian sages say, a state of Sat Chit Ananda – being, consciousness, bliss. This is a state of the recognition of the essence and the interconnectedness of all being.

It has also been my experience that the more we bathe in this inner plane, the more aligned our energies become to its essence. It changes us – just like adding dye to water alters its colour. It is an experience of being realigned, reawakened to our true nature, stripping away the veils of illusion that allowed us to feel separate from our own divinity in the first place.

Many individuals report that when they first begin to meditate, they feel calm, peaceful and more detached. However these changes happen gradually even with regular practice. When they stop for a while, old feelings and behaviour patterns creep back, but are experienced as unacceptable as they have experienced something different. So once again they *consciously* continue the inner journey.

It really is about forming new habits. If we want something enough, and can see or are confident of the benefits, we will put in great effort. How much pain or discontent must we experience before we seek lasting change? Jesus and all the masters, new and old, have told their disciples to look within, that the kingdom of Heaven was within. Unconditional love, joy, harmony, lasting fulfilment and happiness are found by aligning with the energy that created those aspects – the God being within.

Beyond meditation – the eternal in the now.

Ancient wisdom shares that God is omnipresent, omniscient, and omnipotent. Its pure energy is formless, though it dwells in form, creates form, flows through form. We are God in physicality. It is within, it is without. Meditation allows us to experience the God within, to know ourselves as vast, unlimited, multidimensional beings. Regardless of our attention to it, it still exists, it just IS. Though it is not separate from us, we allow ourselves – due to our beliefs of limitation – to feel separate from the God within. If we truly understood, then we would not be separate, we would just BE in every moment. We would BE the All That Is. The ego, the I, the individual would disappear as our conscious awareness merged with and became the creative force. We would BE the creative force.

Having utilised the art of meditation from one to seven as outlined, we can then begin to train ourselves to simply let go and BE in each moment so that our lives are one continual meditation – where meditation truly is pure and perfect concentration on the pure and perfect point. This state of BEingness has been called *enlightenment*. It is a state beyond the love, beyond the joy, beyond the bliss. For to feel any of these aspects would mean we are still filtering experience through the physical senses, and while our awareness is tuned to physical senses we are still separate and operating as individual units of expression.

The power and potency we experience when all our attention is focussed is literally mind-blowing. Generally, we operate on many split levels of conscious awareness. We can be sitting watching TV, reading a book during the commercials, talking to someone, thinking about our day at work. Very rarely do we find our attention 100% focussed on BEing perfectly focussed in each NOW moment; and when we do, we literally move beyond the dimension of time and space. If our BEingness is 100% focussed on a book we move into other worlds, the world of the story, of the book. We welcome it, the scenes and characters are real. We feel their pain, love, victories etc. Imagine if we gave the God within 100% of our focus 100% of our time? Due to the nature of what we are merging with, what would we be?

The following is written in the »Keys of Enoch« under prayer/meditation: »The use of positive energy for the benefit of humanity; the invocation of the light to provide balance and harmony between the worlds. When a thought or idea is concentrated upon, it tends towards action and self-realisation. However, when a person wishes to accomplish something but does not believe he will succeed, the harder he tries, the more impossible it becomes. When a thought or idea of a »revealed sacred name« is linked with emotion, it will surmount and supersede any other conscious suggestion.« Of the myriad forms of prayer/meditation, there are five general practices that should be kept in mind according to Enoch:

1. Hold fast to the holy way of life.
2. In your dealings, honour all with the radiance of love.
3. Look within and look without and see yourself as your own bridge between Heaven and Earth.
4. Behold the palace of the universe and the myriad spheres of the organic balance of nature.
5. Know that you can always rejoice in the Godhead and in the myriad radiations of the living light. I feel that the above are self-explanatory and are easily open to suitable personal interpretation.

»There is but One Source and Principle of Life to which we should give our undivided attention, and that is the God Self within every individual. To the Great Harmonious Self, the personal self should give conscious recognition at all times, and keep in constant Inner Communication with It, no matter what the outer activity of the mind is. The One Great Self is the life energy flowing through every human body each moment, by which all are enabled to move about in the world of form. It is the Wisdom flowing through the mind, the Will directing all constructive activities, the Courage and the Strength sustaining everyone, the Feeling of Divine Love with which all force can be qualified, as it flows through the individual. The Only Power that can ever accomplish any good thing. It is the All-Victorious, Conscious Dominion over every condition of human activity, when released through the personal self without resistance or interruption. This Mighty God Self within you is the Supreme Ruler of all Creation, and the only dependable, permanent and Eternal Source of help in existence. Only through Its Love, Wisdom and Power can anyone ever rise into the Ascended Mastery for constant, conscious communion with It is Freedom and Dominion over all human creation. When I say human creation, I mean all that is discordant and less than perfect.«

St Germain

Creative Visualisation 4
Tuning with White Light and Breath

The following exercise is virtually the same as the one at the end of chapter 7 and can be used to control emotions, de-stress in traffic, or simply calm and »tune« you to begin meditation for the day.

- Get comfortable, close your eyes, establish your breathing pattern using deep, fine and connected breaths – inhale slowly to the count of 7, exhale to the count of 7. Breathe through the nostrils. Make sure there are no pauses between the inhale and the exhale. First practise breathing that is cyclical and rhythmical. Do five minutes of keeping each breath connected, where each inhale flows gently into each exhale, and each exhale flows gently into each inhale.
- Then, when the circular breathing pattern is established with an even number of inhales and exhales, find a depth of breathing that you can sustain. Count to seven in then out, then to ten in then out – breathe in and out as deeply as you can in a manner that you can keep even for at least five minutes. If you get dizzy, nauseous or short of breath or the breath becomes uneven, drop back your count from say ten to nine. Practise until you find your rhythm. Remember, you need to exercise and stretch your lung capacity. You may only be able to sustain a count of seven initially, but with practice this will become ten or 15 or even 20. The deeper you breathe, the healthier you will be. Breathe from deep within the abdomen, not the lungs.
- Next, breathe so finely, slowly, deeply and connected that it feels like a gentle river of energy flowing through your being. Practise holding a candle flame in front of you – your breath in and out should be so fine that it does not flicker.
- When your breath is connected, deep and fine, then you may feel heat or tingling through your body as you are being retuned electromagnetically to a different vibration level.
- Next visualise a cylinder of pure, white, golden light energy coming from the purest energy source and encircling you.

Imagine it has no beginning or end as it touches the ground around you, anchoring itself and engulfing you.

- See this cylinder filled with the most intense, pulsating, electrically vibrant energy. Know it to be healing and transforming – living, liquid light energy.
- Breathe this light into your body. Feel it fill your lungs and imagine it filling all your cells with its healing force.
- On the inhale, feel this light being absorbed through the pores of your skin. Feel as though every part of your being is sucking this light into itself like a giant vacuum cleaner. Feel yourself expand your lungs and your entire being as you inhale.
- On the exhale, imagine you are releasing from your cells, out through the pores of your skin, light from the inner realms. Remember that Supreme Energy is within and without, living in the »empty« space of each cell. So visualise that each cell's light is being switched on like a light bulb, then flooding out into the organs, through the body and out from the pores of the skin. Continue this rhythm until you feel relaxed.

Creative Visualisation 5
Opening to Inner Guidance

Before starting this meditation, I recommend that you read the chapter on telepathic communication as the techniques used are the same for all forms of communication, whether it be with your own inner teacher, guides or others. The meditation and five step program at the end of that chapter will stimulate your intuition and open you up to inner guidance when practised regularly.

Inner guidance comes in many forms, from telepathy and clairaudience, to visionary images, strong emotional feelings or intuitive knowing and even physical discomfort. Your inner being communicates with you in many different ways and, again, self-knowledge – gained by spending time in inner silence – will allow you to ascertain the most direct and powerful way these messages are being sent.

· Firstly, tune yourself with breath and light as this makes you more receptive.
· Next create the inner sanctuary and call to yourself the image of the guide, your Inner Teacher or Higher Self or the being with whom you wish to communicate.
· Then simply ASK and LISTEN. Allow images to drift into your mind and pay attention to how your body feels – do you feel joy in your heart or a tightening in the chest area or flutters in the stomach? Learn to listen to your body as it will respond directly to the mind and emotions.

A second technique to use for clarification to a particular issue is as follows:
· Think about the question or problem.
· Tune yourself.
· Visualise yourself going down a flight of stairs, counting down backwards and taking one inhale and one exhale between stairs, relaxing deeply as you descend.
· At the bottom of the stairs see three doors (or more depending

on your options or potential solutions to your »problem.«) The first one has written upon it – »Insert your question and first option.« Open this door. Step inside and allow the vision to unfold, or feelings to flow, as if this option has been chosen and you are witnessing the results of this choice. How do you feel? Listen to your body. Are you joyous or tense?

· Then go out and look at the next door. It has your second option written on it. You open it and go in. Again the second option is already in place, existing behind this door. Again »see« and »feel« your bodily and emotional responses. Then go back out.

· The third door has »Spirit suggests« written on it. You step inside and again let the vision flow. Again, tune into yourself for clues of physical, emotional or mental reactions. Be aware of your responses and trust what »pops into your head«. Good, clear, positive inner guidance is always recognisable by the results in your life when you follow it. Remember that many beings work with us for our growth and are more than happy to give guidance when it is requested.

Creative Visualisation 6
Healing Relationships

The title is self-explanatory. Many of us have relationship issues that may need resolving or healing. The following guided meditation is one way of allowing us to do so. Interestingly enough, many who have used this technique, myself included, have reported that when they met again with the person they had contacted in their visualisation and healing, the relationship had changed. This is a result of the energetic change between the two individuals involved. Surprisingly, it suffices if one of the two is active on this level. If we release our anger, sadness, fear etc. it changes our energy field and, consciously or subconsciously, the other party automatically responds to the change in our vibration or resonance towards them.

- Again get comfortable, be undisturbed and tune yourself with breath and light work.
- Visualise your inner sanctuary. Allow yourself to let go of all tension and be still.
- Visualise in front of you now the individual that you wish to heal your relationship with, whether you need their forgiveness or need to forgive them or whatever.
- Visualise or imagine a powerful column or cylinder of pink golden light descending and entering your crown chakra, the top of your head. Feel it descend into your torso and settle at your heart. Feel its energy fill your heart and chest area, expanding it, transforming any sadness, frustration or negative emotions that you may hold in your lungs, heart or stomach area.
- Imagine this soft pink energy of love flooding through every cell of your body and dissolving anything that no longer serves you – negative emotions, limited beliefs, feelings of lack or of unworthiness. Ask your I AM to aid in this release and realignment, to fill your heart with love, compassion and forgiveness – towards yourself and others.

117

- When feeling full of love and forgiveness and full of the desire to heal and mend any rifts, visualise the individual/s before you. Ask their I AM Presence for permission to heal the »rift« between you. (This is virtually always given. If you get a clear »no,« then just release your own emotions without seeking for them to do so also.) You can also visualise yourself standing before you – you may need self-forgiveness. This also works for those who have passed away.
- Send a beam of pink love from your heart. See it enter theirs. See the two of you connected by this beam of love. Watch it fill their body, every cell, and melt their heart with love, and melt any blockages in their electrical circuitry from unresolved negative emotions that they may have held towards you.
- See yourselves like the letter »H« – a beautiful large pink »H« with the energy of love and forgiveness flowing freely between you. Share from your heart. Say what you always wished to share. Offer your forgiveness or accept their forgiveness, then be silent and receive words or energy from them. Visualise, and know that it is their inner desire to heal this relationship.
- When this process is complete, see them fade from view. In your mind's eye, call forth the next person you wish to contact.
- If there are many, see yourself in the middle of a circle with these individuals on the perimeter and a beam of pink love coming from your heart centre like a lighthouse beam going around and around or focussing on one at a time until they are all filled with love and all the rifts are healed.

Esoteric Influences on Relationships

Human relationships are formed under genetic, cultural/environmental, astrological and past life/karmic influences. Relationships across the globe are as varied as we are. For example, in the New Guinea highlands, in one tribe, men and women have little to do with one another. They work their own fields and live apart. The young boys move in with the men at six years of age. The missionaries tell them that couples should sleep together, but they don't want to. The women meet their husbands in the fields during the day, which is the only time they can have sex. However, as with many indigenous cultures, modern civilisation is arriving and throwing these arrangements into confusion.

The Ascended Ones share that global unity and harmony will come when we learn to honour the gifts of all cultures. There are wonderful ways of being in all societies, as well as evident imbalances. Being open of mind and heart will allow us to learn of others« ways and then utilise discernment and choice to integrate the best of everything – *a synthesis of the best to create something even more powerful.* The best is what is evidently and demonstrably working for the benefit of all. Imagine humanity absorbing and blending the best from all societies to create a new harmonious way of being, instead of operating from the greed and power-based lower emotions which run rampant in the »civilised« world today.

Ancient wisdom offers that individuals share both individual and group consciousness and that prior to incarnation we choose our sex, culture and country, parents and even siblings. We also choose the lessons that we need to evolve as a soul: lessons to teach us compassion, patience, understanding – the list is as long as is the depth and potential of humanity's emotional and mental capacity.

The main reason for groups of people continuing to incarnate together at the same time is to rebalance past energy exchange, often called »karma«. Karma simply insures the rebalance of energy in the cosmic energy pool.

There are three main types of karma: that accumulated from past lives, that created in the present life, and the portion of past karma which has been selected to be resolved in this life. Ancient wisdom shares that there are usually either 700 or 1,200 years between incarnations, the time difference depending on the individual's personal capacity to handle more concentrated bliss. The more consciously tuned people are to the universal beat, the more bliss they can handle. Bliss is an aspect of pure conscious awareness.

After a degree of spiritual advancement, the Lords of Karma arrange the time appropriate for associating those with whom matters are to be resolved. Some schools of thought claim that we are usually born not less than three and not more than seven times in the one gender before switching over to the other.

Acting in a manner where we desire no personal acknowledgement or reward – as in selfless service – with detached behaviour creates no new karma.

Entering into the question of fate and free will, some ask why is it that so many people work so hard and try for so long and are still disappointed. To understand this we need to look at Divine Will, Divine Timing and the internal saboteur and how these influence relationships. This is discussed in the chapter on mind power – beyond motivational psychology, where we look at specific programming that will guarantee limitless ease and grace in life's journey if practised.

Another interesting point of discussion is the fact that we start each new life with exactly the same lower mental and full emotional bodies as we possessed at the end of our last life. If we are aware that we are systems of energy, then consciously TUNING ourselves through life's journey means that we will re-enter the wheel of life and death on exactly the same vibration that we exited on. This simply ensures that after a »period« of rest, we can continue our journey with the same level of consciousness that we attained in the life before. Like school where if one learns basic mathematics in grade two, then in grade three we can go on with the basic understanding in place to learn the next level.

Those well-tuned and awakened may now be embracing physical immortality and have completed the requirement of both karma and reincarnation that evolving souls must traverse through.

As we begin to consciously tune ourselves through acknowledging the Inner Teacher, many of us may find that we are developing at different rates to our partners. We may ask, »What are the alternatives to ending the relationship with someone with whom we feel we now have so little in common?« Again, the use of programming as in the mind power section, is most beneficial in enhancing the quality of a couple's interaction.

People reincarnate together to bring the previous energy exchanged into balance. Once this has been completed, it often happens that they drift apart as they are no longer bound together electromagnetically. However, once the »karmic slate has been cleared« they can, as awakened ones, decide to begin a new chapter together and build on their shared history and the bonds of love that they have formed.

As discussed previously, thought is a force, and creates either beneficial or negative experiences, whether verbally expressed, or acted upon, or not. What we focus on becomes our reality. By eliminating judgmental thinking and by being more unconditionally loving and limitless in our thinking towards all life forms, we will become more unified. This is a time for humanity to learn to co-exist harmoniously, simply enjoying the uniqueness of all expression.

We live in a plane of duality. This applies to men and women. Esoterically, this duality is symbolised by the Star of David – the triangle with its apex upwards is the male principle – active, yang, day, fire, hot, positive electrically. The triangle with its apex downwards is the female principle – passive, yin, night, water, cool, negative electrically. The double triangle illustrates androgyny, our past and our future. It is also a state of balance.

One way that we can bring balance to ourselves, which then flows into all our life's relationships, is through the use of meditation. Dreaming can also be a bonding agent if the ability to recall dreams is acquired and we can give impressions of the dream to others.

When human beings co-exist we are automatically involved in the process of the sharing of life atoms. Living in close proximity, sleeping together, sharing the same food and environment actually produces a blending of energy fields that can either empower or disempower us.

As discussed in the chapter on the I AM Presence, humans have 144 monadic extensions. So there is always the possibility of a couple, or relatives, or friends being from the same monad or soul group. This is also why we feel some people that we meet are soul mates or we feel like we've always known them, even though we may have just met them for the first time in this life.

Coming back to what's actually occurring in the day to day reality of humanity, personally and globally, we find that recent research and surveys regarding modern »civilised« and industrialised societies report the following information and statistics:

· Dual income couples spend an average of 12 minutes a day talking to each other. Maintaining or creating quality relationships with so little time shared becomes an art or act of magic.

· Many parents feel guilty about not spending enough time with their children and growing youth often feel disenchanted with life.

· Youth suicide in industrialised countries is reportedly much higher than that of indigenous peoples. However, indigenous infant mortality, due to lack of adequate living standards, is much higher than that of industrialised nations.

· It is said that all classes of workers are now working harder and longer. In both the US and Australia, many companies have retained the same level of business revenue with half of the staff they had four years ago. This is creating enormous personal pressure in relationships as there is so little time spent with the enjoyment of family, friends and basic solitude and personal time out. So we become unbalanced.

- Alternative therapists have found that all disease comes from stress and emotional dis-ease from imbalanced lifestyles.

- Advertising, plus the inner drive to find happiness, adds to the pressures of modern society for people to be enthusiastic consumers. One in 100 Americans go bankrupt each year, not from business failure, but because of over-extending themselves via credit spending.

- Pressure on relationships caused by financial strain is great. Consider trading down in material lifestyle to enhance your enjoyment of life.

- A new word called »caroche« describes death from overwork in Japan. To leave home at 5 a.m. and return at 11 p.m. is not uncommon. The Japanese are now rethinking their position because productivity has been falling in recent years and is now behind the US.

- In medieval times, the working day was nine hours, but it was leisurely and there were 150 vacation days each year. In the Renaissance period when clocks became widespread, people's work could be more efficiently organised. In the industrial era, 14 hours a day was the average worked. Children worked from age ten – a maximum by law of 16 hours a day. In 1933, Kelloggs introduced a 30 hour week, reduced from a 40 hour week, to increase the productivity of people it employed during the depression, and found that productivity doubled. The firm retained the 30 hour week until 1985 when management reverted to an eight hour day. Today, overtime is up and at the same time unemployment is high. The efficient German workers at BMW work a 36 hour week with six weeks paid annual vacation, compared with two weeks vacation in the US.

All beings have the right to enjoy the fulfilment of basic requirements such as clean water, food, shelter and clothing. Once survival issues are taken care of, individuals can begin to focus on accessing their »higher aspects« for full expression.

To maintain quality relationships and quality lives, it is necessary to develop and tap into the four-fifths of the brain that houses higher consciousness and utilise both the power of creative imagination and limitless thinking.

Again, bridging cultures and blending the best of all societies would allow for a more equal distribution of wealth from industrialised societies to nations still struggling for their basic requirements such as food and shelter.

Vigilant thought control for »limitlessness« thinking, which brings an understanding that quality thinking produces a quality life, plus working consciously with the Inner Teacher, will allow humanity to move from poverty consciousness to wealth consciousness as they come to understand that we live in an abundant universe. Poverty consciousness is not just about finances. It is about lack generally. It is about lack of self-esteem, lack of self-worth. Abundance consciousness is about freedom and abundance in love, health, creativity and wealth – working for the good of the whole, not just the one.

Chapter 15

Maximising Energy Flow for Meditation

While it is understood that intention and desire are powerful factors in the experience of the inner realms, it is also beneficial to cleanse the energy fields of the lower bodies so that this experience may be intensified.

It can be likened to having chunky soup from the same container, day after day, and never washing it so that all sorts of matter accumulates and then deciding to drink water from the same cup. If you give it a good clean, the water will taste better and be purer. Your thirst will still be quenched if the cup is not cleaned and it is up to you to decide whether you wish to clean your container – *consciously* or not. I personally prefer to have the finest, purest and most intense experience I can, so preparation of the vehicle is natural and not an issue to me.

The energies that are being activated upon this planet at this time are ensuring all the energy fields of all beings are being realigned anyway. However, there are many tools and techniques that we can use to aid this cleansing if we desire to enhance and quicken the process.

Cleansing the physical body

Basically, what we eat and what we think are made manifest in the physical body. The chain of command is as follows: Physical body > emotional body > mental body (higher and lower) > soul or Higher Self > monad or I AM Presence. The physical body is like the private in the army or pawn in a chess game and takes orders from, or is manipulated by, the emotional and mental body. As discussed in chapters 8, 9, 10 and 11, what manifests in the physical body is a direct result of the influence of the mind and the emotions.

It is our mind, supported by will power and self-discipline (or lack of discipline), that chooses the food for the body to be sustained by. There is so much literature and research available in Western society about food and healthy diets to maximise health and vitality that I will not elaborate further here. Suffice to say that the energy field of the physical body is the first to break down in direct response to the toxicity of our thoughts, food and long-term choices.

Repeated research has shown that most individuals consider premium health to be of maximum importance to enjoying quality life. Yet choices are often made, through lack of self-discipline or ignorance, which lead to the breakdown of this vehicle through disease, decay and premature death. The physical body is a most amazing, complicated system of energy and operates far beyond the comprehension of many – it heals itself, regenerates cells, produces new life and new organs and tissues at will, all seemingly by some unknown coding, like a computer program that is built to run indefinitely until invaded by a computer virus. The equivalent of this virus is our thoughts and limited beliefs. Belief in death and ageing as inevitable, coupled with choices of inadequate nutrition, contribute to the breakdown of the physical vehicle.

It is important to understand that the energy fields of the physical, emotional, mental and spiritual bodies are interrelated and consequently affect each other. When the energies of these bodies flow harmoniously, the experience of the inner world is intensified. When energy blockages are present, we are out of alignment with our true nature and this is reflected in the quality of our life.

The simplest way to cleanse the physical body is as follows

1. Drink lots or pure, fresh water – preferably not from the tap with its inherent chemicals.
2. Do regular stress-free exercise like tai chi, swimming, dancing, yoga and walking. I also recommend that you be a *conscious breather* when you exercise so that you tune to the energy as it moves through you and enhances your experience.
3. As a conscious breather, do deep, fine, connected breathing everywhere – in the shower, in traffic, when exercising, when eating (between mouthfuls) – always being aware of the energy

that drives your breath. This keeps your awareness in the NOW and helps to eliminate ageing by the non-recognition of time.

4. Eat light and live food. Remember that unless you are an expert at transmutation, then alcohol, sugar and red meat keep your vibrations dense. The lighter and finer your vibrations, the better the quality and quantity of life. Most individuals eat according to the dictates of the emotional – not the physical – body. Eating junk food and overeating are emotionally-based habits. The body requires small amounts of pure food and *derives no benefit* from processed and refined foods.

5. Learn to listen to the body. The cleaner it becomes, the clearer the messages it will communicate. The physical body has the capacity to be completely self-sustaining and to do so without physical nourishment. It can be refined and tuned to live off prana alone. That is how miraculous it is, and how perfectly designed it was by the Creator. Some religions say we were made in the Creator's image, so surely we are inherently perfect?

6. Master the emotional body by mastering the mental body. This will keep the physical vehicle free from disease and perfectly tuned and self-sustaining.

Cleansing the emotional body

While you are doing 1 to 5 above, you can also be cleansing the emotional body by using the specific visualisation technique mentioned in the last pages of the chapter on the power of emotions, plus any other techniques you may be attracted to that will achieve this. This cleansing also can be done as you sleep, as mentioned in chapter 10, plus also utilising specific healing modalities as also outlined in that chapter.

The storage of negative emotions in the physical body creates energy blockages which, if unresolved, will lead to decay and disease. It is not in your interest to hold onto negative emotions. These need to be dealt with effectively – again refer to chapters 9, 10 and 11. Sometimes when you consciously begin this work, it is like opening »Pandora's box,« but remember that for short-term pain there is long-term gain. »Sweeping our rubbish under the carpet« does not heal, resolve or cleanse – it is still there, and in the meantime, its existence allows for, and promotes, the deterioration of the physical vehicle.

The two most powerful ways of cleansing the emotional body is by *meditation,* as it will alter the vibrational frequency and cause or stimulate a natural realignment, and through *past life regression.* Although past, present and future exist simultaneously, most of us live within a linear and sequential timeframe of events which is our day to day reality. As discussed in chapter 9, our emotional body knows no time. Its hurts, angers and sorrows have been accumulated and stored from the mental body's *perception* of an event *at that time.* So while we grow, learn and evolve in consciousness and awareness, the emotional body may have energy blocks dating back eons of time that are currently unjustified and often irrelevant to current day events – if viewed dispassionately and objectively. This explains our over-reaction to people, places and things when deep memories are triggered.

Another regression session I experienced explains the above quite simply. I »saw« myself, standing alone on a cliff top, feeling immensely sad. I knew someone I loved had been sent away via sea. It turned out to be my sister (a dear friend now in this life). She had fallen pregnant and as it was socially unacceptable in that day and age to be an unwed mother, she was sent away and I never saw her again. I was never told why and I held both sadness and anger towards my father for his actions. In regression I was able to see the bigger picture: to witness the event, feel my sorrow again, but then stand back, tune into my father and his own sorrow and also understand the situation. From today's understanding of times past, I could see that the »blame« lay in the ignorance of society and so I could release my anger towards my father and also my sorrow.

I felt my heart open and energy flow out. The energy of my body realigned itself to this new understanding as the emotional body understood from this »new« perception, and so dissolved energy blocks. Simple, but powerful and very healing. Karma is just a readdressal of energy imbalance. When we can retrogress and release disharmonious energy patterns, karmic imbalance is neutralised and additional pain for the others involved is often avoided. This rebalance may not be possible if they still have valuable learning to do. In that life my father had inadvertently created a karmic debt to me for I held great anger towards him which needed rebalancing. By releasing the power or energy of this anger through my »new« understanding, this debt was forgiven and released. My father then is my father now.

It is interesting to note that this life, for many, is one of having all with whom there is an energy imbalance from times past reincarnate now with us – like our soul family or group – as it is a time of healing, cleansing, realigning. We cannot carry our emotional baggage with us and all energy blocks must be freed to move into the higher octaves and dimensions of existence that have been preordained for humanity at this time.

Cleansing our mental body

This can only be done through mind mastery as covered in chapter 9. It is one thing to understand intellectually, but it is another to *live* these understandings. The idea that our »thoughts create our reality« is well understood. When assimilated into the various levels of our being, our lives will become abundant and rich on all levels – physical, emotional, mental and spiritual. This is governed by the universal Law of Creation – as you sow, so shall you reap – also known as the Law of Fulfilment. When our bodies are tuned and resonating in perfect harmony with each other – they all vibrate at their own unique rate – we will experience complete fulfilment and at-one-ment with all creation.

If every time we go within or tune our conscious awareness to the inner God, we go with a cup that is half full (of ego, desires, negative emotions, cellular baggage etc.) then that same cup can only be half filled. The mixing of the old contents with our new awareness results in a diluted, less effective mixture. However, a little diligence – a little care to present a pristine, empty vessel – will mean that the vessel can be filled with the purest energy.

Being the God that we are is like peeling away the layers of an onion to reveal the pure essence within. Each layer represents a veil of separation, be it belief in limitation, belief in mortality, or simply garbage that has accumulated over lifetimes on all levels.

To simply state that »I AM God« does not necessarily make it a conscious reality, for deep within, on a cellular level, may be lifetimes of denial of that statement even being a possibility. So we must peel away the layers until our reality manifests itself – until it just IS, or until we just ARE.

»When a person individualises within the Absolute, All-Pervading Life, he chooses of his own free will to become an intensified individual focus of self conscious intelligence. He is the conscious director of his future activities. Thus having once made his choice, he is the only one who can fulfil that destiny, which is not inflexible circumstance, but a definitely designed Plan of Perfection. It is a Blueprint which he elects to express in the realms of form and action. A human being may at any time determine to rise out of his human qualities or limitations and if he will give all of his life, his energy, to that determination, he will succeed. Those of us who have raised the body, accomplished the »Ascension« by giving all unto the God Self within – and hence It expresses through us Its Perfect Qualities – »The Divine Plan of Life«.«

St Germain, »Unveiled Mysteries«, through Godfre Ray King.

Chapter 16

The Chakras – The Body's Energy Centres

Chakras are the doorways through which energy is attracted into the body and then dispersed. In a healthy person these seven main energy centres are open and spinning. When a person is ill, blockages can usually be found in the chakras. Everything in the body is connected to these energy centres. Chakras absorb universal life force (prana, chi) and send it along the body's energy rivers (nadis) to the nervous system, the endocrine glands and blood to nourish the body.

Excerpt from »Other Kingdoms« by Hilarion: »Chakras are essential to life on the physical plane because they are the doorways through which energy from the Higher Self is allowed to pass down to the lower. In the absence of this energy transfer, life would cease ... a person whose chakras are strong and open will be very much in touch with his/her true being ... Chakras can be seen as coruscating (flashing) shimmering wheels of beautiful colour, ever moving and dancing, singing the glorious songs of life ... but only in the spiritually developed person do they appear thus.«

In the human body there are seven main chakras plus numerous minor chakras. Above the head there are known to be at least five transpersonal chakras that connect us energetically to our monad or I AM Presence. The energy fields of all our bodies are anchored by the chakras: the physical body is anchored in the base chakra, the emotional in the sacral, the mental in the solar plexus and the spiritual in the heart chakra.

There is abundant literature available on chakras, so I will not elaborate too much here. However, I wish to make it clear that by tuning, cleansing and fully activating these energy centres with colour and light we can create vibrant health, energise ourselves, and also learn to move our consciousness from within the confines of the physical form, i.e. bi-location etc.

I would also like to mention that blockages in these energy fields occur through lack of mastery of the mental and emotional bodies. Techniques to clean, energise and realign the chakras are like taking a pain killer for a headache. They are effective but it does not always address the problem, only the symptoms. These techniques need to be used in conjunction with mind mastery to produce long-term optimum health.

Techniques to work with the chakras are covered at the end of this chapter and should be part of your regular maintenance program, carried out weekly or monthly. In the initial stages, the exercises can be done daily until these centres are spinning, rich in colour and activated to their full potential. Chakras respond to toxicity of thoughts and emotions and change in colour to reflect these imbalances.

Let us begin with the seven main chakras located in the physical body. The three chakras in the head and throat govern reason, the chakras on the front of the body govern the emotions and the chakras on the back govern the will. Chakras are cone-shaped as in the diagram at the end of the chapter. As they spin, they attract energy in through the front and the back, or through the top and the bottom in the case of the base and crown chakras. Each chakra has small rotating vortexes spinning at very high rates, and each vortex metabolises an energy vibration that resonates at a particular spin frequency. The pelvic chakra has four small vortexes and four frequencies of energy. The colour observed in each chakra is related to the frequency of energy being metabolised at its particular rate. Consequently, as we increase the light quotient within our beings and also our vibrational frequency, these energy centres unify and become one column of light. The brow chakra has 96 small vortexes and the crown centre has 972. Each chakra has a different number of vortexes and consequently its own unique spin rate and frequency.

1. The base, or root, chakra

This is the location where the Christ love facet of mankind will manifest as the human race learns to love without selfish or romantic motives, to love merely for the joy of seeing the loved one happy. Purity, restoration, resurrection, ascension and hope are also associated with this chakra.

On a more »earthly« level, this chakra is related to the quantity of physical energy we have at our disposal and the »will to live« in physical reality. It is the location of the first manifestation of the life force in the physical world. It acts as a pump on the etheric level helping direct the flow of energy up the spine. Its colour is red and it is perfectly tuned in resonance to the musical note of »C«. This cone of energy spirals downwards from the pubic centre and connects us energetically to our personal »earth star« chakra which is located about six inches below our feet in the Earth. Our sense of touch is associated with this chakra.

This first chakra is also associated with the first auric layer which is the etheric body working with the automatic and autonomic functioning of the body. The etheric body is composed of tiny web-like energy lines and is blue/grey in colour. The chakras of the etheric body are also blue/grey in colour: blue in a sensitive person and grey in a more athletic individual. The cells of the physical body grow along the lines of energy of the etheric matrix which is present before the cells grow. This »body« is made up of pulsating light waves and generally extends from one-quarter to two inches from the physical body.

Energy work is now being done by various healers to instruct the body to grow a new limb where one has been destroyed, for example, by accident. This can be done only due to the existence of the etheric matrix. The etheric blueprint can be perceived as an energy field that holds fourth (astral), fifth and sixth dimensional structures. The majority of karmic patterning is stored within the etheric body. It also keeps the DNA functioning. The fifth dimensional lightbody structure usually lies dormant in the etheric blueprint and holds etheric crystals which block certain energy flows to prevent the lightbody from activating too early. Its sixth dimensional structure holds the templates set for the formation of matter and lightbodies and the DNA codes which determine the shape of the physical form.

2. The sacral, or naval, chakra

Located just below our navel, the energy of this chakra can be used to enliven and balance out other centres. It tends to lend its super-abundance of energy to the head centres to enhance wisdom and clairvoyance, to the throat centre to promote the verbalisation of truth, to the heart centre to encourage the outflowering of love for all creation and to the solar plexus to lend physical drive and strength to the body. It is also active in the sex experience of the race and can be used for the coming together of all that is beautiful in two mated souls. It is the seat of forgiveness, mercy, compassion, transmutation and freedom. The front of this chakra is called the pubic centre which is the feeling centre and is related both to the quality of love for the opposite sex, and the giving and receiving of physical, mental and spiritual pleasure. The back energy vortex of the sacral centre is related to the quantity of sexual energy and is a centre of will. Its colour is orange and its musical note is »D«.

This second chakra is associated with the second auric layer and grounds and anchors the energy field of the lower emotional body. The structure of this auric layer is more fluid than the etheric and does not duplicate the physical body. It appears as coloured clouds of fine substance in continual fluid motion and usually extends from one to three inches from the body. Its colour reflects the individual's feelings. Highly energised feelings – love, joy, excitement, anger – give clear hues and confused feelings reflect a dark, murky colour. The chakras in this energy field also follow the rainbow in colour like the ones in the physical body.

The emotional body is made up of geometries. When we get stuck in our emotion and do not allow its energy to flow freely, we lock the geometries into patterns which create limitation of expression and hence discomfort.

3. The solar plexus chakra

Physical energies stream into the body from the highest planes through this centre. Its main function at present is to allow the body to be energised, but in the future it will be the centre that will allow an object to be moved through space merely by concentrating and willing it to move. Combining visualisation, will and solar plexus energy will create many phenomena when used in conjunction with universal laws. It is also the seat of healing power, devotional worship and ministering grace.

The solar plexus is the name for the front centre and it has to do with expansiveness and spiritual wisdom. It is a seat of will and the emotion understanding of who you are in the universe. The back is called the diaphragmatic centre and is said to be related to healing and one's intentions towards one's health. The colour is yellow and the musical note is »E«.

This third chakra is associated with the third auric layer of lower mental activity and consequently with linear thinking. This chakra also anchors the energy field of the lower mental body. This body appears as a bright yellow light generally three to eight inches from the body and is made of the finest substance of thoughts and mental processes.

The mental body is also made up of geometries. The function of this body is to determine our reality and it generally believes it is »running the show« and operates best when it feels it always knows what is going on. The mental body, as boss, does not like change motivated by »other« forces. Consequently, it tends to dispel or ignore impulses from Spirit as »not real«, as these are vast and unlimited and cannot be understood intellectually or controlled.

The three lower auric levels metabolise energy relating to the physical world and are active in the game of karma. They can be seen fifth dimensionally as double tetrahedrons. The upper three metabolise energy in relation to the spiritual. The heart chakra is the transforming crucible through which all energy must pass when going from one world to another. The majority of humanity operates from the energy fields of the three lower chakras but are now being prompted by their inner Spirit to activate and utilise their higher chakras.

4. The heart chakra

The human race has worked with this energy vortex from the very beginning. It is the chakra that connects the lower bodies with the higher bodies. It is also the conduit through which love flows from the Higher Self. When blocked, it often creates diseases of the heart. It is humanity's connection to the unconditional love of God. It also metabolises and expresses this Divine Love. When we express love and devotion our heart centre is activated. The colour of the heart chakra is emerald green and it best resonates to the musical note of »F«.

In her book »Hands of Light«, Barbara Brennan states also that the heart chakra anchors the astral body. All the chakras in this auric layer – which generally extends six to 12 inches from the body – are infused with the rose pink colour of love, although their rainbow colours predominate.

5. The throat chakra

This chakra is intended to allow each soul to give to others in words that which his/her wisdom has absorbed or that which her/his clairvoyant gift has revealed. The centre will be harmonious when used with purity of words and will be open to allow great inspiration from the higher planes to come through. This chakra is associated with Divine Will, power, protection and illumined faith. It gives energy or power to words and »speaking things into being«.

The front is associated with taking in and assimilating, and is also associated with taking responsibility for one's personal needs (learning to speak up). The back is associated with a person's sense of self in society, her/his profession, and the desire to succeed on the material plane. Its colour is sky blue and it resonates to the musical note of »G«. This chakra is also associated with the senses of hearing, smell and taste.

The throat chakra anchors the etheric template (physical aspect) which corresponds to the fifth auric layer. The etheric template is the template form for the etheric layer – which is the template form for the physical body. It is the blueprint for the etheric body and generally extends 1.5 feet to two feet from the physical body. It is the level at which sound creates matter. Healing can occur at this layer by using sound. For males, deeper voice pitch usually means healthier lower chakras and corresponding energy fields.

6. The brow chakra

Also called the »ajna« or »third eye«. It is the organ of sight on a psychic or etheric level and it can be raised in vibration to a point where auras and etheric shapes and beings can be seen. It corresponds to the mental quality of »seeing« as opposed to wisdom. This chakra is the seat of clairvoyance. It connects the higher emotional body with its experience of celestial love and encompasses all life and knows all life forms to be precious manifestations of God. When it is fully activated we can »see« with these spiritual eyes, not just the physical ones.

It is also associated with truth, consecration, dedication, concentration and inner vision. It is the place of the manifestation of divine light which is only visible to our spiritual eyes. It gives us the ability to understand mental concepts. The ability to project thoughts and ideas and create reality comes into play through the »executive« centre at the back of the head. The ability to create ideas through vision is at the front. The ability to carry these ideas into fruition is at the back. The colour of this chakra is indigo and its musical note is »A«.

The sixth auric layer, or celestial body, is anchored in this chakra. This is our higher emotional body or the emotional level of the spiritual plane and it generally extends two feet to 2.75 feet from the physical body. This is the level through which we experience spiritual ecstasy: a point of being and connectedness to All That Is. Unconditional love flows when the celestial chakra and heart chakra openly exchange energies resulting in a shimmering light body of pastel colours with an opaque, silver/gold shine. It is composed of light radiating out from the body.

7. The crown chakra

As the centre governing the faculty of wisdom and understanding, it allows a grasp of spiritual truth at a level usually inaccessible to man while in physical incarnation. It is connected to the seventh auric layer, the higher mental body, the »knowing« and integration of our spiritual and physical make-up. It is the source of enlightenment, universal wisdom, understanding and illumination. When activated it allows us to go beyond the physical world and creates a feeling of wholeness, peace and faith, plus a sense of purpose to existence.

Its colour is violet or pure white light and its musical note is »B«. The crown chakra brings in the higher energies and connects this energy through the other chakras down to the base and into the earth. It is cone-like in shape, as are all the others, but like the base chakra it is vertical. It faces upwards, like an inverted triangle standing on its tip. The other chakras are like horizontal triangles that connect in the centre like an »x«.

The seventh auric layer is the ketheric template or causal body which generally extends 2.5 to 3.5 feet from the body. This is where we *know* we are one with all creation. It is egg-shaped and contains all auric bodies of the current incarnation an individual is undergoing. It is »seen« as tiny threads of golden light, a grid-like structure that vibrates at a very high frequency. This golden template also contains the main power current that runs up and down the spine. It also is the main power current that nourishes the body and also holds past life bands. The band found near the head/neck area contains the past life we are currently trying to clear in present life circumstances. For more information on this refer to Barbara Ann Brennan's book »Hands of Light«.

The spine is the main vertical power current. It is our central channel of light. The nerves from the spine have direct contact with different parts of the body, and thus disorders of the body will affect the spine. Cleansed and fully activated chakras will allow for pure energy transfer throughout the spine and the body and, as a consequence, health and vitality within the physical vehicle.

Chakras can be cleansed and activated by many methods. While some texts differ, it is generally understood that when cleaning and activating, the rainbow colours be visualised and the chakras be spun and activated in a clockwise manner. Diagrams of the chakras can be found in numerous texts on the subject. For other work, such as bi-location etc., the chakras can be spun in an alternating fashion: i.e. crown – anti-clockwise, brow – clockwise etc. The correct sequence is ACACACA for women and CACA-CAC for men. The colours used will also be different, depending on the exercise.

Many individuals are now working with the thymus chakra, located between the heart and the throat. When activated, it allows for verbal expression with love to create harmony and balance. Its colour is magenta. We also have higher chakras that are located in finer energy bands within and around the body.

There is much information on the higher and lower chakras now available, with more information for the lower, as humans have known of, and worked with, these energy centres for much longer. There are also many guided meditation tapes available (also from S.E.A.) on chakra work. However, as we raise our vibrations closer to the speed of light, all the chakras will unify into one column of light.

It has been said that chakra work can be likened to the healing modalities of homeopathy, chiropractic and other alternative therapies: useful and powerful, but soon to be replaced by light energy work, and work with sound and colour which will be the new healing methods to be utilised in the coming millennium. Similarly, the »new« chakra work will be done with golden white light only, as this is the purest energy in all the universes.

Regarding the higher chakras, the only detailed information I have been able to obtain is from »The Complete Ascension Manual« and »Beyond Ascension« by Dr. Stone. These texts, which form part of his series »The Easy-To-Read Encyclopaedia of the Spiritual Path« have been graciously donated to S.E.A. by Dr. Stone. In these works, Dr. Stone talks about chakra grid systems where chakras one to seven relate to the third dimension; eight to 15 to the fourth dimension; 16 to 22 to the fifth dimension; 23 to 30 to the sixth dimension; 30 to 36 to the seventh dimension, and then once we have left the energy fields of this planet and move into still higher dimensions of light, we anchor and activate chakras 37 to 43 and 44 to 50 which connect to the eighth and ninth dimensions respectively.

Information from my Inner Teacher, my I AM Presence, further elaborates that these grids are connected to the initiations and the higher dimensions as energy matrices of finer frequencies that resonate to the speed of light and beyond. Further checking with the Ascended Masters reports that we are connected through all the vibratory levels to the Source by an energy vortex or chakra. All the chakras have a different frequency and spin rate. »As above, so below« is also applicable to the chakra grid system as the system manifest in our physical form mirrors those in other dimensions. Overlaying is done by *implosion of energy* where we are magnetised and reabsorbed back into the next frequency band. Again, all this occurs via a state of resonance.

These energy matrices are like fine webs that are overlaid on top of each other. We merge into them like an opening flower bursting towards sunlight. So as we literally raise our vibrational frequency through increasing our light quotient, these grids are overlaid, anchored and activated. Full activation and utilisation of these grid patterns and energy fields automatically bring abilities such as teleportation, dematerialisation and so on. But these abilities depend on the grid system that is in place, e.g. 30 to 36 must be anchored and activated for teleportation. Dr. Stone states that when the full 36 are anchored, actualised and opened, the 12-strand DNA moves from the etheric vehicle into the physical vehicle. He also states that the invocation of key codes, fire letters and sacred geometries opens all chambers in all the chakras.

The anchoring and activation of these grid systems needs to controlled by our monad or I AM Presence so we do not overload the electrical circuitry of the physical vehicle. The light quotient in our being is actually the amount of light from the monad that has been released through, and anchored in, the physical vehicle.

So before moving on to the full installation of all chakra grid systems, I recommend unified chakra exercises. However, any chakra work will be beneficial as healthy, fully activated chakras keep the body from ageing and decay. The unified chakra meditation is described on the next page.

The Chakras

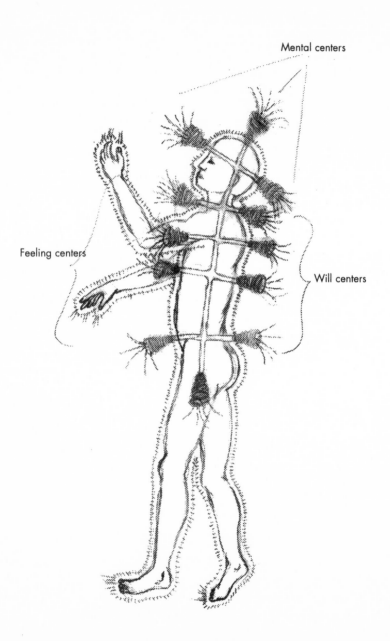

Mental centers

Feeling centers

Will centers

The Auric Layers

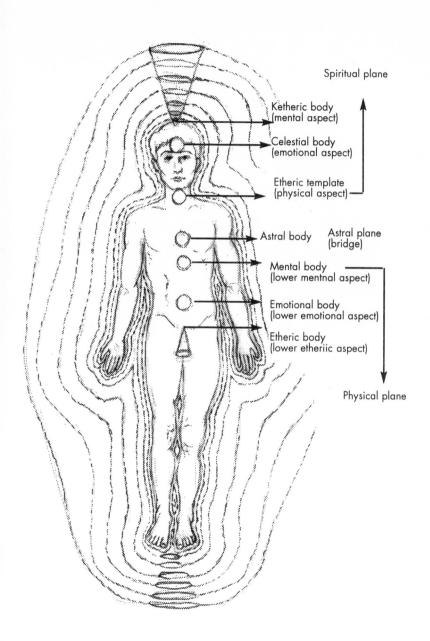

Spiritual plane

Ketheric body
(mental aspect)

Celestial body
(emotional aspect)

Etheric template
(physical aspect)

Astral body   Astral plane
(bridge)

Mental body
(lower mentnal aspect)

Emotional body
(lower emotional aspect)

Etheric body
(lower etheriic aspect)

Physical plane

Creative Visualisation 7
Invocation to the Unified Chakra
From Tony Stubbs, »An Ascension Handbook«

I breathe in light through the centre of my heart
opening my heart into a beautiful ball of light,
allowing myself to expand.
I breathe in light through the centre of my heart
allowing the light to expand,
encompassing my throat chakra and my solar plexus chakra
in one unified field of light within, through and around my body.

I breathe in light through the centre of my heart
allowing the light to expand,
encompassing my brow chakra and my navel chakra
in one unified field of light within, through and around my body.

I breathe in light through the centre of my heart
allowing the light to expand,
encompassing my crown chakra and my base chakra
in one unified field of light within, through and around my body.

I breathe in light through the centre of my heart
allowing the light to expand,
encompassing my alpha chakra above my head,
and my omega chakra below my spine
in one unified field of light within, through and around my body.
I allow the wave of Metatron to resonate between them.
I am a unity of light.

I breathe in light through the centre of my heart
allowing the light to expand,
encompassing my eighth chakra above my head, and my thighs
in one unified field of light within, through and around my body.
I allow my emotional body to merge with my physical.
I am a unity of light.

I breathe in light through the centre of my heart
allowing the light to expand,
encompassing my ninth chakra above my head, and my calves
in one unified field of light within, through and around my body.
I allow my mental body to merge with my physical.
I am a unity of light.

I breathe in light through the centre of my heart
allowing the light to expand,
encompassing my tenth chakra above my head, and below my
feet
in one unified field of light within, through and around my body.
I allow my spiritual body to merge with my physical.
I am a unity of light.
I breathe in light through the centre of my heart
allowing the light to expand,
encompassing my eleventh chakra above my head, and to below
my feet
in one unified field of light within, through and around my body.
I allow my oversoul to merge with my physical.
I am a unity of light.

I breathe in light through the centre of my heart
allowing the light to expand,
encompassing my twelfth chakra above my head, and to below
my feet
in one unified field of light within, through and around my body.
I allow my Christ oversoul to merge with my physical.
I am a unity of light.

I breathe in light through the centre of my heart
I ask that the highest level of my spirit radiate forth
from the centre of my heart,
filling this unified field completely.
I radiate forth throughout this day.
I am unity of Spirit.

Chapter 17

The Higher Self and the I AM Presence

Research into the Alice Bailey material reveals there are 60000 million individualised spiritual sparks (monads or I AM Presence) of the Creator. Each monad put down 12 fingers of fire (Higher Selves) and each of these created 12 individualised souls. These can also be called our »soul extensions« or »personalities« which are our physical form. Not all soul extensions may currently be in embodiment.

There are many, many accounts about how sparks of the Divine came to be in physical embodiment and about the origins of humanity. I feel that if this is of interest, it can be researched and models or conclusions formed to suit the individual. I do not wish to embark on any in-depth explanation or analysis at this point as to me the issue at hand is why we are here and not how we got here, although both are fascinating. Discovering why we are here automatically improves the quality of individual life.

»The Prism of Lyra« by Lyssa Royal and Keith Priest presents an interesting account from a galactic level. This book puts forth suggestions like future selves where, because past, present and future exist simultaneously, a being may contact parts of itself across the expanse of time. Extraterrestrials are said to be humans of the future who wish to establish contact with their past lives, such as time spent on Earth, to create a connection which will heal their own past. It has been suggested by those who understand the illusion of linear time – which is confined to the time/space continuum of the third and fourth dimensions – that not only are many extraterrestrials just humans of the future, but that the concept of Higher Self or future self is interchangeable since a future self is an evolved version of the present or past self. This book also explores the planetary systems from which all human life is reported to have come, i.e. our galactic heritage.

Many »New Age« books and channelled writings touch on the story of creation to various degrees. At the end of this book, I have included an excerpt from the »Aquarian Gospel of Jesus the Christ« by Levi which is an account of creation that may interest some. The general consensus of opinion is that we are spiritual beings trying to be human and that we »devolved« into a denser expression and vibration so that we could experience life in form, through the senses, grow and learn and evolve back into our purer form when the timing was right and the »experiment« complete. Most agree (including the Bible which calls this period »the Fall«), that at some stage we forgot that we were spiritual beings trying to be human and started to believe we were only our physical form, our minds and emotions and no more. In some religions, our beliefs in our limitation created feelings of separation and of a God external to ourselves.

All sacred scripts, texts and teachings and prophecy talk of a time of awakening, although they use different labels: Armageddon followed by the 1 000 years of peace, the dawning of the Golden Age after the birthing pains of Earth, the age of Aquarius etc. Much has been foretold of this time. It is a time of great awakening as humanity releases itself, first individually then collectively, of its beliefs of limitation and realises its true divine nature.

This divine nature has been called our God Self, our Higher Self, our I AM Presence, the Inner Christ etc., all of which refer to that pure energy force that sustains us. Higher Self refers to that aspect of ourselves that resonates to a purer frequency or clearer energy band (i.e. more in harmony with our God self). The Theosophists refer to the Higher Self as our soul and the connecting link to the God I AM within. The I AM or monad, is the purest aspect of ourselves and is the spark of the Divine. Consequently, our conscious alignment to these higher energies allows us to be »impregnated« or infused with the Divine so that our lives can be expressed in greater harmony, joy, love and true fulfilment. It can be likened to a lost child who is tired, hungry and generally unhappy at his/her state of being. Coming home, being loved and cared for is like the connection made when we »find« our true state of being – not lost but very loved and joyously welcomed home.

As previously mentioned, connecting with our God essence, the I AM, is like peeling away the layers of an onion to reveal a beautiful core. The core is the I AM, and the layers are the veils of illusion we have collected through eons of time spent in the density of this planet – our fears, emotional scars, belief in death, ageing, disease, limitation, and so on. Eventually ALL evolve to a point of understanding that not only there *must be* something more but that *yes, there definitely is* something more. It is said that the Higher Self and the I AM – because of their vast, multidimensional nature and existence on many other planes of being – do not concern themselves with the soul extension or personality until the soul extension (us in embodiment) seeks to know them. So the first step is simply the sincere heartfelt desire to know more.

It is like the parent who watches the child in the playground, aware of its movement but preoccupied with reading the paper, until the child says that it is tired and wants to go home. Then the parent assumes responsibility by gently taking the hand of the child. Yet the child must still walk. It must still choose to »make the journey«. Free will allows choice for the child to whine and drag its feet or to walk quietly and happily. So it is with our evolution. No one can walk our path to reunification with our Inner God but us. The journey is an inner one and only we can fine-tune our frequency in alignment to our pure essence, for our frequency responds to our thoughts, and who thinks our thoughts but us? Our frequency is altered by our words, our actions, every choice we make from a dietary level to a perception level to so much more. The impact of thoughts and unresolved negativity is covered in previous chapters and how to consciously change the vibrational frequency and the energy signals we transmit is covered in chapter 23.

148

The I AM, the Higher Self and the personality each have three levels as follows:

The I AM or monad has:
· Will or power – the Father principle.
· Love and wisdom – the Son principle.
· Active intelligence – the Holy Spirit principle.

The Higher Self, soul or superconscious mind has:
· Spiritual will.
· Intuition – love/wisdom, the Christ principle.
· Higher mind.

The personality has:
· The mental body.
· The emotional body.
· The physical body.

The spiritual body, or energy field, connects the personality with the Higher Self. The merging of the Higher Self with the personality is where a state of consciousness is achieved of living in unconditional love for self and others, of desiring to always be of service, of recognising the Oneness of all and the God in all.

The merging of the I AM occurs after the merging of the Higher Self and brings with it a state of complete self-realisation (enlightenment) and self-mastery. It brings a state of existence where a being is free from karma, free from the wheel of life and death. At the completion of this integration a being is also an immortalist, able to dematerialise and rematerialise at will and is completely limitless.

As we have covered in previous chapters, we are systems of energy. All is energy which is neither created nor destroyed but simply changes form. Energy is consistent and cannot be graded as pure or impure. It is the consciousness of the vehicle, through which the energy expresses itself, that can be graded. The type of expression of consciousness is detailed in the chapter on vibrational frequencies where awareness moves from a single point of expression in an atom to the actual »cosmic glue« of the vibration of pure love that binds the molecular structure of All That Is. In essence, the Creative Force is pure love and all who have ever tapped into, or merged their awareness with, the creative force that sustains them, will attest to this.

The evolution of consciousness can be likened to being given the role of a gardener in the garden of creation. When we first arrive to take our post we may find that all we see are large, brilliant yellow sunflowers which, for various reasons, captivate our attention. We nurture them, weed around their bases, water them, talk to them until one day we decide there must be more. More what? Variety? So the search begins. We wander around the garden and one day stumble across a patch of beautiful yellow daffodils. They have always been there but, maybe because their colour blended so beautifully, we never saw them. So we begin to nurture them also. They grow with our loving care and multiply and soon we have created a bed just for daffodils! We are aware now that if the daffodils were there all along then maybe other flowers are also. So we learn to be constantly on the lookout for new species to enhance the garden. As time passes we find roses, petunias and orchids. All require specialised care and attention, but bloom at our efforts. We feel expanded at these discoveries and ask ourselves what other rare flower may exist for us to stumble upon.

Now and then we meet other gardeners, and when we share our story some become excited and go in search of other flowers in their garden (for they have always thought there were only sunflowers). Others tell us that only sunflowers can grow and nothing else exists, that it is all our imagination. Even though we show them, they cannot see or hear. They are so absorbed with their sunflowers and the time and effort required for their care, that they have no energy or desire to look for more. It may be easier to tend to what they have. Or perhaps they have searched their gardens before but have not found anything to their liking, only weeds. So for whatever reason, your stories fail to excite them. Now and then you find a gardener who has not only discovered what you have discovered, but more species, for every garden has the same range, the same potential. In this sharing you become inspired, excited, and so your exploration continues.

When we have discovered as many flowers as we wish for now, we may rest – enjoy the fruits of our labour, watch all blossom wondrously, or develop one aspect of the garden. Perhaps roses are a favourite, so we make the rose bed the central feature. For our fellow gardener it may be orchids, and so forth. All has been made manifest by our awareness. We have enhanced what was there, made it visible to others and to ourselves to enjoy. It was there all along, but not found until we consciously looked, although now and then we would discover something by seeming accident. Everything grows if we pay our attention to it. The same is true of consciousness. Awareness creates awareness. Being alert for opportunities allows us to recognise them.

As consciousness is attached to energy, everything is always evolving, like a river that winds its way back to its source, the ocean. The water is then absorbed by droplets into clouds. Clouds are blown across mountains, then become rain that fills streams and rivers that flow back to the ocean. The hermetic saying »as above, so below« simply states that all is a reflection. When one flows with the energy of creation, one is led into creation itself through defined pathways: from creator to creative expression to co-creator to creation – where the creator and creation knows no separation. All are necessary steps in the evolution of consciousness. Humanity was once formless, creative energy. Its expression became »solid,« and we are now becoming conscious of our limitless nature, of the energy that sustains us and of our inherent ability to create. We create through thought. *What* we create depends on the purity of the thought, the consciousness attached to the thought. As we live, we learn and become more aware. We seek self-knowledge, the reason for our existence. We call in our purer aspects – our Higher Self and we become co-creators in this play of life. As we merge with our Higher Self, we call in our I AM – the monad, the divine »spark«. As we merge our consciousness with our I AM, we become again creation as we no longer know separateness, only Oneness.

151

Information on the Five Higher Bodies

From the »Keys of Enoch«

I have included this information as it relates to consciousness that is attached to the energy fields of our higher bodies, and while this information is related to the higher bodies as discussed in the chapter on chakras, it comes from a different source and throws a different light on the subject of higher energy fields and the inherent natural abilities of the consciousness of our Divine Self.

1. The Electromagnetic Body

»This vehicle body codes your physical body directly into other consciousness regions of the local universe through the whole array of electromagnetic waves. The E-M vehicle must work with its »Christ Overself Body« or a Master of Light if it is to work with the many electromagnetic spectrums ... One must first illuminate the E-M vehicle with light before one can cross the threshold of negative mass.«

2. The Epi-Kinetic Body

»The biological plasma used by the energy-vibratory body for projection and teleportation within a singular dimension, the Epi-Kinetic Body is the consciousness vibratory vehicle which can pass through the common kinetic paradigms of velocity and mass. Great energies of vibratory projection, inspiration, and the balancing of the creative consciousness levels with the unconscious and subconscious levels can take place through this vehicle of vibratory synthesis.«

3. The Eka Body/Bodies

»There exists a substratum of direct current potentials in the body which precedes the action potentials of biological reality. This is a Higher Consciousness Body/Body Two substratum which can co-ordinate the inner realities of each consciousness vehicle through an interconnecting clock manifold, whereby consciousness time can be in perfect control of the biological clocks and common/mundane reality. Enoch calls this vehicle the »Eka Body« which is a collection of many plus and minus relativities, depending on the nature of the consciousness levels. The consciousness vehicle is used for time travel while sustaining a direct relationship to the physical vehicle which is left at some point in biological time.« This is the body we use to time travel into past or future lives as all exist simultaneously and dimensions can be entered into by a shift in conscious awareness and perception.

4. The Gematrian Body

»The vehicle of light synthesis in the body formed by the Shekinah's »life force«, which controls all the inner relationships of light. This body prepares the human vehicle to be connected with the Christ Body Overself. On the physical plane, it can control the ratio between the plasmic state of living things and atomic-molecular matter. The Gematrian Body is made up of »light geometries« used in consciousness creation, inspiration, healing etc., which can mathematically arrange each of the energy meridians of the human system to make them available to guide and energise the body.«

5. The Zohar Body

»The body vehicle of the »outer light« that permits the body to go beyond the light cone of immediate relativity. This body places a band of light around the four other energy vehicles of »Incarnation« so that the physical body can distinguish between the sacred space of »light« and the profane space of »light« ».

Chapter 18

Destiny and Service

There seems to come a point in our evolution where higher mind prompts questions as to our role, destiny or reason for existence. Regardless of whether we are *consciously* motivated, we are all driven by a desire for happiness and a feeling of purpose.

Discovering the purpose to our life can be likened to finding our own piece of a giant jigsaw puzzle where the only one who has seen the complete picture is the creator of the puzzle. Each life we are all assigned our own piece which may represent part of a garden, a river, a mountain. All make up the puzzle, all pieces are unique and perfectly formed to fit together to create the whole.

This puzzle is called the Greater Plan, or the Celestial Plan. Destiny is recognising our unique place in this puzzle. Service is allowing perfect alignment so that all pieces fit together to complete the whole. Now, our piece of the puzzle may be a flower in a bed, in the bottom left hand corner, but there may be numerous pieces of a smaller puzzle that make up the whole of our piece. So as we experience life in the »classrooms« of Earth, we may find the stem of the flower in one life (where we have learnt lessons of patience or compassion etc. that has allowed the stem to be strong yet flexible); the next life we have may be to find a leaf. Each piece of the puzzle is already complete and perfect and it is our awareness and perception that is growing and unfolding. As our awareness of our divine nature grows and our consciousness expands, so does our ability to recognise the perfection that is inherent in all.

Sometimes as we learn and grow, we may find a piece that doesn't seem to fit until we have learnt and discovered something else. Then, suddenly, bingo! It all makes sense. It's like finding a root and a blossom but no stem, so there appears to be no connection, yet all belong together eventually. So, as you can imagine, there is no room for judgement of others. They may be forming a

154

cloud or a sun, while we form our flower or garden bed. All of us are unique. All fit perfectly in the Divine Plan.

So what is this Greater Plan? Firstly, it is my understanding that the scope of creation is so vast that it is beyond mental comprehension, although we may have a deep, inner *knowing*. Secondly, what is taking place on Planet Earth at the moment is like one small speck of an even grander plan. We play our destined role as a speck within that speck (not underestimating how unique and divine we as specks are!).

Let us narrow down the field and zoom in on the part of the Greater Plan for this quadrant of this universe at this point in linear time. From my research and personal communication with the Ascended Ones, it has been put forth that the planet is ascending and is being reawakened to her true divine nature. This change and awakening is causing a domino effect, as all who reside in her energy fields will also awaken and ascend. This discussion is elaborated upon in the chapter on ascension. Suffice to say it is not only a grand awakening but it is a time of grand celebration, like a coming of age party!

As with any party, there is much planning and organising and many roles to participate in. There are the decorators, caterers, the musicians, the Masters of Ceremonies, the guests, the waiting staff to »serve« and so on. It could be likened to the opening night celebrations that take place when this giant theatrical production (the play of life discussed earlier) has been a »raging« success, after surviving a few minor, or even major, mishaps. So in a linear time frame, Earth in its unfoldment is going into grand celebration mode – a new birth.

In the above context, *destiny* is where we discover that we have been invited to the party and *service* is when we care enough to ensure that all the guests are having a great time. Service is where we put ourselves at the disposal of the Master of Ceremonies (Divine Will) and do as we are directed to benefit the whole show. The catch to service is that the master always makes the best servant, and we cannot truly serve until we have learnt to thoroughly enjoy ourselves and fulfil our roles in the play, the success of which the party is celebrating! The servants at this party can serve by example only! Remember, the party is held for the benefit of those in the play of life – the actors, support crew, audience etc.

As Lord Sananda said, Earth is a gigantic library and school of learning. Each lifetime has a destined purpose. We may spend an entire lifetime studying religion and/or science, art, music or any combination of these. These subjects may not teach us much, but *living* – as we learn to attain and understand – does. So one life may emphasis the experiences of compassion, another perseverance, and so forth.

Destiny is then a multifaceted process. We may spend eons of time, in a linear time frame, training for our destined role. Part of our training is to learn to enjoy each step along the journey and not just focus on the goal at the end. If we can trust this process, then we can learn to love, honour and enjoy all of life's experiences. Trust allows us to recognise that *all is here to teach us, to inspire us* to play our part to perfection as was preordained by the Greater Plan.

As we trust and open up to the guidance of the Inner Teacher, our Higher Self and I AM Presence, we find ourselves flowing through life in a joyous and synchronistic fashion. The Inner Teacher received the invitation, knows the address, what »role« we will play this time around and will guide us accordingly. So destiny is preordained. Free will allows us our choice of training methods for this »role«.

Service is also multifaceted, and is defined by the quality of our intention. However, many are now aware that it is simply more effective to align their will to that of the will of the Creator of the Plan, who obviously has the full picture. Our direct link to the Creator is the Inner Teacher who we access through regular meditation and contemplation.

At this point in linear time, these lifetimes in learning and training is now culminating for many in a grand awakening and celebration. For some their learning must continue, for, although they will receive their invitation, they may not recognise its significance and may decide not to attend. These individuals will continue the cycle of rebirth and will enter into a similar institution of learning on another planet whose frequency aligns with theirs. So again, all is valid and all will gently unfold, perfectly and rhythmically.

Chapter 19

Balance and Integration – Empowerment and Enlightenment

Although there are said to be many steps on the homeward journey, I feel that they can be broadly classified into four main areas:

· Balance.
· Integration.
· Empowerment.
· Enlightenment.

Balance: The ancient symbol of the square has long represented balance. Balance of east, south, west and north. Balance of opposite forces. Divided into two triangles, this square represents two halves to a whole – the dual nature of life on this plane. In order to move beyond the consciousness of duality we must have balance. Balance of male/female energies within and without; balance of positive/negative; balance of light/dark. The diagonal line symbolically cuts the square and represents the duality united by four corners. Once we have united the two halves, or the two complete triangles, we become integrated or whole. (This is covered further in the chapter on androgyny).

Integration: Is represented by the circle. The ancient symbol of the circle represents wholeness or completion. When we are fully integrated, we become whole. Wholeness is attained when we integrate all aspects of our being – which occurs when we learn to love and honour all within, knowing that it has brought us to this point in our evolution. We use methods – like the ones covered in previous chapters – to break through the habitual »I« to find the Divine Consciousness, knowing that wholeness results in our alignment with our pure essence after the release of all that no longer serves us.

Integration and balance of all aspects of self, are what humanity is now undergoing collectively – the journey into wholeness through balance. When we have integrated all aspects of our being, our resonance is set at a pitch that allows for higher communication.

Empowerment: The triangle is also a pyramid. It has been said that pyramids were a communication device to bridge into other realms. The triangle represents two facets. The first is the opening to higher guidance. This guidance, due to its pure source, further enhances integration and balance in all aspects of life. So, as we move inward – square, circle, triangle; so we move outward – clear, solid integration of this guidance which then creates perfect inner and outer balance. The rhythm is established like the expansion and contraction of energy, or the out-breath and the in-breath of creation. All flows naturally. The second symbolic representation of the triangle is the holy trinity. The symbolism of the trinity is self-explanatory. Suffice it to say that complete union is empowering. So these aspects of the triangle symbolise the empowerment which always comes with clear and strong inner guidance and wholeness and balance.

Enlightenment: The two triangles represent the male/female aspects of our being fully merged, integrated and harmoniously aligned. The merging of the two triangles also forms the Star of David or the double tetrahedron. It symbolises the Merkabah – the vehicle of light allowing for interdimensional travel and freedom. The six-pointed star also symbolises enlightenment. Through balance, integration and the empowerment of clear, inner guidance from the Inner Teacher, we attain enlightenment.

Enlightenment can only be attained through the process of going within. Without balance we cannot integrate. Without integration we cannot receive the purest guidance (the purity of the message is dependent on the purity of the channel). Pure guidance results in empowerment and when we are fully empowered we will attain enlightenment.

Chapter 20

Meditation for Empowerment and The Violet Flame of Freedom

This meditation, I believe, was first channelled through by the Ascended Lady Master Kwan Yin in 1982. It is covered in the initiation process into the healing modality of Magnified Healing which is again »overseen« by Kwan Yin. She is known as the Goddess of Mercy and Compassion and has been revered in Eastern cultures for eons of time. With her permission I have elaborated upon this meditation so that it can be used to allow beings to step into their true power – the God/Goddess state of being.

The common inhibitor of the majority of individuals with whom I have worked has been lack of self-worth and doubt of their true divine nature. Often, this lack of self-worth manifests as their inability to regularly find time in their busy schedules to BE with themselves in silence. If we truly loved and honoured ourselves, we would put as much effort into our relationship with ourselves, and the Inner Teacher, as we do with our loved ones. We would then find that loving and honouring ourselves is a natural by-product of spending time with the Inner Teacher!

So as with all previous guided meditations in this manual, I suggest you record onto tape a version of the following meditation that works for you. This meditation can also be obtained on tape from S.E.A. Listen and meditate on it regularly until the desired result is attained. This meditation is designed to empower us in the inner realms of being to step into our queenly/kingly selves, to open up to inner guidance after being realigned energetically using the three-fold flame of love, wisdom and power which blends together to form the Violet Transmuting Flame of Freedom. (I have also included a simple meditation using the violet flame before the meditation for empowerment.)

Before we elaborate on this meditation, I would like to cover a little information and background on the Chohan of this ray and the violet flame. The Ascended Master St Germain is of the Seventh Ray of Spiritual Freedom, and he works with this flame, which is one of the most powerful energies in the universes. St Germain is known as the Comte St Germain and he has identified himself with the outgrowth of consciousness particularly in Europe. He is known also as the Master Ragoczy and it is said that he has enjoyed previous embodiments as the disciple Mathias, Merlin and even Christopher Columbus (these reports sometimes vary with the channel).

St Germain's energy was prevalent in the early Americas over-shadowing the writing of the Declaration of Independence. He also channelled the I AM discourses through medium Godfre Ray King. In my personal dealings with him, he advises that he is now overshadowing many to utilise the media in a positive manner so that information can be brought through that is inspirational and also illuminating.

Archangel Zadkiel works beside him in assisting in ushering in the new Golden Era by teaching humanity how to transmute the negative energy we have accumulated into light. They do this by using and upholding the radiance of this flame of forgiveness. St Germain is also known to use the amethyst jewel which is the condensation of the violet ray.

The freedom brought by working with the seventh ray is the freedom from the cycle of life and death; the freedom to do the will of the Mother/Father Creator God; the freedom to rise above earthly limitations; the freedom to recognise the divine life force that exists within all of creation and the freedom to relate to this divine force with peace and love and understanding. Freedom is to recognise that this divine life force is God expressed in countless, myriad's of individualised form and then to further recognise the wholeness of which everything is a part. Freedom is to release the veils of separation and ignorance and to know that *in joy, in safety and in harmony, we can step into the unknown*!

»The Eternal Law of Life:
What you think and feel you bring into form;
where your thought is there you are,
for you are your consciousness;
and what you meditate upon, you become.«

St Germain

Affirmations for Freedom by Forgiveness using the Violet Flame

Through the power, love and mercy of my beautiful I AM
Presence,
I call upon the Violet Transmuting Flame
to blaze forward within me
to transmute all that is not of the highest flame of light.
I forgive ... I forgive ... I forgive ...
through my compassion, love and mercy all that is
tangible and intangible
that has ever wronged me in any way,
and through this Violet Transmuting Flame of Forgiveness
I am now freed and liberated to move forward
within the love of the violet ray of God's Holy Spirit
so that I am forgiven and freed from the cycle of karma
from the constraints of the laws of cause and effect.
I thank the beloved Source of life
for this flame of forgiveness
this flame of freedom.

I am new and today I shall bring newness to my life
and I shall express as spontaneously as I can
my power into this world as it presents itself to me.
I call upon the forces that work with my soul
to create my world.
I call upon these forces now to bring to me these elements
that would draw forth my talents,
that I may discover it.

Merlin

Creative Visualisation 7
Meditation using the Violet Flame

· Get comfortable where you will not be disturbed.
· Tune yourself with breath and light work as previously suggested.
· Take deep breaths, then visualise yourself standing in the Great Silence and see yourself in the centre. Visualise a pillar of golden yellow light of Divine Wisdom.
· To the right behind you, visualise the pink light of Divine Love.
· To your left behind you, visualise a blue light for Divine Power.
· Now envision the three flames or pillars of light blending into a circle around you, with the gold in front, the pink on the right and the blue on the left.
· Feel the energy and the activity as these three aspects penetrate every cell within your physical system, and as it does so, focus your attention in your heart where the three-fold flame sits as that spark of divinity within you.
· Now see the three-fold flame expanding to meet the pillars of light around you, blending all harmoniously within and without.
· Now with your heart centre visualise a large disc of golden pink light expanding from your heart flame.
· Affirm to yourself three times – »I AM the Ascended Master Freedom«.
· Now in your mind's eye, in the third eye of your sixth chakra, visualise a large disc of blazing white light from the ascended realms.
· Feel it expanding into your very being.
· Affirm to yourself three times – »I AM the Ascended Master Consciousness«.
· Now visualise the golden pink light of wisdom and love within your heart, rising up to your third eye and see it blend with the blazing white light.

- Visualise a beam of light extending now through your crown chakra right up to your beautiful I AM Presence, connecting all in unison.
- Now repeat three times – »I AM that I AM.«
- Feel the Ascended Master Consciousness and Freedom and envision it coming back down through your sacred spine, through your chakra system.
- Picture the light blazing forward now into your beloved Earth Mother, to all humanity, to our continent, to any beloved group, family, and friends.
- Visualise this light circulating around each person within this group and connecting the flame within your hearts as one.
- See one big circle of great white light combining all energies and know that you are the perfect God essence, that you are made in the perfection of God's image.
- See this thread of light connecting back to your heart, back up to your third eye, returning to your I AM Presence.
- Now pour forward to your I AM Presence the gratitude and the love that you have for yourself and ask by the grace of God that your I AM Presence continue to pour forth this perfect activity into daily life and your physical vehicle.
- Now through your beloved almighty I AM Presence call forward the invincible Violet Transmuting Flame asking for purification and transmutation.
- And so it is!

Creative Visualisation 8
Meditation for Empowerment

This meditation is designed to connect you with the God/Goddess within, and to be empowered using the violet flame.

· Again get comfortable where you will not be disturbed.

· Let us begin – close your eyes.

· We are about to commence the journey to the inner realms.

· Begin to tune yourself with light and breath work.

· Breathe slowly, rhythmically and deeply

· Feel this breath moving through your physical body and release all tension.

· Imagine that you are in a tall building on the tenth floor.

· As you step into the elevator and begin to descend, you count backwards, breathing one connected inhale and exhale between each count, allowing yourself to relax deeper and deeper as you descend ... 10 ... 9 ... 8 ... 7 ... 6 ... 5 ... 4 ... 3 ... 2 ... 1 ... 0 ...

· The doors of the elevator open.

· You find before you a most beautiful sanctuary.

· Let your mind wander and create as you open up your inner senses.

· The sky is a brilliant blue. The breeze is gently blowing, birds are singing.

· You see before you a crystal stairway and you begin to climb, slowly leaving your cares, worries and concerns and even the planet behind. You seem to be climbing into the centre of the very universe.

· As you absorb its vastness, you begin to feel so small – like a speck, an ant, an atom .... so small that you can now simply step into the chambers of your own heart.

· As you stand now in the inner heart chamber, you see before you the three-fold flame of pink, golden white and blue.

· You move forward gracefully and step into the pink flame – the flame of Divine Love.

· Feel its soothing energy whirl around your feet, moving up around your body like a gentle mini tornado. It engulfs you and then infuses through your body, through all your energy fields.

· It fills every cell with its soft loving pink energy, its vibration of love. It is as if you are standing in a shower of love. It surrounds you, moves through you, realigns you to its vibration.

· Breathe its energy into the very heart of your being.

· As you exhale, release the energy of love from within your cells, for it resides there also.

· When ready, you step into the flame of Divine Wisdom, its golden white light wrapping itself around you – around your feet, up over your head.

· Then it also infuses through you, and as it does so it activates all the positive cellular memory that you need to utilise in your life now.

· It aligns you with Divine Intelligence, reawakens you to the knowledge of all universes – to sacred wisdom, to higher knowing.

· You feel alive, loved, connected to all.

· Breathe this energy into every cell as you stand within this flame.

· Take three deep breaths.

· You feel the blue energy of the flame of Divine Power now begin to encircle you.

· As it does so, and as it moves through the centre of your very being, you feel empowered – as if you can do anything, achieve anything, you feel determined, filled with love, filled with wisdom, filled with a strength of purpose.

· Breathe this new-found awareness and inner strength and power into every cell.

· The three flames dance around your being, blending their energies into one powerful vortex – its colour becomes violet in hue. It is the Transmuting Violet Flame of Freedom.

· As it swirls around you, you begin to dance, to spin – clockwise, anti-clockwise – the direction does not matter.

· You feel yourself becoming freer as you spin around, as if all

- unwanted matter, negative energies, psychic bonds are being broken or simply jettisoned from your energy field.
- Visualise yourself to be spinning in the centre of this mini tornado of violet light.
- Visualise all emotional baggage and limited belief systems being flung off into the atmosphere around you and dissolved by light. All that no longer serves your highest good and divine unfoldment leaves you now.
- Feel this flame move through your cells as you dance – realigning you, freeing you, dissolving all dross, pollutants and negativity in your cellular structure. You continue this spinning dance until you feel so light you could float away – so free and unencumbered, joyous.
- Breathe deeply of this new energy that engulfs you now.
- So you have been bathed in Divine Love.
- You have felt the flame of Divine Wisdom activate all higher knowledge within you, have been empowered and then set free.
- As you step beyond this flame, you see before you now a most beautiful throne. Notice its colour, its texture – perhaps it is crystal or gold and bejewelled.
- Pause for a moment.
- You have a sense of a robe being placed around your shoulders. Feel the texture on your skin, notice its colour.
- A crown is placed upon your head. Is it plain or jewelled or crystal inlaid? This is your coronation. You are the king/queen, God/Goddess of your inner realms. As you sit upon your throne, you feel as though you have stepped into your true divine nature – your God Self.
- You contemplate any problems you had before entering this magical place.
- You ask for guidance.
- You are still and listen.
- You breathe slowly, deeply and connectedly and begin to visualise how you wish your life to be – knowing you have the love, wisdom, power and freedom to create wisely.

- Allow your mind to drift, to fantasise.
- Allow higher vision to click in and reveal itself to you.
- Take deep, connected, fine breaths.
- Feel your Divine Self alive and activated within you.
- Feel it grow and expand with every inhale and every exhale.
- As you breathe, you feel yourself becoming larger and larger and, still seated on your throne, you find yourself now once more on top of the crystal stairwell in the centre of the universe; for not only are you the God/Goddess of the inner realms, you are empowered to rule wisely over your universe, over all aspects of your life.
- As you rise and begin to descend this staircase you affirm what it is you wish to create in your life with each step down ...
- I AM healthy, I AM vibrant, I AM radiant.
- I give and receive love easily in all aspects of my life.
- I enjoy loving, positive relationships with all in my life.
- My life is joyous and abundant.
- Affirm what you wish with each step. Feel more empowered as you do so.
- You see Planet Earth before you. You look upon it with eyes of love and compassion knowing that the God/Goddess within you is also within all sentient beings. You send powerful beams of loving healing energy into the Earth and into the hearts of all her inhabitants.
- Finally, you step back into your garden.
- You pause to remember your experience, any messages your Divine Self may have whispered to you, any visions you have accessed and any decisions you have made stay fresh in your memory.
- You feel a deep sense of love, of peace, a quiet inner knowing of true empowerment.

Creative Visualisation 9
Meditation for Manifestation

If you wish to manifest something in your life, you may wish to apply the following guidelines and then try the meditation for abundance that follows.

- The first requirement for manifestation is to be clear about what it is you wish to attain.
- Next, write in ink the »activity« or »thing« you wish to manifest in your life. This anchors the application in the etheric as well as in the physical.
- Let it sit for 24 hours (one cycle) undisturbed. This allows the energy to go forward into the universe to build enough momentum to attract the Law of Manifestation back to you.
- After 24 hours burn the piece of paper and recite this decree: »My beloved magic I AM Presence, through the power of your flame bring this application into physical manifestation. I now release this into the three-fold flame of my heart.«
- Have no attachment to it or to the outcome – this is called the »ritual of completion« where the burning releases the energy.

Meditation for Abundance or Manifestation

- Get comfortable, close your eyes.
- Tune yourself with breath and light work.
- Visualise yourself standing on top of a tall mountain overlooking everything.
- Feel as though the air is super-charged with electrical, magnetic energy. Breathe this air into you slowly, feel it filling every cell. Feel as though you are becoming more and more charged, more energised as you breathe this air into you.
- Breathe it through the pores of your skin.
- As you exhale, breathe back out into the atmosphere love and gratitude for all that you have in life. Feel as though you are giving love to the world.

- Continue breathing in and out, feeling empowered, energised on the in-breath.
- Visualise on the in-breath that whatever it is you are seeking, is attracted to your electromagnetic force and gently flows back to you with each inhale.
- Then as you exhale, send back love and gratitude for the receipt of your desire (if we wish to receive something we must keep the energy balanced by giving in return. Sending out the energy of love into the world is very empowering to the sender and receiver.)

Practise the above visualisation for five minutes morning and night. Some say that for manifestation to work all you need to do is to be clear about what you want, ask once and then let it go, assume the message has been received and *do not doubt* that it will be attended to. However, it is also good to create the habit of seeing yourself »tune up« magnetically and attract to you what you wish, as this vision lays the seed in our mind that we are creative beings. Try both and see what works for you.

Apart from doubt that many have about their ability to manifest, the next most limiting factor is the belief of lack of deservability. When we can overcome these two factors, manifestation becomes automatic and faith in our ability grows with success. When we also truly understand the Law of Resonance, where like attracts like, we also realise we can manipulate our energy fields to create the life we desire. True manifestation is the ability to create via thought alone without physical action.

In summary:
1. **Intention:** Think it and make sure your intention is for the highest good for you and others.
2. **Definition:** Say it clearly and specify a time frame you wish to achieve this. Spirit knows no linear time so it may be brought to you years hence!
3. **Deservability:** Know you deserve all you desire if your intention is pure.

4. **Desire** it: Write it down in a positive format.
5. **Action:** Do it. Do all you can do yourself to make it happen, then let it go and trust it will be done. If you always act with *integrity* and do not doubt you will succeed. If we are tuned in synchronistic alignment with Divine Will and have no internal saboteur programs running, then anything we wish to make manifest must come to pass.

The Abundance Bank and the Kosmic Koffers

Understanding universal law and assuming that we exist in an abundant universe, then it stands to reason that poverty and lack must stem from the uneven distribution of existing resources. What attracts abundance to some and yet is kept at bay by others? We say »kept at bay« as the Law of Resonance states that like must attract like – lack of abundance mirrors a lack of acceptance of abundance within us.

The Master Alchemists have often said that the last great test for the lightworkers is the release of poverty consciousness; which is often particularly difficult as we have had many lifetimes as monks and priests where we have repeatedly taken many vows of poverty, chastity and obedience. Consequently in the deep, dark recesses of our minds we may often still believe that it is not possible to be spiritual and ... have money, have great sex lives and loving relationships, follow our own hearts and only do work that we looove etc etc .... Releasing these thoughtforms and old patterns is essential for our progression into abundant lives. To do so effectively we recommend the following:

1. Be aware that there exists the Universal Bank of Abundance – or what I often cheekily prefer to call the KOSMIC KOFFERS!
2. Be aware that the Master Alchemists, who run the Bank of Abundance, are happy to arrange a permanent line of credit for any individual who is in committed service in the fulfillment of the Divine Blueprint on Earth. The universe exists in an ebb and flow of energy, so in order to be in perfect balance, the line

of credit must be paid back through the rewards that come with being the Divine Ambassadors committed to the plan. Giving and receiving are to be always eventually balanced.

Receiving funds from the Kosmic Koffers is only possible when:

1. You open to attract, receive and hold abundance so ....

    a) Be aware that affirmations alone will not work if there are any »internal sabotage programs« running from cellular memory. To clear these we need to say to our Divine One Within (our DOW): »I now command that all discordant energy patterns that are blocking me from receiving all the abundance that is mine, be now released from my being. I ask to complete* any learning around these issues in joy, ease and grace so that I may be free to accept universal abundance and fulfil my Divine Blueprint here NOW on Earth«.

    b) Know that once an individual has aligned their will with Divine Will, and is totally focused on their Divine Service, they have a right to expect to be paid for this service work. In the game of Divine Alchemy, God is your new employer. If you do not *expect to be paid and accept your divine salary* – with all its »lurks and perks« like a suitable home base, suitable transport, even a decent office, assistants etc – then you cannot receive what is rightfully yours. So remember, EXPECT TO BE PAID from sources known and unknown and you will be.

    c) Once you have cleared limiting beliefs, and signed onto the divine payroll – then *the final step is be vigilant in your thinking* patterns. Watch your thoughts – be aware every time you have a limiting thought about abundance, particularly around money. When each limiting or »negative« thought that arises, immediately reprogram it with »Yes, I

---

* Patterns cannot be released from our field until we have completed our learning around why we created the issues in the first instance.

used to think like this, however I NOW ACCEPT AND
GIVE THANKS FOR ALL THE ABUNDANCE THAT IS
MINE. So be it, so be it, so be it!« Or use any other affirmation that comes to mind. Reprogramming in this manner
signals to the universe that you are now open to receive
your abundance.

2. Asking your DOW to: »Bring me NOW all the people, all the
resources and all the information *relevant* to fulfil the next
piece of my Divine Blueprint« is also a most useful program of
intention.

Chapter 21

Androgyny – Our True State

Regardless of physical expression, i.e. whether the energy that sustains us inhabits a feminine or masculine form, energy is by nature androgynous. It may express itself to be of masculine nature or feminine nature, but it is – in essence – the union of the two.

It is our culture that encourages predominance of expression. Genetic encoding also gives particular leanings, but inherently we all have within us male and female, positive and negative forces. As previously explained, what we pay our attention to grows. Society deliberately cultivates aspects of our nature to suit fashionable beliefs, current rules and to promote certain balances of power.

In a paternalistic society, males are encouraged to express leadership, assertiveness and competitiveness. Females in that society are expected to develop the submissive, nurturing aspects of their nature. Both males and females have all of the above characteristics and many more qualities inherent within them. Which characteristics come to the fore is largely determined by environmental influences, culture, society, teachings and expectations of family and peers.

Research into the supposed mythological time of Atlantis, via the Edgar Cayce writings among others, reveals a predominantly matriarchal society, particularly in the later stages. As with any imbalance, the pendulum must swing the opposite way in order to find its centre. Consequently, many cultures have now become predominantly patriarchal. Currently the pendulum has begun its downward swing and will achieve equilibrium and balance.

Western society has recently witnessed the advent of feminism. This is basically the readdressal of the forces of energy. The pendulum must return to centre whenever there is imbalance. The follow-on from feminism is »peopleism,« or individualism, where we can all express and utilise our potential and fully develop all aspects of our nature, both masculine and feminine.

It is important to note that we are working with energy fields, and that energy rebalance is the motivating factor for all change. The advent of the feminist movement, for example, was simply the answer to a need for the influx of more feminine energy to re-establish balance as the pendulum had reached its highest point in patriarchal societies.

If the energy that sustains us is androgynous, then it is obvious that the more we merge or align our conscious awareness with this divine aspect of our nature, the more we will manifest androgyny ourselves. True freedom comes with balance, self-knowledge and recognition, exploration and integration of all aspects of our nature. The planet is on a »homeward« course back to the Source and the completion of a cycle. Completion comes with wholeness, and wholeness comes with balance.

Society reflects the consciousness of its people. Beings who have balanced the male/female aspects of their nature will create a balanced society. This is a state of existence where both the masculine and feminine are honoured and co-exist harmoniously in mutual pleasure and mutual empowerment.

Creative Visualisation 10
Meditation to Balance
Male and Female Energies

Although the following is a very simple visualisation, it has surprisingly had quite profound effects on many who have utilised it. Perhaps because of historic conditioning, few individuals are completely in touch with both the male/female aspects of their nature, and this exercise creates an opportunity for inner guidance from both. It also allows for the merging of both aspects of your being as the male represents the left side of your brain and controls the right side of your body. The female represents the right and controls the left side. The following energetic merging again further enhances inner balance of energy and communication.

· Tune yourself with breath and light work.
· Visualise yourself to be in your »sanctuary«.
· Breathe deeply, finely and rhythmically until you are completely relaxed.
· Then visualise a special place within your sanctuary, somewhere where your male/female aspects can be symbolically united – as in marriage.
· Be aware, as you open up all your inner senses, of all that surrounds you.
· You hear a female voice calling you. You follow the sound, and there before you stands your female aspect.
· Notice what she looks like and what she is wearing (if anything).
· Is she young or old?
· How does her »energy« feel? Is it familiar to you?
· She is aware of the significance of this destined union and, before you leave her to connect with your male aspect, you ask her if there is anything she would like you to pay attention to, to make your life more balanced, to express your female aspect

- more fully or harmoniously. Be still and listen for any inner guidance she may wish to impart.
- Breathe deeply, connectedly. Allow your »supersensory« senses to be activated.
- You hear a male voice calling, but before you follow it, you thank your female aspect for her wisdom and guidance.
- There before you now stands your male aspect.
- Be aware of how he is presented to you. Is he young or older, naked or dressed?
- How does his energy feel to you? Is it familiar?
- Again you ask for any guidance from this aspect of yourself, that will again allow for a fuller, more balanced expression of the masculine aspect of your nature. You listen in stillness, absorbing through all your inner senses all you have »envisaged« around you.
- Breathe deeply, connectedly. Allow your supersensory senses to be activated.
- You take his hand, thank him for his wisdom and lead him to your female aspect.
- Notice how they greet each other – shyly or comfortably, like long-time companions.
- Perhaps they have both had equal expression in your life, perhaps not.
- Because this is the inner world where thought creates instantaneously, you see them now »appear« in their robes of union.
- As they hold hands, you notice a beam of light connecting them energetically – first at the base chakra, then connecting their sacral centres.
- A beam of golden white light connects them at their solar plexus chakras.
- Then a beautiful soft pink beam of light connects them heart to heart.
- Then a blue beam throat to throat,a violet beam from forehead to forehead.
- Then a rainbow arc that blends to pure white light connecting energetically their crown chakras.

- As you witness this beautiful display of light, notice how your body feels, for this is also a merging taking place within you on the inner planes.
- Standing back you see the light at their crowns getting brighter and larger, becoming a huge ball of energy that encases them both as they begin to merge into each other like a film negative that was double exposed and is now forming one clear visual image, surrounded and encased in pure white light.
- You watch this scene of their merging as a detached observer, then you »see« this beautiful God/Goddess being emerge from the light, walk towards you, then merge into your own energy fields.
- You feel a powerful current of energy surging through your body and yet you feel complete, balanced, an inner harmony.
- Take a few deep breaths. Breathe deeply, connectedly, finely.
- You feel as though this inner merging has realigned you electromagnetically.
- When you are ready bring your attention slowly back to your body, to where you now sit. Feel your legs, your arms.
- You feel at peace, a deep sense of inner contentment.
- You open your eyes.

Creative Visualisation 11
Visualisation to Increase Energy Flow
Left/Right Brain

Many beings find themselves often to be predominantly »left« brain oriented i.e. analytical, easily grasping mathematical and scientific data etc.; while others have tended to be more intuitive and creative, predominantly using the right side of their brain. Society also encourages specific male/female roles, and subsequent brain use, which I have covered in the previous pages. This visualisation exercise is perfect to use for migraine headaches or to clear confused thinking. It is designed to free and maximise the flow of energy through the electrical pathways and circuitry of the brain. It allows for maximum energy flow between the left and right hemispheres of the brain, and consequently more »balance« in life.

· Tune yourself with light and breath work.
· Close your eyes and visualise that you are holding your brain between your hands as your palms face each other.
· Visualise a beam of pure, golden white light entering your crown and filling every cell of your body before flowing out through the palms of your hands.
· Imagine that this light is an intense, highly charged healing laser light that is designed to dissolve any blockages in its path, designed to heal and repair, as it begins to flood into the cells of your brain which you still imagine yourself to hold between your hands.
· You may feel resistance as you begin to draw your hands together as if they are invisible and can pass through every cell of your brain.
· See your hands – like a concertina accordion – coming together, sweeping their energy through the brain then pulling apart like an elastic band being stretched, then returning once more to its natural position.

180

- Do this exercise numerous times.
- Every time you bring your hands together, imagine the light that is intensely flowing between them is activating, healing and clearing all the pathways of the brain, is switching on the electrical circuitry between the left and right hemispheres as if someone has switched on a thousand light bulbs of intense energy, or as if electrical storm type currents are surging through the brain, energising it, activating dormant cells, dissolving old ones, allowing your full brain potential to be utilised.
- If you feel resistance in bringing your hands together, just slowly continue. It simply means you are encountering energy blocks which need to be cleared.

I once did this exercise with a student who said his brain felt very »sloppy.« I laughed and said he'd probably »sauced« it too much with alcohol in his younger days! He then admitted he had been an alcoholic and this was very evident by the structure of his brain. As he continued this exercise he felt his brain become firmer and gain elasticity. Other people have also reported great relief from migraines using the above visualisation. The Ascended Ones say that fully illuminating our brain regularly with light has innumerable benefits we have yet to even discover!

Chapter 22

Meditation and Crystals

Crystals have been utilised for eons of time to maximise and amplify energies of the human body as well as for healing. Consequently, due to these inherent properties, many individuals choose to select either a variety of crystals or one particular crystal to work with in their times of meditation. I personally love to work with crystals, so I have included some basic information for those who are interested in the power and properties of crystals. Detailed information can be obtained in Katrina Raphael's books »Crystal Enlightenment« and »Crystal Healing«.

It is said that in the times of Lemuria and Atlantis, crystals were used as generators for all sources of power. Many indigenous people are familiar with the »sacred« properties of crystals. In healing, crystals can be used to realign the energies of the body's power centres, the chakras. Each chakra has a crystal with which it particularly resonates. This type of work can be done in your meditation/contemplation times and will maximise the flow or intensity of energy as crystals are, by their very nature, amplifiers of energy. For working with the higher chakras, the following crystals are recommended.

Clear quartz crystal: This crystal vibrates clear, white light which contains all other colours and is used to balance emotions and also to amplify thoughtforms. It is always associated with the crown chakra and receives, stores, activates, transmits and amplifies energies. It can be used to dispel negativity in our energy field and environment. Clear quartz is excellent for meditation and enhances interdimensional communication and communication with our I AM Presence, Higher Self and/or guides.

Clear quartz crystals are known to work subliminally through the subconscious and stimulate the finer, more subtle realms of our being. Clear quartz can be male or female. The female crystal is cloudy and rarer to find. The male crystal is good for clearing emotional confusion, and the female for stimulating mediumistic qualities.

Amethyst crystal: One of the best stones for meditation as it helps open the third eye, also known as the brow chakra, and stimulates clairvoyant capacity. Its colour reflects the purple/violet ray which has the highest vibration and it aids in stilling mundane thought processes and promotes mental tranquillity. Amethyst energy shows the mind how to be humble so that the door to the higher mind can be opened. It also calms and heals the nervous system. The amethyst initiates wisdom and greater understanding and is here to teach humility. It is good to use when overworked or overstressed and if placed on the brow upon retiring will promote deep, peaceful sleep.

Blue lace agate: Along with the crystal crysocholla and turquoise, it is associated with the fifth chakra, the throat chakra, and allows for the peaceful, melodious flow of expression, clarity in communication and speaking our own truth. This blue stone is associated with the energy of Venus and was used extensively by the American Indians. Its energy is peaceful and feminine. It works well with the thyroid gland to promote emotional balance and sensitivity.

Rose quartz crystal: Is associated with the heart chakra (along with the green tourmaline). Its energy is essential to self-fulfilment and inner peace. It comforts and heals any wounds the heart has accumulated. This crystal promotes calm and dissolves any accumulated burdens that suppress the heart's ability to give and receive love. It teaches forgiveness and reprograms the heart to love itself and tap into the infinite source of Divine Love. It clears the channel for the flow of energy from the higher consciousness into the lower bodies of man via the heart chakra to the lower chakras. When used in healing, it helps clear stored anger, resentment, guilt, fear, jealousy and reduces stress and tension. The rose quartz crystal also enhances self-confidence and creativity and aids in the development of forgiveness and compassion.

Those interested in working with and amplifying the energies of higher consciousness can combine the energies of the clear quartz, the amethyst, the lace agate and the rose quartz to maximise Divine Wisdom (crown chakra), Divine Seeing or clairvoyance (brow chakra) with Divine Expression (throat chakra) and Divine Love (heart chakra).

Chapter 23

Understanding and working with Vibrational Frequencies

I remember standing on the sidewalk one sunny Brisbane spring in the mid-eighties and intuitively realising that I needed to understand more about vibrations and frequencies. At that time I had been regularly meditating for 15 years and, although I had experienced many powerful benefits from this practice, from somewhere deep inside came a knowing that the next important step in my »spiritual« journey involved understanding energy bands.

It was at this time in my research that I understood that our four lower bodies – physical, emotional, mental and spiritual – could be likened to a four-string guitar. When each body or energy field is tuned, our life flows harmoniously and when any are »out of tune,« life is not as harmonious. I realised also that we have the free will to consciously tune ourselves, or not. Being aware of the bodies as systems of energy gives us choice to be tuned instruments and create life as we wish rather than have events in life occur randomly.

As Annalee Skarin writes in her book, »Ye Are Gods«: »Learn to control vibrations by controlling thoughts and you will hold the keys of Eternal Life in your hands. The eternal energy surging through all matter, the power of existence in atoms with their whirling molecules and electrons in all earthly substance is nothing more or less than vibrations condensed to the point of slow, heavy, mortal tangibility. Control the vibrations and the power to control substance and material energy will eventually be given, that is the keys to handling Eternal Life, for energy is life, and life and light and love and energy are the eternal elements and are vibrations created by mental thinking.

Every thought sent forth is a never-ending vibration winging its way across the universe to bring us back just what we sent forth. We can control the vibrations that emanate from us – and we can thereby control our destinies. Thus science and religion can at last join hands and step into the spiritual realms of eternal progress and happiness together.

Further, Dr. Norma Milanovich explains in »We the Acturians«: »We discovered that the frequency at which a being vibrates is directly related to the command it has over its thoughts, words and emotions. When a being vibrates at a lower frequency, it permits many other forms of energies to mix and mingle with its pool of energy and its cycles. When this happens, the thoughts have a tendency to get confused which causes a being to experience frustration. In this state of BEingness, one who is operating at this frequency can get very discouraged and depressed, which in turn has the tendency to keep the vibratory level at a constant lower level.

When one increases one's frequency to that of the speed of light, then the mastery of the process begins. This means that the being now has access to more information in the universal consciousness ... that being ... can dictate what will or will not come through the filter ... In this transformation process, the being becomes centred and the energy patterns are more ordered, holistic and harmonised.

When we are centred, we access the universal code and when we tap into this frequency, we understand another's frequency patterns too. That is, again, because we are one. In the Oneness of this existence we are able to transmit and receive messages; and more importantly, we can become the sender and receiver of messages in perfect understanding.«

In the text »Revelation from an Archangel – Ascension to the Twelfth Dimension«, Archangel Ariel states: »Matter, as you know it from the third dimension, is densification of light ... When you have a process of densification such as your universe, you reach a point when it has gone to maximum separation from the purest form of light. At that point of maximum separation, a shift occurs, and the planet begins to reverse its process and start on what we would term a homeward route i.e. back to the one point.«

Each time a planet ascends it changes its vibratory rate to be less dense and lighter and it undergoes this process in its own unique way.

Certain evolutionary cosmologies talk of seven bands with seven sub-levels each. The first may be seen as seven planes of the solar system plane with seven sub-planes and is known as the cosmic physical plane. There are said to be seven cosmic planes – physical, astral, mental, Buddhic, atmic, monadic and Logoic. The planes of our solar system belong in the cosmic physical. Once we complete these seven sub-levels we move onto the bottom level of the next cosmic plane, and so it continues, slowly evolving back to Source. It is said that one day of God, which is an out-breath and in-breath, lasts 4 billion 320 million years. We still have 1.2 billion years left in our time until the in-breath is complete and then the cycle will start again. This is an interesting concept and one well-explored by the Theosophists among others.

The exact mid-point between the in and out-breath is said to be in the year 2012. This date is the last date of the Mayan calendar and is foretold by the Hopi Indians and many other civilisations. This year marks a time of wondrous change with multitudes awakening to their true divinity.

The in-breath phase takes place more quickly than the out-breath: just as a rubber band stretched tightly and slowly to its maximum capacity has tremendous tension and when released returns to its original condition incredibly quickly. Due to the change in the vibrational frequency as we pull back in, our experience of time is also affected. Consequently, even though we have passed the mid-way point in linear time – 1.2 is not half of 4.3 – the passage of time is speeding up with the increase in the rate of oscillation. Similarly, as we »get older«, time seems to »fly« because in comparison we actually have less time. If we were to live to 80, at eight we have nine-tenths (90%) of our »time« left. At 40 we have 50%. It has been said in channelled information that due to the change in frequency and faster rate of vibration, comparatively speaking, our 24 hour days are now experienced as 16 hour days.

The discussion of the dimensions, or planes, as frequency bands is not the subject of this book. One word, however, about the cosmic physical plane. It is only in the »top« frequency band, the seventh, that awareness is a multidimensional experience. Once awareness reaches this level it is capable of passing into the next frequency band – with its seven sub-levels. It is said that individual consciousness no longer exists at this point. It is the plane above the monad or I AM consciousness. The seventh dimension is pure light, pure tone, sacred geometry, pure expression and creativity: a plane of infinite refinement.

Our planet is said to be currently vibrating at the top of the astral plane. As it continues to shift and ascend, the lower dimensions will »be rolled up into the higher dimensions and cease to exist« – Archangel Ariel. The dimensions below the fifth are known as the »lower levels of creation«. Those from the fifth to the ninth, are the mid-creation realm.

The sixth dimension is the Christ consciousness, or Buddhic, state of awareness where responsibility is taken for the whole rather than the self. It is where the monad is anchored. This is said to be the level of consciousness that existed in Jesus when he became the Christ. The sixth also holds the templates for the DNA patterns of all creation. It is made up of colour and sound (tone) and it holds all the light languages. It is where consciousness creates thought and where one goes to work and learn while asleep. Beings here are pure energy but can create a body by choice if required as in the fifth dimension.

The fifth is a plane of experiential awareness of »I« as a group identity and is not bound by linear time. Beings on this plane may take physical form when, and if, they choose. The fifth is the dimension of light where all are masters, multidimensionally aware and totally dedicated to Spirit and service to Divine Will. According to the »Keys of Enoch«, the fifth dimension is the next »garment of light« that our matter-energy body will enter.

The fourth plane is a state of superconsciousness and of the reintegration of group identity without the loss of the individual or ego identity. It brings the ability to interface with multidimensional realities. It is the last density requiring a physical body. The fourth dimension is said to be emotion-based and is also known as the astral world. It is said that we are entering into the energies of the fourth dimension and many individuals have already moved beyond the third dimensional consciousness. The transition, or Harmonic Convergence, has brought about a major energy alignment and shift in the vibrational frequency of both our planet and the beings living on her. On the 12 of December 1994, the gateway to a further influx of energies for planetary realignment was opened and these influxes of energies will continue in greater or lesser degrees.

The third dimension is matter-based and is a state of volumetric awareness, as well as of ego awareness. The vibration of this plane creates the illusion of separation and is thus a challenge to individual awakening. It presents humanity with the opportunity to discover that we are spiritual beings trying to be human rather than human beings trying to be spiritual.

The second plane is the density of the plant and animal kingdoms although these, too, have become more refined in frequency due to the changes in planetary vibrations and are moving into the third. Self awareness and ego are usually absent from the second plane.

The first dimension is that of minerals, water, atoms and molecules that make up the basic genetic codes. Just as the second dimension was the plane of linear awareness, this is the plane of point or unidimensional awareness.

As a being evolves spiritually, this is reflected in both his/her vibrational frequency and molecular structure. Regarding molecular density, the Ascended Masters have explained that the space between the electrons, neutrons and protons in atomic structure becomes greater as the »light« expands within an atom. This »light« also reflects a being's conscious awareness of its inherent divine nature. As this light or awareness grows, it expands to fill the space in each atom thereby changing the frequency or rate of oscillation of each atom. As a being expands its awareness and increases the light quotient within its cellular structure, it becomes multidimensional i.e. able to move into other dimensions of reality. Again, it is simply a matter of shifting one's point of conscious awareness and »switching« channels.

Various reliable channelled sources report that as we evolve further into light, our DNA is undergoing modifications to accommodate these changes and is in the process of becoming 12-stranded. The influx of higher energies at this time will allow for humanity to evolve faster in the next 40 years than it has in the last 3 billion. These higher energies are also responsible for the speeding up of time as we know it.

Also as our frequencies change, abilities such as telepathy, healing by touch, clairvoyance, teleportation etc. will become completely natural. As tuned instruments operating at our highest maximum potential, our life will become harmonious, joyous and filled with synchronicity, grace and magic. Even though we cannot avoid this process of change – as due to the Earth's evolution, we must also change – we can consciously be aware and accelerate these changes if we wish to.

Well-researched information plus practical techniques for changing vibrational frequencies by conscious choice are outlined in full detail throughout this book. Succinctly put, it can be achieved by the following:

· Most importantly and powerfully by meditation – breath and light work – especially when meditation is used to increase the light quotient in our cellular structure.
· By the fuel chosen for the maintenance of the physical body. We can treat the vehicle like a Porsche for peak performance or like a jalopy – the choice is ours.
· By mastery of the emotional body and cellular memory.
· By mastering the mental body via intention, programming and accessing the four-fifths of the brain that house higher consciousness.
· By mantras and toning using sonic waves.

The conscious process of tuning brings also strong feelings of empowerment as we literally understand the practical game of reality creation through signals we transmit as energy centres.

33 – the Universal Beat

To deepen our understanding of vibrational frequencies and the power one can hook into when one is tuned, we can to look at what are termed beats and octaves.

Esoteric research discloses that physical reality operates in bands of seven, with seven sub-planes or sub-levels (octaves) in each band. There are seven chakras, seven colours of refracted white light and so forth.

It is also held that the beat of the solar system is ten, with ten sub-levels in each energy band. The beat of the galaxy is 12, with 12 sub-levels. The highest and most refined beat one can obtain or tune to while still retaining physicality is 33 – the universal beat. Again, this beat fragments or refines into 33 sub-frequencies.

When we embark on the journey of refinement, we gain an understanding of the various dimensions and parallel realities. If, for instance, people focus on physical realities – those who adhere to the »I'll believe it when I see it« school – the result will be the limitation of their field of reality to the seven x seven dimension and they will not be able to move beyond that field until they consciously refine themselves to the next higher beat.

Conscious refinement takes place as one undergoes the process of involution, inner reflection, contemplation and connection with the Divine One within. The beat of the Divine One is 33. It is the backdrop upon which all creation is manifested in its various forms.

As a being consciously »refines« and tunes itself, it can gain access to higher realities and tap into the ten x ten, 12 x 12 or even 33 x 33 levels. Hence, we have many people now feeling expanded and multidimensional as the Inner Teacher begins to share the delights of all that we are – beyond just the more dense aspect of ourselves housed in a physical vehicle witnessing and enjoying physical reality of the seven x seven paradigm.

Conscious refinement brings great freedom and limitless being. Freedom from the need to eat. Freedom from the need to sleep. Freedom from utilising the Gregorian time of 12:60 or the

Mayan time of 13:20 and moves us into the divine time flow where one finds themselves always in the perfect place at the perfect time.

The subatomic particles or »soft particles« of the quantum field – also known as prana, chi or the universal life force – beat to the octave of 33 x 33 in their most refined expression.

When we tune to this beat, in a manner similar to turning the dial of a radio to pick up a specific frequency, we literally move into the paradigm of Oneness. We see the divine perfection in all. We lose all feelings or interpretations of separation.

It is a fascinating journey for me. When people ask me questions, I now find I have to ask, »On what level do you want that information?« The correct answer depends on their beat and their ability to access various levels of reality. The simplest way to tune in is to ask that all our sharing with other people be for their highest good and your highest good. This guarantees that the interaction is energetically matched and synchronised to the highest possible paradigm that the combination can possibly access.

Conscious tuning is like practising scales on a piano. At first the scales are basic and then rhythm or beat combinations are introduced. Similarly, as we expand our consciousness – through the desire in our heart to realise our full potential – we attain different levels of refinement which can be likened to advanced note combinations.

Eventually we realise that we have the power to create or access any level of reality we wish – and that we have been constantly creating to learn and evolve through all our embodiments – even to the creation of parallel realities.

The Universal Mind guides us to simplify the game and tune to the highest paradigm that is accessible, namely the Divine Rhythm. This is the symphony that is driving the unfoldment of the Divine Plan and when we become part of the orchestra by aligning our free will with the Divine Will, *all doors are guaranteed to open.*

The only catch to this – as many have found out – is Divine Timing. One can be an instrument in the Divine Orchestra and still be either out of step or synchronistic. The program of »*Dear Mother Father Creator God, I ask that the next perfect step of my piece in the Divine Blueprint clearly reveal itself to me and bring with it the perfect people required to make this piece manifest into physical reality NOW!*« as many have now experienced, will guarantee alignment with Divine Time.

So one literally flows in a sea of Oneness. As Sai Baba says, »For the individual and the universal are One; the wave is the sea. Merging fulfils. When merged, the ego is dissolved; all symbols and signs of the particular, like name, form, caste, colour and creed, nationality, church, sect and the rights and duties consequent therein, will fade. For such individuals, who have liberated themselves from the narrowness of individuality, the only task is the uplifting of humanity, the welfare of the world and the showering of love. Even if they are quiet, the state of bliss in which they are will shower bliss on the world. Love is in all; love is of all; love is all.«

The vibrational aspect of the feeling of this beat is pure love, Divine Love with variations of this from the 33 x 33 to the coarser seven x seven vibration and lower emotional body expression. Divine Love is not only the source and building block of all creation energetically, but also the most powerful transmutational force available. When tuned to, accessed and focussed upon, it absorbs, refines and realigns all lower emotions to the most refined beat possible while in a physical body. Again, it brings freedom.

Commanding the Divine One to align our energy fields and express full embodiment in our physical reality automatically tunes us to the universal beat. All veils of illusion and separation fall away – like the peeling of layers of an onion until all that remains is the perfectly tuned pure essence.

This is what I have come to term »plugging into the cosmic circuit board«. This is where the discussion of breatharianism and liquidarianism leads us in the end. For the ability to live on light is a natural by-product of giving ourselves permission to be sustained by the divinity within. Similarly, we can tune ourselves to do without sleep, or tune ourselves to no longer feel temperature extremes but simply adjust our body temperature so that we can be comfortable in every physical environment – an ability I am still developing.

All this is just raw human potential – to get to a point where there is no difference whether we are in our physical bodies or »sitting on the lap of and wrapped in the arms of God,« for all is one. We are one with all. This is what the Indian sages term »Sat Chit Ananda« – being, consciousness, bliss. I see myself in you. This is the paradigm of oneness and limitless being.

The Seven Elements And The 33 Beat

The following information flows naturally on from the previous chapters. I had been programming that »the next piece of my part in the Divine Blueprint NOW CLEARLY reveal itself to me AND bring with it any beings who would aid in the physical manifestation of this part into physical reality NOW« when who should be magnetised to my field but Leonard Orr.

For those unfamiliar with Leonard's work, in 1974 he founded the rebirthing movement, now some 10 million strong world wide. In Australia on tour, we managed to connect and discover each other's work. We swapped books and agreed to co-facilitate through Europe and part of South America. We now include some of his work on spiritual purification in the chapter on the great immortalists.

Reading Leonard's work has allowed me to understand another perspective of my own by recognising the connecting links. I have discovered that I am being intuitively guided to *build bridges*. I knew that I liked to network, to discover, share and enjoy brilliance and limitlessness. So, adding a »rebirthing flavour« to our understanding, let's look at effective bridge-building via tuning: tuning to the elements and also energy field purification utilising the elements.

What I call tuning the four-body system – physical, emotional, mental, and spiritual – Leonard calls »spiritual purification« which is achieved by utilising the four elements.

The following information continues from our previous discussions on vibrational frequencies and the universal beat.
The first element is fire – the »learning to live with an open flame« practice. This corresponds to the physical field of the seven x seven beat. Fire can be used to burn accumulated emotional dross from any energy field we wish to cleanse.

The second element is earth – tuning to the earth element involves the practice of fasting, food mastery and exercise.

The third element is air – tuning to this element is done through conscious energy breathing. Each breath is connected, the inhale followed by the exhale and is deep and fine until one clicks into the experience of *being breathed.* In its finer expression this is an experience of Akasha – the sixth element. Conscious connected breathing bridges the physical and etheric by bringing an experience of refinement into the physical vehicle.

The fourth element is water. Long hot baths tune all the chakras, especially the sacral or »muladhara« chakra. The latter is the connecting link between the energy fields of the emotional and physical bodies. Baths also realign and rebalance the body's energy fields and dilutes, what Leonard terms, emotional »energy pollution« accumulated within the morphenogenic field of mass consciousness. Even long hot daily showers clean your auric field but, according to the rebirthers, not as powerfully as baths. They say that daily baths and rebirthing sessions can clear cellular memory on many levels.

The fifth element is astral light. This is of the solar vibration ten x ten, and is the vibration of living from the pranic field – utilising photon energy to sustain the body.

Vibrating at a galactic frequency of 12 x 12 is the *sixth element or Akasha,* the first element beyond the void or Source. It is semimanifest and is the matrix in which our universe is embedded.

Cosmic fire, alternatively known as the Principle, is *the seventh element vibrating to the universal frequency* of 33 x 33. It is the first element in the expanding beat, and the seventh element in the contracting beat.

The five elements, including astral light, also correspond to our five senses: fire = sight; earth = smell; air = touch; water = taste; astral light = hearing. The sixth element, Akasha, corresponds to intuition, our sixth sense. The sense for the cosmic fire element has yet to be revealed. I think that it is, perhaps, the sense of just *knowing.*

When we bridge the worlds, we discover the three subtle elements, enjoy the exploration and experience of their power and then consciously direct their flow back into linear time and physical reality.

Tuning the four-body system with the four elements empowers us in the physical plane, provided mind mastery is adopted and demonstrated. It also brings into our cellular awareness a strong elemental force that will tune us to the heartbeat of the Mother Earth. The more tuned we are to the heartbeat of God – then allow the forces of the elements to tune us to the heartbeat of our planet – the stronger and more effective our bridge, between the differing vibrations of these worlds, will be.

Bridging the worlds occurs when the inner doorways have opened through the practice of »spiritual purification« or through tuning the four-body system to its synchronistic and »Divine beat«. When these doorways are open, we can direct the resulting flow of opened, pure consciousness.

Masters are aware that only an aspect of their consciousness is expressed into physical reality. A master is consciously aware of all levels of creation, both in the microcosm and the macrocosm.

Utilising the universal Law of Resonance,
the »as you sow so shall you reap« paradigm,
we realise that the more we consciously tune to the universal beat of
33 x 33 – Oneness – the more we draw to us the mirror image of these elements.
This is then what brings Oneness into evidence in the physical as it is mirroring our vibration and our creative power.

Vibration and Sound – Toning and Mantras

»Toning is a technology and language for the multidimensional transmission of light, colour, motion and geometries. Toning breaks up dysfunctional patterns, transmutes lifetimes of karma, infuses new patterns and feels good,« writes Tony Stubbs in »An Ascension Handbook«.

My personal experience of toning has been primarily to use it for shifting and breaking down energy blocks in the physical body. The physical body often has weaknesses in certain areas due to cellular memory held there from previous life experiences.

We can change our frequency by toning and using mantras. According to the »Keys of Enoch«, mantras are »sacred syllables; a contracted form of the Dharanis (Sanskrit – syllables as prayers) for mental and spiritual expansion ... A set of sound patterns and thoughtforms which can code consciousness into the consciousness of light. The mantra are holy energy forms of meditation which are used to change the body with the powers and rapture of the Divine Mind. The greater the thoughtform, the greater the mantra in opening the mind for real disclosure of knowledge«.

All great avatars and masters have recommended the use of sound and mantras in spiritual practice. It has been said that if we have the name of God on our lips in the last moment of life, our spirit will pass directly to that sacred space of being. That is how powerful the sacred names and sounds are.

In his book, »The Complete Ascension Manual,« Dr. Stone writes: »The ultimate purpose of reciting names of God is to blend your consciousness with God-consciousness«. He says that constant chanting of power names and words tunes your frequency to the particular mantric resonance being used. The discipline required builds spiritual force and power in your aura, cleanses your four-body system and brings your energy fields into alignment with the energy of the sound being used. Dr. Stone devotes a chapter to these power names that is well-researched and worth reading.

Sound is vibration and use of sound realigns vibrational frequencies. White Eagle says: »The word was sound, vibration and the vibration created by the Word started life in form. The Scriptures of the world all contain this same truth, they all tell of the Word, the sound, the vibration, the activity of the atom which created form or life on the Earth.«

AUM. In the beginning was sound – the Word – and the Word was God. AUM. The word AUM creates a powerful vibration throughout the whole of a person's being when used repetitively. All religions use mantras, from the chants of the Jewish »Yod hay vod hay«; the Hindu »AUM« or »OM«; the Islam »Allahu Akbar«; the Western »I AM that I AM«; the Egyptian »Nuk-Pu-Nuk«; the Christian Lord's Prayer and the Jesus Prayer; the Tibetan Foundation chakra mantras; the Buddhist »Om Mani Padme Hum«; to Djwhal Khul's mantra »I AM the soul (or I AM the monad), I AM the light divine, I AM love, I AM will, I AM fixed design,« plus many more variations.

An ancient mantra currently used in New Age circles is, »Kodoish, Kodoish, Kodoish, Adonai, Tsey Beyoth (pronounced Ka-doi-sh, Ka-doi-sh, Ka-doi-sh, ah-don-ai, Sey-bey-ot). The »Keys of Enoch« say that this is the universal greeting in the mother tongue of the civilised worlds – its origins being Sumerian-Hebrew. It is a mantra of prayer and protection which immediately balances and repels negative forces on all levels. It is said to be a sound code and the frequency signature of the universal hologram that encodes the rhythm and beat of all energy and matter. It is also said to be the sound of the human heartbeat and synchronises the left and right hemispheres of the brain within the overself body (our higher brain function) engendering not only spiritual focus and discernment, but extraordinary flashes of insight and clarity.

Mantras to use for expanding interdimensional consciousness

One of the most powerful mantras one can use is described in »Keys of Enoch« and is as follows: »Amen- Ptah, Phowa, Kwan

Yin, Gabriel, Buddha«

This mantra interconnects languages of Egyptian and Chinese to unify all the biochemical languages within the body on a horizontal level. Sanskrit and Tibetan fire letters will unify all vertical levels. Hebrew fire letters, sacred energy sounds and thought-forms of light connect us with the intelligence of the Pleiades and Orion, unifying all crystalline languages of the third eye and opening the template of the mind for eternal light.

When the above names are spoken simultaneously, the mantra will activate the pictographic communication of the Brotherhood within the brain. These languages form a grid connecting the higher I AM with the human I AM through a cosmic light vibration.

The Egyptian-Chinese grid pattern (horizontal) interchange with life situation through a series of light pictographs which allow for multi-levels of external knowledge to be internalised and encoded beyond that which is normally spoken (through the mental process).

The Sanskrit-Tibetan grid pattern (vertical) form connecting links from the lower planes to higher dimensions of an infinite quality of joy. These two grid patterns continually realign to accommodate changes brought by reincarnation cycles.

When you reach a point where higher soul transplant can take place, the grid opens to the presence of a third grid pattern – the divine light pattern (the Hebrew connection) which allows for complete bliss and freedom – a total cosmic spiritual connection.

The flame scripture, or *sacred fire letters*, is an ancient, cosmic language of geometries that, according to the »Keys of Enoch«, are designed to »open the eyes of Man to behold wondrous things of Divine Wisdom«. They are also »specific letters of a sacred language shaped in »fire script« so that the consciousness of the sacred letters of spiritual writings can actually penetrate the soul of the reader so that the soul of the reader comes to behold the Deity«.

As with some of the other topics in this manual, I have only touched on mantras briefly and recommend that, if it is of interest, research this area until you find one that feels right for you to work with.

Creative Visualisation 12
Breath Technique to Consciously Raise our Vibrational Frequency

This technique was taught to me by Commander Korton of the Space Command while under instruction in telepathic communication. He stated that it was a quick way of tuning ourselves energetically into higher frequencies.

Firstly we must change our mindset to truly understand that we are not sustained by oxygen, but by energy. This technique is designed to change the resonance or vibration of our energy fields. As long as we believe we need oxygen to sustain us, practice of this technique may leave us literally »gasping for air«. So firstly, we must be disciplined and exercise mind control over matter and trust that the body's »watcher« will ensure our oxygen requirements are met.

· Know that this technique will »elevate« your frequency.
· After you have settled yourself via »tuning« with breath and light work as discussed previously ...
· Change the rhythm of your breathing so that your exhale is less than your inhale. For example, if you were to count seven on the inhale, then seven on the exhale – as in the first breath technique which establishes an even rhythm – then change from seven on the inhale to five on the exhale.
· You need to »play« and experiment with this to find your perfect rhythm. Just as different individuals may have different counts e.g. ten in and ten out, or 15 in and 15 out for technique one, similarly with this technique, you may have ten in and five out, or 12 in and eight out etc. The requirement for both is to be able to practise in a regular, even, *sustainable* manner.
· You may find that after a few minutes you need to exhale as completely as you inhale. That is OK. Do so, then start again.
· It should feel like you are climbing up a mountain range, a peak then a valley, up to a peak then a smaller valley and so on.

- It is as though you are being dragged upward energetically.
- When this rhythm is sustainable, be still within. Look and listen with spiritual eyes and spiritual ears and »see« what visions unfold.

I use this technique to quickly tune myself into a state of higher receptivity. It can be likened to where one uses the energy of the chakras to build up energy and move beyond the confines of this physical body. By using the breath as a mechanism to control the energy, we can quickly and easily alter our frequency to a finer, higher resonance.

Chapter 24

Channelling

»Channel – a path along which signals can be sent e.g. data channel, output channel, in the education of the soul via spiritual commands ... The portion of a storage medium that is accessible to a given reading station e.g. track band ... A unit which controls the operation of one or more units ... A band of frequencies used for communication« – thus the interpretation of the word »channel« from the »Keys of Enoch«.

I have included this chapter on channelling as it is a great method of opening up to inner guidance and guidance from our Higher Self, I AM Presence, guides or beings of light. Apart from aiding in obtaining clear personal direction there are various side benefits we gain through the action of written, verbal or telepathic channelled communication. One of these benefits is the regular alignment to a higher frequency which is said to increase our spiritual growth 1 000-fold.

If we can move our point of awareness to »tune« into another station – e.g. channel 11 – when we've only ever watched channel four, then not only can we »see« and have visions of these other realms of existence, but we can also »hear« them and receive telepathic communication from beings who reside in these other frequency bands. Channelling and communicating with other intelligence's from other dimensions of time then becomes as simple as making a phone call from Australia to Europe.

One of history's most famous channels was the »sleeping prophet,« Edgar Cayce. He was called the »sleeping prophet« because he would go into a deep sleep-like trance and then, when required, would make incredibly sophisticated medical diagnoses. As he had no medical training and was educated only to the sixth grade, this astounded the medical fraternity at the time. Cayce also moved on to do well-documented past life readings, many of which were historically confirmed upon investigation. It is said that he had the ability – while in deep trance – to access the Akashic Records where all the events of life are recorded. There are reports that Cayce, in a previous incarnation, was also the great Egyptian prophet and priest, Ra-Ta who escaped the downfall of Atlantis and brought much knowledge to Egypt.

Edgar Cayce was classified to be a deep trance channel. Research has shown that the deeper the trance, the purer the transmission, as there is minimal interference from the conscious mind and the filters of perception of the personality. However, conscious channelling is becoming more commonplace as more individuals open up to higher guidance. We should keep in mind, however, that all channelled information is only as pure as the channel. The level of information a channel can access is a direct reflection of their own conscious awareness, as like can only attract like.

If you seek guidance from channels, be aware of how they live their life before you give much credence to their reports. Is their life abundant, loving and joyous? Are they healthy and do they practise what they preach? Positive guidance is always evident by the fruits in our lives. If channels have clear inner guidance it will be evident in their own life. Also be aware of channelled information that is judgmental, negative or disempowering, as it will not be coming from the purest source. *All beings of light seek only to inspire, to serve and to empower.*

I personally feel that the only true guidance we can depend upon is that given to us by the Inner Teacher. Due to our uniqueness there can be no one set of »rules« to be adhered to and no one knows us like the Inner Teacher – our own God Self or I AM. The more we focus on opening up to and strengthening the inner connection to the infinite source of knowledge within, the more purposeful, aligned, joyous and abundant our lives will be. Once a strong connection is established, it becomes irrelevant if we put labels of »our Higher Self, our I AM, beings of light, guides« etc. on the source of this guidance – what is important is the quality of the fruit of this guidance as it manifests, when followed, in our lives.

Well worth reading is the book »Opening to Channel« by Sanaya Roman and Duane Packer whose own guides write: »Most souls exist in the astral plane when they die, for they are not yet evolved enough to live in the causal plane. Many high guides come from the causal plane and beyond, from what is called the multidimensional reality. To live in these other dimensions requires mastery of the polarities, an advanced level of control over the emotions and mind, and skill at using energy. Some guides have lived on Earth, evolved quickly, mastered the lessons, are now pure spirit in the causal plane, and are evolving further through serving mankind. Others come from the multidimensional realities and are extremely high beings in their own systems.«

Their guides Orin and DaBen continue to explain: »Guides make contact with your soul, and their information then flows through your soul (the Higher Self) to your consciousness, translated through the words and concepts that you have available. There are an infinite number of ways a guide may transmit information to your soul ... To channel, you step up your frequency as you achieve a trance state, and we lower ours to match. It is not an exact energy match, but a complementary one. We create electromagnetic fields in our dimension that are similar to yours in your dimension«.

They say that these transmissions are monitored and adjusted accordingly and as we become more »aligned« and open the easier it becomes. Again, trust is of utmost importance. Most transmissions are received through the right side of the brain and then computed and spoken/written using left brain function. They also state that new pathways through the neurones of our mind are laid, developed and utilised as we open to, and practise, channelling which changes our normal mode of thinking.

Orin and DaBen go on to say that we must learn to trust and honour our imagination as »your imagination can link you with other universes. It can take you backward and forward in time. It can link you with higher minds, and create anything it focuses upon. The imagination can help you journey out of body. If you desire, you can project your consciousness and use your imagination to view places and people even while you are far away from them. As your imagination opens, you can travel into many realities. It is your imagination that transcends matter. It is one of the highest abilities you have. It gives you visions, dreams, and perceptions in consciousness that transcend your normal awareness.«

Confirming what Grace Cooke shares in her book »The Jewel in the Lotus«, DaBen and Orin continue: »Just because you feel you made something up doesn't mean it isn't real. Reality begins within you. When you first experience channelling, it may feel as though you are using your imagination. The imagination is at a higher vibration than the mind, and it is freer of the limits and constructs of physical reality. It is able to hold thoughts that may appear impossible or unusual to the mind. Your imagination is the touchstone to the higher reality.«

From my own experience and research, I have found that when you channel you not only bring more light and higher vibrations into your body, but that you also begin to change the molecular and cellular structure of the body. This in turn may heighten your awareness and physical senses. Channelling allows us to awaken our connections to Universal Mind, the Divine Intelligence within. Throughout history there have always been individuals who have been in contact with worlds beyond our known universe. Shamans, seers, prophets, oracles, psychics, mediums, channels – of all religions, cultures, and creeds – have been sought out by the masses for their ability to envisage or tune into other realms, and/or bring through great vision for their people.

With the changing energies upon this planet, more and more people are now able to connect with that same source of eternal knowledge simply by going within as all our inherent psychic abilities now come to the surface of our awareness and recognition.

Shortly after I underwent the process that I describe in the chapter on prana, I found myself getting headaches and neck aches and experienced an intense build-up of energies in the back of the skull area. I had no desire to channel as I preferred to sit quietly in the back of the room, where this phenomena occurred, and watch. I was definitely not interested in being in »the public eye«. I had also been getting many voices in my head which I felt were just my own self-talk or my imagination and, as they continued, I began to joke that perhaps I was becoming schizophrenic.

Over the previous years I often experienced communication with the »dead«. Information that made no sense that would pop into my head, along with the name of the person who had just died. Or I felt their energy field and just »knew« who it was – so I would shyly pass this information on to the party for whom the message was intended. I had been told that the reason »they« came to me was because they knew I was open and receptive and would not dismiss it and that their loved ones were often too emotional to receive messages directly. I always doubted this communication but passed the information along regardless – just in case.

I had also received clear names and some positive guidance from »guides« Elijah and Samuel who had made themselves known to me in my meditations in the mid-eighties. They advised that they were always there to communicate if I required it, but most of the time I ignored them. Again my logical mind dismissed it as a product of my overactive imagination – but I was also secretly pleased!

I would like to share that while I believed in guides and higher communication, I didn't believe that it could happen to me or that I was psychic or able to communicate this way. I felt that only »selected« individuals with the correct training or who were »born« psychic could communicate with guides and »dead« people. I began to realise that it is all to do with vibrational frequency and that we all have telepathic abilities that would come to the fore if we refined our frequency and energy fields.

So naturally then, with the intense change in my vibrational frequency due to the realignment from the 21 day process (as outlined in chapter 27), I began to get regular messages and voices that seemed to have different energies attached. Some came in gentle and soft, others more powerful and strong. My body felt different and I was telepathically told that the activity, and subsequent discomfort of headaches etc. was due to a build-up of energies in the hypothalamus area, and if I opened my mouth and allowed these voices to express through me, the energy build up would be dissipated.

I was also advised that some of the physical discomfort was due to the activation of the »ascension chakra« which is at the back of the head, ponytail height. This chakra allows for the influx of higher communication, the energies of which then begin to activate not only the hypothalamus but also the cerebrum – the four-fifths of the brain we do not normally use, but will use for interdimensional communication.

Friends who could see energy fields reported a strong ball of concentrated energy at the base of my skull and no amount of healing, Reiki or energy manipulation made it feel better. I decided to take the plunge. I issued the invitation to beings of light, who operated only for the *highest good* of myself and all humanity, could come through and express. So began a wonderful journey and experience for me of channelling.

Again the book »Opening to Channel« covers the feelings one has when beginning this journey quite beautifully. Feelings of doubt, of disbelief that then move into joy and exhilaration. I have often found that the times I have not felt connected, yet have offered myself in service for a message to be purely expressed, that it was as if an invisible hand reached down through my crown chakra and lifted my energy and frequency up to a more in tune, perfect resonance in an instant. This change has been equivalent to hours, or sometimes weeks, of regular concentrated meditation to realign myself and its instantaneous nature has been gratefully received.

Obviously the more we align ourselves willingly, with dedicated effort and pure intention, to higher energies of light, the more we will become that energy with which we align. This is the universal Law of Resonance in action. Channelling is a simple way to do this. We do not have to channel for anyone but ourselves and having clear, inner guidance simply makes our journey here less confusing and more enjoyable!

While we can study the phenomena of channelling and do guided meditations and visualisation practices to open up these »extrasensory« abilities, know that all these things will *naturally* present themselves to you as you align your energy to the force that sustains you.

While I am not sure whether this applies to all telepathic levels of communication, the Ascended Ones advise me that when we tune ourselves to channel, we connect into Universal Mind. Information comes from that source – either the Akashic Records when we are working with past, present and future linear time-frames or simply Infinite Intelligence. Truth is truth and we can feel it in our own heart by using our discernment.

A suggested practice for anyone channelling for others is to program the following: »Dear Mother/Father Creator God, I ask that I be utilised as the clearest channel for your love and wisdom. I ask that the energy and information moving through me be of the prefect vibration for the consciousness of the individual/group present. I ask that the perfect being of great light and great love that is tuned to the highest good of all, come through me NOW«. By asking for the perfect vibration, we are more harmoniously aligned to the needs of the group present. Asking for the highest vibration may bring through an energy that is too intense for the group to integrate.

For those attending channelings, we recommend that you sit in the seat of discernment in your heart and remember that we are all divine beings. There are none greater than the Inner Teacher within us all. The most important gift that we can give to ourselves is to learn to hear and trust the voice of the God I AM within.

Often during my travels I have been amazed at the willingness of people to give their power away – to a teacher, a guru, a channel or some extraterrestrial identity. It is as if many people still expect some external source or force to create change in their life, to wave a »magic wand« and make all the bad in their life good again.

There is no guru like the Inner One. Within us dwells an enlightened being – our ascended self – it knows all about our past, present and future and holds the key to all we desire. Learning to tune ourselves to its beat, and then to trust and listen to its guidance is a far more powerful, fulfilling and satisfying journey than finding an external teacher to tell us what to do. Self-mastery is about self-knowledge. Knowing fully the Divine Self.

Chapter 25

Ascension

Ascension is simply a name given to building the light quotient within – merging with our true nature. There are no rules, only guidance from the Inner Teacher as to what is right for us alone. It is our journey. No one knows the way like we do, for our path is not new – just forgotten.

Ascension can also be described as raising the vibrational frequencies of our energy fields to the highest octaves of light in perfect resonance with our Higher Self, God essence or the pure energy source that sustains us. In Eastern philosophy it is described as the state of »soruba samadhi« where divinity descends and transforms the spiritual, mental, emotional and physical bodies into perfection – where we can enter and leave the body at will and control the ageing/youthing process as well as rearrange our molecular structure via dematerialisation etc. The beings who choose this state of ascension and subsequent immortality do so in order to be of continual service to humanity – as they have escaped the cycle of life and death and have gained »supernatural« powers.

The Siddhas (holy immortal men) used the science of Kriya Yoga to rejuvenate the physical body and gain self-mastery. They slowed down the ageing process through the use of mineral, herb and salt formulas. They also practised Kriya Yoga and specific breathing techniques which maximised the intake of prana and aided in the control of longevity. When their »role« was complete they would leave the physical body at will and move on to serve in other planes, or take their physical body up into light.

No longer are these things available to just the select few. Nor are we required to sit in a cave for 50 years and meditate to achieve this state of perfection. As both the vibrational frequencies of the planet and humanity are raised, these »supernatural« powers will become commonplace.

As discussed in previous chapters, consciously raising our vibrational frequencies allows us to attract – via the universal Law of Resonance, where like attracts like – the finer things that we desire such as joy, balance, harmony and unconditional love. If we feel the need for more of these experiences on a consistent basis, we can do practical things to attain them.

What we can consciously and practically do to raise our vibrational frequencies has been discussed in detail in both chapters 15 and 23. However, to recap briefly ...

On the physical, practical level:
· Eat light and live food – fresh fruit and vegetables, grains, nuts and legumes. Unless we have developed the power of conscious transmutation, it is said that sugar, alcohol and red meat keep our vibrational frequencies dense. If we wish to tune the physical vehicle to a higher resonance, it is recommended we eliminate these from our diet. As we fine-tune our frequencies, we can actually attain a point where we no longer need to eat or drink and can be sustained by light (prana) alone.
· Drink lots of water. Water is a wonderful conductor of energy and is the basis of our physical composition. It also flushes out toxins from the cells and organs and helps keep the physical system pure. Eventually, as our bodies become light-based rather than water-based, we will need to drink very little fluid.
· Partake of gentle, stress-free exercise. This oxygenates the blood and also allows for the free flow of energy. Yoga, tai chi, swimming, walking – combined with deep, connected breathing – are most beneficial. Highly recommended is dancing, especially with our eyes shut and blocking out external stimulus, as this allows the energy to flow more freely throughout the body and helps us to generally *let go and loosen up*. Dancing in this manner allows us to feel as though we can move beyond the limitations of our form.

On the emotional level:

· Dr. Deepak Chopra says that cells are just memories that have clothed themselves in matter. We are the sum total of everything that has gone before us, this life, previous life experiences, genetic encoding, environmental influences – all these are held in cellular memory. As we relate in a linear timeframe, we tend to view events as being sequential. When we move our awareness beyond linear time we realise that everything occurs simultaneously – past, present and future co-exist in what are termed »parallel realities« that constantly feed into each other.

· Energy blockages occur in the body's electrical circuitry from many different influences and directly affect our resonance or vibrational frequency. These blockages occur because of poor diet, lack of exercise, toxins, pollutants, unresolved negative emotions, negative beliefs and limiting thought patterns. Cellular cleansing can be achieved through a suitable diet as well as through various alternative therapies such as kinesiology and homeopathy.

· More importantly, we can use specific meditation, breathing and creative visualisation techniques to realign our energies to light and cleanse the cells with light daily. Self-healing is the most valuable tool of all, and we can also ask for our Higher Self and/or guides to cleanse the emotional body in our dream state by working through our subconscious mind – all cellular memory is held within the subconscious mind. (See the chapter on the power of emotion).

On the mental level:

· By understanding that our thoughts create our reality and being vigilant with our thinking patterns, we learn to attract the experience we desire by monitoring the energy of our thoughtforms. Energy follows thought. (See the chapter on the power of the mind).

On the spiritual level:

· Meditation and spending time in the Great Silence with the Inner Teacher is the most powerful way to realign our frequencies to the higher octaves of light. Meditation can be split into seven specific categories that we can work with or tune to. (See the chapter on meditation).

As we exist within the energy fields of a living being – Planet Earth – we will find that our own energy fields and vibrational frequency will automatically change in accordance with the planet as she undergoes her own ascension into higher vibrational fields.

Planetary ascension is a natural phenomena that occurs to all planets at a certain stage within their evolution where their base changes from carbon to silicon. Also as their frequency is refined, or evolves to higher octaves, the beings within and on its surface also change. So personal ascension is a natural consequence of planetary ascension.

Personal ascension is something that will be undertaken either with full conscious awareness and participation of an individual, or not. It is happening regardless. However, it is as if a grand ball were taking place. Some of us have our invitations in the mail or are shopping for appropriate attire. Others are on their way via car or carriage, or have already arrived and are dancing and having a wonderful time. The planet is awakening and so are her inhabitants as an increasing number of people seek the answers to the purpose and meaning of existence and sense that there must be something more to life.

As we align the frequencies of the lower bodies (the physical, emotional, mental and spiritual) in perfect harmony to the higher octaves of light, abilities such as telepathic communication (clairaudience), healing by touch, clairvoyance, physical immortality, and bi-location (the ability to be in two places at once) become completely natural and accessible. Inner guidance becomes a strong and clear force and reveals our destined role and purpose.

214

There may be a variety of reasons for choosing the path of ascension at this time. They may vary from the desire to experience more joy and purpose in life, to wanting to serve Divine Will and improve the quality of life for all beings on this planet.

To me, ascension is also *descension* – the descent of spirit into physicality. When we access our Divine Blueprint, discover our life purpose and fulfil that purpose, we realise that ascension is the act of tuning the vibrational frequencies of the four-body system to resonate in complete harmony with the I AM within so that the light and the I AM may fully express themselves through us. In the descent of the light we are fulfilling our divine purpose as we anchor and ground the energies of light to manifest through our being for the good of the whole, and not just the good of an individual.

Ascension is the natural consequence of bringing our energy fields into complete and perfect alignment. The more intense and pure the alignment, the more intense and pure will be the energies that move through us while on this plane. As we then emit these pure energies, so we attract pure and perfect life experiences back to ourselves. We then find that we literally are existing in a state of Heaven here on Earth. The general commitment for those on the ascension path is to be the purest vessel for divine expression that they can. Their recognition is that as they serve Divine Will, they are in turn serving humanity and the good of the whole.

We are here for a purpose: at this moment in time, to make manifest the Golden Age. Ascension is not about being carried away in a spacecraft and escaping this »crazy three D world«. Craft visitation is a reality for those who choose it to be, and at some point in the acceleration of our frequencies, regular communication with beings of light (e.g. the Intergalactic Federation, the Great White Brotherhood etc.) is a natural occurrence. These beings of light are simply here to serve humanity since in the greater universe it is well understood that the most powerful tool of spiritual evolution is service to the First Cause.

»The Ascended Masters« way of life is to give, give, give;
first Love and Adoration to His own »Mighty I AM Presence«
and then expand Love and Perfection by pouring It out to every-
body and everything. To send out Divine Love without limit all
the time, is the whole of the law applied.

If mankind could only understand this, the individual would
realise that he must pour out this

Flame of Divine Love, before the Perfection he desires can
flow into his world,

and release things into his use.

Divine Love is a feeling, an actual Ray of Light, which flows
out from the Flame within the Heart.

It can be sent forth so powerfully, that this Ray of Light
substance is both visible and tangible.

It is the most Invincible Power of the Universe.

Use It Beloved Ones, without limit, and nothing is impossible
to you.«

St Germain

Initiations

I have been guided to write this chapter on initiations for the purpose of inspiring individuals to refocus and recognise who they truly are.

Ancient wisdom and channelled material received from the late 1800s to current linear time reveals that, basically, there are two systems used for the measurement of esoteric initiations.

According to Dr. Stone's study of the work of Alice Bailey, Dwhal Khul and the Theosophical school of thought, a seven level system can be applied to measure the spiritual progress of an initiate. This can also be interpreted to mean the degrees of awakening a person has attained in the recognition of his/her true identity.

Some ancient schools utilise a 12 level system that Dr. Stone explains can be classified as sub-levels to the seven level system others utilise. When an initiate has completed either system, he/she is then released from this plane of physical existence.

It is now a time to consciously rewrite the scripts, individually and globally, in alignment with the Divine Blueprint. One of the scripts we need to rewrite is that of *self-worth*. Many have been workshopping, reading, de-programming and re-programming, and »realigning« themselves for so long. Often the focus has been so much on what they wish they *were not*, that they have not fully yet recognised that which they *are*. (And remember – universal law governs the energy of thought. What we focus on grows.)

Many people have no conscious awareness of the role they play and yet are active on the »inner planes«. They are brought into intuitive and telepathic contact on etheric levels and are under direct tutelage of the Spiritual Hierarchy of Ascended Masters.

Recently, the Ascended Ones gave a simple exercise designed for me to really acknowledge just what has been going on during my own intense focus on enlightenment/ascension during this embodiment. Like myself, all who have participated in this exercise since have been amazed at the results – mainly by the shift in their attitude towards themselves.

Firstly, just what are »initiations«? The next section from »Conversation with Reac« will provide the reader with some information. Basically, however, initiations can be likened to the setting of, then the acknowledgement of, the passing of tests.

Throughout history both the ancients, the indigenous peoples and the world religions have utilised initiations as a test/reward system. As with everything, initiations can be perceived on many levels from the highest spiritual/esoteric initiation to a physical plane initiation.

Tribes use the passage of rites, rituals and initiations. Universities and schools use the exam system of initiation, and life utilises the »learning from our trials and tribulations« form of initiation. These initiations can occur on the physical, mental, emotional and etheric/spiritual levels. They can be »little knowings« to »big bang awakenings«.

The exercise is simply this. Go into contemplation and focus on all the insights and/or gifts that you have been given from all the workshops, meditations, etheric/dream experiences that you can remember. You will find that these were actually initiations. Under inner guidance I remembered when, at 14, my brother died and I was given the gift of *insight,* a glimpse into the »after-life« through my first telepathic contact. It also brought the intuitive gift of *faith* in a Greater Plan, then simply a way to ease the pain.

Then at 17, my physical and spiritual initiation, through my Indian guru's Mahatma, into the ancient art of meditation after waiting and preparing for two long years (it seemed like an eternity!). It later brought the gifts of further *discipline, devotion and dedication.*

My physical initiation into motherhood brought the gifts of *patience, persistence and the recognition of purity and innocence.* An initiation, via dreaming and later repeated on the physical, with the cetaceans, gave me the Sirian connection; with Sanat Kumara on the etheric level: a crystal in my brow centre for clairvoyance; with Kwan Yin, the initiation into the art of Magnified

Healing; and then Reiki with the Master Usui; the 1994 etheric initiation at Joanna Cherry's workshop via bi-location to the Ascended Master retreats, and so the list goes on.

Again in Mt. Shasta, another instant and physical initiation, via the work of Jo Dunning (then Hazur) – experienced in full only weeks after the event. An etheric initiation in meditation where I saw that to accept the honour and the mantle bestowed upon me, regardless of whether I felt I was worthy, was the only way to BEing it; that if I continually identified myself as being in a »process of becoming«, then I always would be; that if I accepted that I was All already, then I could simply BE and allow that to manifest fully.

So take a moment to honestly, without false humility; recognise your training and the gifts you have been given. Write them down. Savour them. Honour yourself and know we already are all we could ever wish to BE.

Initiation

Excerpt from the book »Conversations With Reac« by Eltreya

Eltreya: How does the self come into physical incarnation?

Reac: The Self creates 12 souls as extensions of itself, to better know itself. Each soul incarnates 12 personalities or soul extensions, all in simultaneous time, not in sequential time. That is, some of the personalities may be spread over linear time, in the Lemurian, Atlantean, in the present, or in a culture yet to occur, but co-existing from the soul's higher view. This provides multiple opportunities for each soul to work out particular problems. The soul acquires through its 12 extensions the knowledge of itself that it is seeking.

Individual personalities succeed in merging with the soul, accepting its full expression, when they effectively instruct their physical, emotional, mental, and spiritual bodies to rotate synchronistically. The nature of the soul is then demonstrated, being: will, love/wisdom, and intelligence.

Eltreya: Could you explain the various levels of evolvement?

Reac: First degree initiates have control on the physical plane. Second degree initiates have control on the emotional plane. Third degree initiates have control on the mental plane.

Only third degree initiates have the possibility of correctly demonstrating the soul, that is, the personality is at one with, and is totally infused by, its soul. When an individual passes the third initiation, the soul begins to call back its soul extensions to the spiritual realm and focuses on the more advanced soul extensions.

Fourth degree initiates in incarnation have achieved self-realisation. The fourth initiation is when the soul merges with the Self. At the fifth initiation, the soul, the intermediary between the Self, and the personality is no longer needed, and the causal body, which is the body of the soul, is destroyed. A new, direct relationship between the Self and the individual is established, and the person is described as an adept.

Eltreya: Can you expand on the nature of the soul?

Reac: The soul exists at the causal level, vibrating at a very high rate. Its nature is fire. The personality is the reflection of the soul on the physical level. The physical, emotional, and mental bodies are the vehicles which the soul uses to experience its becoming in time and space. The goal of the soul is to create vehicles through which it can act without any kind of limitation, without blockages, or any lessening of its spiritual energies.

Eltreya: What counsel can you provide for advancement?

Reac: Service and detachment are the prime attributes to develop, and meditation and dreaming provide the detailed guidance.

Eltreya: Many people are working on esoteric matters in groups. I understand that group initiation is possible. Could you comment on this?

Reac: Initiation through a group means the individual becomes so fused and blended with the consciousness of the group that they do not see themselves as separate. It is experienced as a group expansion of consciousness, which is a gradual process in which the consciousness expands progressively.

Group initiation is achieved by creating and sustaining spiritual tension, which is generated by an impersonal focus on the work to be done.

Eltreya: Can you advise how this should be conducted?

Reac: For advancement using a group structure, certain procedures should be followed:

- Impersonal, detached, non-sentimental relationships must apply.
- Individual ambition and personal ties must be obliterated to ensure the necessary detachment.
- The strength and ability of individuals must be recognised and utilised, retaining unity through recognising diversity, and

- Occult silence must be observed, effectively controlling and directing streams of thought by limiting speech.

Eltreya: So co-ordinating the physical, emotional, mental, and spiritual bodies is essential?

Reac: The Lemurian race focussed on physical development, the Atlantean on emotional, and the current Aryan race on mental. Advanced humanity is now working on its spiritual body. Advancement involves correct balancing of the physical, emotional, mental, and spiritual bodies, without excessive emphasis on one in particular. All are of equal importance as a vehicle for the Self to express itself and to better know itself. The four bodies are like musical instruments, which are being played together by the Self, and need to be maintained and tuned to produce quality music. One of the bodies may require more attention for a period, but balance and co-ordination are essential.

Eltreya: How are individuals who are said to be »twin flames« related?

Reac: Twin flames is a description of the relationship of two soul extensions from the same soul. This meeting is very rare, but does happen infrequently. Monadic mates is a term used to describe the relationship of an individual with another of the 144 extensions of the same Self. Twin flames or monadic mates may be different ages, gender, culture, and may not be personally compatible, but will have a powerful connection. A search for this elusive person is a waste of time and energy, since success is an extremely unlikely possibility, and synchronicity will provide the connection if it is required.

Ascension Acceleration Techniques

For those who are already committed to the ascension path, I have taken the liberty of transcribing recommended Ascension techniques, to be done in meditation, from the book by Dr. Joshua David Stone »The Complete Ascension Manual«. This is a book well worth reading as it details the seven initiations required for full merging with the I AM Presence. He states that ascension is the sixth initiation and that »the consciousness of ascension is that of total joy, total unconditional love, and the complete, full recognition that you are God and everyone else you meet is God walking on Earth«.

Please note that I have streamlined these techniques for simplicity and grouping of similarities. I suggest these be utilised according to your desire and heartfelt resonance to the technique. For me, the common element in all ascension research and channelled information is the need to build the light quotient within our four-body system which, in turn, affects our vibrational frequency and will allow for ascension to flow naturally.

There is no need for me to completely duplicate Dr. Stone's work* but I feel that background knowledge of the beings he recommends to »call down« may be important to some, so I have drawn up a glossary of terms used, for reference, at the end of these techniques. However, the techniques and suggestions can be just as effective if you go through your I AM Presence (monad). I also feel it important to not give your power away to anyone, including the Ascended Masters, so working directly with the I AM Presence is preferred.

*Dr. Stone asks that these techniques be regularly practised and distributed.

Creative Visualisation 13
Some Ascension Acceleration Techniques

- Ask in every meditation for your I AM to prepare the four-body system to accept and anchor its full descent and to build the light quotient so that this is possible.
- Ask your I AM for a permanent dome of white golden light to be placed around you – or create it using visualisation techniques discussed previously. (I recommend an open-ended cylinder connecting all the way to Source energies, rather than a dome.)
- Ask your I AM to seek highest assistance to remove any energy blocks or discomfort in meditation or to keep the physical body balanced while meditating.
- Ask your I AM to spin all your electrons in perfect resonance with the Ascended Masters – this will allow for greater telepathic communication and guidance.
- Bring down the golden white ascension energies daily through the crown chakra, start every meditation with this tube of golden white light, calling in Metatron or the Mahatma energies to build, and increase by 100%, your light quotient.
- Call forth for the complete merger of all aspects of your being on Earth, your personality, higher self (soul) and I AM (monad) and for your I AM to be fully anchored. (This will only occur when your light quotient is high enough.)
- Call forth in meditation for the experience of rapture, of being taken up by a pillar of light.
- Call forth the Ascended Masters or your I AM to purify your entire four-body system and remove all negative, ego, fear, limitation and feelings of separateness.
- Call to the seven ray masters to shine through the third eye centre and connect the force of the *antakarana* into the ascension light column and through the entire chakra system through to the monad or I AM.
- Permanently anchor a column of white golden light over your personal meditation area and where you may hold group meetings.

- Regularly each day ask for perfect integration and alignment of all your energy fields with the highest of cosmic energies.
- Team up with other beings on the ascension path, meditate together as group energies create acceleration.
- Visualise your higher and lower energy fields merging into completeness and oneness.
- Ask in meditation that you be put on an »etheric drip of liquid light« while you sleep to build your light quotient.
- Ask that the monadic (I AM) blueprint body replace the previous blueprint that we have worked with in previous lifetimes.
- Ask the Ascended Masters and your I AM to prepare your physical and etheric nervous systems so that you can fully express your Divine Self in the physical realms now.
- Ask your I AM to build the 12 strand DNA in your etheric physical body.
- Call for the construction of your Merkabah and ask in meditation that it be spun to raise your frequencies. Learn the Merkabah breathing and vehicle creation as it will allow those who tune to it to do soul travelling in meditation or at night.
- Call forth for the anchoring and activation of the unified chakra (this meditation is covered in the chapter on chakras) – with ascension, the seven chakras become one unified chakra, one inner column of light.
- Call forth for the permanent anchoring of the Cosmic Heart – this step is self-explanatory in its intention.
- In meditation connect with Sanat Kumara (the Planetary Logos) and ask to make your ascension, plus any other ascension requests. You may also state your preferred service and ask for guidance and training to fulfil this service.
- It is said that there are 60 thousand million monads (I AM Presence) who have put down 12 souls (Higher Selves) each. These souls each have 12 soul extensions (personalities) which may not all be in physical embodiment. So in meditation you may seek connection with all 144 of your soul extensions as this will strengthen and accelerate your ascension.
- Meditate. Ask to go to the ascension chamber of your I AM's

choice, then go for a walk. This is good practice for bi-location, as your consciousness will be split.

- Ask to go to the golden chamber of Melchizedeck for initiation to this order by the Universal Logos, Melchizedeck. This order is the basis of all spiritual teachings on Earth and this being ensouls the entire universe.

- In meditation, prior to sleep, ask to enrol and participate in classes on the inner plane for you to fulfil your Divine Blueprint in physical reality now. Information and training is held in cellular memory for future access.

You may also like to call in Archangel Metatron – the creator of the electron and the creator of all outer light in the universe – to help increase the light quotient in your body. It is said that we need a minimum of 80 – 83% light in our cellular structure to effectively radiate the Supreme Splendour.

Creative Visualisation 14
Ascension Acceleration Meditation

Based on the work by Dr. J D Stone from the »Complete Ascension Manual«, with some additions by Jasmuheen.

- It is recommended that this meditation and affirmations be practised every day for 90 days – or until you are intuitively guided to stop – to gain maximum benefit and transformation.
- Sit comfortably where you can be undisturbed.
- Keep your mind and attention focussed on each instruction.
- Tune yourself with deep, fine, connected breathing. (Take three deep breaths)
- You may repeat each instruction as it is said, or after it is said, or simply instruct your being to absorb into itself all that is for the highest good at this point.

Begin:

- Beloved God most high of the most high universe, beloved mighty I AM Presence, my monad, I AM that I AM, beloved beings of light who work for my highest good and the highest good of humanity and all sentient beings ...
- I am the monad, I am the light divine, I am love, I am will, I am fixed design ...
- I hereby ask and pray for your collective help in the following ascension meditation.
- I hereby call forth an all-powerful cylinder of cosmic light substance to serve as an invincible shield of protection throughout this meditation and throughout my life in general.
- I ask that this cylinder of light be absolutely invulnerable and invincible to all that is not of God and the Christ light.
- Within this large cylinder I now visualise a smaller cylinder the circumference of my head, now moving upward from my crown chakra, up through my soul, up through my monad – my I AM Presence – up through all vibrations of my being back to Source.
- Visualise this connection being made. (Take three deep

breaths.)
- Know that the All is within and is without.
- This tube of light is a rainbow bridge connecting you to all levels of your being from the physical to the vibrational fields of your I AM, your God Self. Visualise it moving down through your seven chakras, then to the centre of the Earth.
- See yourself as a channel, a conduit for energies from the God Source to flow through into the Earth, assisting the planet in her ascension, by bringing into her centre pure frequencies of the Source. (Take three deep breaths.)
- Feel the presence of Oneness in your being.
- Chant the sacred name – AUM – the sacred sound of the creative force of God seven times and send it up through the rainbow bridge back to Source.
- Feel this vibration of AUM throughout your being as you chant it, realigning you, tuning you.
- Chant AUM seven times.
- Take three deep breaths and remain silent as you feel these vibrations.
- Call forth from God and the creative force a pillar of pure golden white light and see it fill your cylinder of protection.
- When it is filled, let the light spill over and fill your physical body, your etheric body, your emotional body, your mental body, your spiritual body, all the energy fields of all your bodies.
- Feel the golden white light of the Mahatma energies flood every cell of your being. These energies are the purest and holiest known in all the universes and embody all consciousness back to the Source.
- Let these energies fill every organ.
- Instruct this light to fill your pineal gland, your pituitary gland, your thyroid gland, your thymus gland, your adrenal glands, your gonadic and sexual glands. Let the Mahatma energies fill your seven glands and your entire being with light.
- Take three deep breaths.
- Affirm: »Beloved God and Mahatma, I choose now to accept

and invoke a deep penetration of Mahatma energy into my entire being, into my entire energy matrix, thereby allowing a full, open radiation of my Divine Self in service to All that is, NOW.

- Visualise now a series of golden balls of light descend from the God Force through the I AM, and enter into the crown chakra and down the chakra column ...
- I let the golden ball of light enter my first chakra.

I now fully open and activate my first chakra.

I AM that I AM – AUM.

- I let the golden ball of light enter my second chakra.

I now fully open and activate my second chakra.

I AM that I AM – AUM.

- I let the golden ball of light enter my third chakra.

I now fully open and activate my third chakra.

I AM that I AM – AUM.

- I let the golden ball of light enter my fourth chakra.

I now fully open and activate my fourth chakra.

I AM that I AM – AUM.

- I let the golden ball of light enter my fifth chakra.

I now fully open and activate my fifth chakra.

I AM that I AM – AUM.

- I let the golden ball of light enter my sixth chakra.

I now fully open and activate my sixth chakra.

I AM that I AM – AUM.

- I let the golden ball of light enter my seventh chakra.

I now fully open and activate my seventh chakra.

I AM that I AM – AUM.

- I call forth my I AM and all beings of light empowered for my highest good, to now enter and balance and perfectly attune each chakra, to remove any unwanted energies or chords of energy that no longer serve Divine Purpose or my true Divine Blueprint.
- Pause, breathing deeply and rhythmically while each chakra is tuned ...

Tuning the first chakra (take three deep breaths).

Tuning the second chakra (take three deep breaths).

Tuning the third chakra (take three deep breaths).

Tuning the fourth chakra (take three deep breaths).

Tuning the fifth chakra (take three deep breaths).

Tuning the sixth chakra (take three deep breaths).

Tuning the seventh chakra (take three deep breaths).

- I call forth the violet flame of St Germain and feel this flame NOW bathe my entire being, transmuting any negativity into the purity and perfection of God.
- Take three deep breaths.
- I call forth the golden twelfth ray and feel it now fill my entire being with the energy of the Christ consciousness. Visualise this energy pouring in and flooding all levels of your being.
- Take three deep breaths.
- I now request that my I AM Presence construct around me my Merkabah vehicle.
- Visualise yourself standing in the centre of a three-sided equilateral triangle, with one apex facing upwards and one down – like a three dimensional, solid Star of David. See it fill with the light of the God Force. Visualise it begin to spin and quicken your overall vibrational frequencies, tuning you to the cosmic pulse and frequencies of the God Force.
- Take three deep breaths.

I am now ready for the ascension process to begin:

- Beloved God Force, I call forth my Higher Self, my soul, to fully descend into my consciousness and four-body system if it has not done so already.

I AM that I AM – AUM.

- I call forth my glorified lightbody to now fully manifest into my consciousness and four-body system.

I AM that I AM – AUM.

- I call forth the full activation and creation of my full potential 12 strands of DNA within my physical vehicle.

I AM that I AM – AUM.

- I call forth the full activation of my pituitary gland to create only the life hormone and hormones that allow for physical immortality.

I AM that I AM – AUM.

- I call forth and fully activate my monadic divine blueprints in my conscious, sub-conscious and super-conscious minds and four-body system.

I AM that I AM – AUM.

- I call forth and fully activate my kundalini energy as guided by my monad and my mighty I AM Presence.

I AM that I AM – AUM.

- I NOW call forth for the perfect spark of cosmic fire from the purest source to illuminate and transform my entire being into the light of God.

I AM that I AM – AUM.

- I call forth my I AM Presence and the light of God to transform instantly into light and pure energy all substances I may ingest in the physical body.

I AM that I AM – AUM.

- I call forth and fully claim my physical immortality and the complete cessation of the ageing and death process.
- I am now youthing and becoming younger every day.

I AM that I AM – AUM.

- I now call forth the full opening of my third eye and all my psychic and channelling abilities, that I may use them in the glory and service of the most high God and my brothers and sisters in Christ on Earth.

I AM that I AM – AUM.

- I now call forth perfect, radiant health to manifest within my physical, emotional, mental, etheric and spiritual bodies. I ask and command that these bodies now manifest the health and perfection of Christ.

I AM that I AM – AUM.

- I call forth with all my heart and soul and mind and might the collective help of my 11 other soul extensions of my monadic group in my ascension process, now.

I AM that I AM – AUM.

- I now call forth the complete balancing of all my karma from all my past, present and future lives.

I AM that I AM – AUM.

· I now call forth the raising of my vibrational frequencies within my physical, astral, mental, etheric and spiritual bodies to the fifth dimensional frequencies.

I AM that I AM – AUM.

· I now call forth my monad, my mighty I AM Presence and Spirit to fully descend into my consciousness and four-body system and transform me into light and the ascended master I truly AM.

I AM that I AM – AUM.

Take a few moments of silence to allow the complete ascension to fully take place while remaining here on Earth. Breath deeply and slowly.

Affirm the following when ready:

· Be still and know that I AM GOD.

I AM that I AM – AUM.

· I AM the mighty I AM Presence on Earth forever more.

I AM that I AM – AUM.

· I AM the Ascended Master *<insert your name>*.

I AM that I AM – AUM.

· I AM God living in this body.

I AM that I AM – AUM.

· The mighty I AM Presence is now my real self.

I AM that I AM – AUM.

· I AM divine perfection made manifest now.

I AM that I AM – AUM.

· I AM the realised manifestation of the eternal self.

I AM that I AM – AUM.

· I AM the embodiment of Divine Love in action.

I AM that I AM – AUM.

· I live within all beings and all beings live within me.

I AM that I AM – AUM.

· I AM now one with the monadic plane of consciousness.

I AM that I AM – AUM.

- I fully affirm my identity as the eternal self, the Christ, the Buddha, the Atma, the monad, the I AM Presence in service to mankind.

I AM that I AM – AUM.

- I fully affirm that I AM physically immortal and I can, if I choose, remain on Earth indefinitely without ageing.

I AM that I AM – AUM.

- I see every person, animal, plant as the embodiment of the eternal self, whether they are aware of their true identity or not.

I AM that I AM – AUM.

- I AM now the perfect integration of the monad, soul and personality on Earth.

I AM that I AM – AUM.

- Kodoish, Kodoish, Kodoish, Adonai Tse Beyoth!

Holy, holy, holy is the Lord God of hosts!

Kodoish, Kodoish, Kodoish, Adonai Tse Bayoth!

Holy, holy, holy is the Lord God of hosts!

Kodoish, Kodoish, Kodoish, Adonai Tse Bayoth!

Holy, holy, holy is the Lord God of hosts!

- I AM that I AM – AUM.

Chapter 26

Immortality

It is interesting to note that ageing and death can still be experienced by both breatharians and those nourished by prana. Humanity has been hooked into the consciousness and belief of limitation for eons of time to the point that glands such as the pituitary and pineal support the belief of death and ageing rather than fulfil their natural life-sustaining and regeneration patterns.

The body is a complex and self-sustaining molecular structure. Billions of new cells are created daily – e.g. a new stomach lining every five days – and it is said that every two years a human being is completely new on a cellular level. Then why do we age and die if we have the ability to renew and create our cellular structure? In his book »Quantum Healing«, Dr. Chopra says that this is because of our programming and belief systems and that cells are just memories clothed in matter. Leonard Orr in his book, »Immortality«, suggests that people die firstly because they expect to.

A decade spent in the business world, sometimes working 50 to 60 hours per week while raising two daughters as a sole parent, and attending to my meditation and esoteric interests, led me to be aware of the virtues of time management. Somewhere along the line I came to the conclusion that physical death was poor time management. After 20 years of a vegetarian diet plus gym work and relevant research to maintain peak health, I realised that the body was a wonderful self-sustaining organism that only wore out due to high levels of toxicity: toxic thinking, toxic feeling and toxic feeding.

The attraction of the idea of physical immortality grew because I did not like the idea of attaining a certain level of awareness and then have the physical vehicle fall apart due to my neglect. To be obliged to prepare a new vehicle and suitable conditions for the next life, then be born, wear nappies, have parents, attend school and go through adolescence again did not appeal to me in the least.

Please note, I had a wonderful childhood, parents etc. and a challenging but instructive adolescence with the freedom to develop and then »flower« as I consciously chose. I was also aware at this time that I had consciously chosen, prior to incarnation, the garden bed my seed of consciousness was to be planted in. To go through all that again and then finally remember what I'd already come to understand through years of research and experience in this life, seemed ludicrous to my logical mind and was poor time management.

At that stage I had been vaguely introduced to the idea of physical immortality and had definitely understood this could be my final incarnation on the Earth plane if I chose. I also knew I had work to do and a role to play. I decided that I wanted to pass on when I'd finished my work and when *I was ready*. I was no longer interested in dying through maltreatment, or ignorance, of the physical vehicle.

Embracing physical immortality has nothing to do with fear of death. All immortalists I know see death as a more gentle, fearless and favourable process than birth – there is certainly less pain involved. Suffice it to say that life on this plane of existence can be likened to school, and the time spent away from physical embodiment is like a wonderful vacation. Often people have claimed an individual's desire for physical immortality was generated by fear of death and the unknown. In some cases this may be so. *However, there comes a point in our evolution where physical immortality is not only good time management, but a natural consequence of our resonance. Physical immortality is not possible without the corresponding resonance or the belief that it is a possibility for us.*

In order to become physically immortal, we need to address the following:

· Let go of the belief that we have to die.
· Release all negativity – of thoughts and emotions – from the energy fields of our bodies.
· Master the physical, emotional and mental bodies.

Letting go of the belief that we have to die is quite simple when we truly understand that we are systems of energy and that the level of cellular degeneration and/or regeneration is dependent on the level of mind mastery that we have achieved. Mastery of the mental body leads to mastery of the emotional body, which in turn masters the physical body.

However, there are also practical techniques that can be practised that are reported to reverse the ageing process, and I would like to explore these in detail. This information is from a wonderful book called »The Fountain of Youth« by Peter Kelder. So under this chapter on immortality let us explore a set of tools for...

Regeneration and Rejuvenation »The Fountain of Youth«

It is my understanding and conviction that the higher the quotient of light within the body, the stronger our natural ability for cellular regeneration on the purest level. Logically, the freer our cellular structure is from all forms of toxicity plus the more light and the higher the vibration or rate of oscillation of the our energy fields, the less possibility of disease, decay and degeneration. Light attracts light – light transmutes and dissolves that which is not of light. Consequently, while we may reprogram our glands to produce only life-sustaining hormones, our main focus must be to increase the light quotient within the cellular structure.

In »The Complete Ascension Manual«, Dr. Stone states that a light quotient of 80 – 83% allows for ascension, 96 – 98% for dematerialisation, teleportation and rematerialisation where we manipulate the cellular structure of the physical vehicle with a single command or intention. In these states, physical immortality is a natural consequence as liquid light flows through the systems and the chakras become unified in one column of light. With the lightbody completely activated and the monad (I AM) fully manifested, everything becomes naturally self-sustaining.

Excerpt from »The Fountain of Youth« by Peter Kelder: »The body has seven energy centres which in English would be called vortexes. The Hindus call them chakras. They are powerful electrical fields, invisible to the eye, but quiet real nonetheless. Each of these seven vortexes centres on one of the seven ductless glands in the body's endocrine system, and it functions in stimulating the gland's hormonal output. It is these hormones which regulate all of the body's functions, including the process of ageing.

The lowest, or first vortex centres on the reproductive glands. The second vortex centres on the pancreas in the abdominal region. The third centres on the adrenal gland in the solar plexus region. The fourth vortex centres on the thymus gland in the chest or heart region. The fifth centres on the thyroid gland in the neck. The sixth centres on the pineal gland at the rear base of the brain. And the seventh, highest vortex centres on the pituitary gland at the forward base of the brain.

In a healthy body, each of these vortexes revolves at great speed, permitting vital life energy, also called »prana« or »etheric energy«, to flow upward through the endocrine system. But if one or more of these vortexes begins to slow down, the flow of vital energy is inhibited or blocked, and – well, that's just another name for ageing and ill health.

These spinning vortexes extend outward from the flesh in an healthy individual, but in the old, weak, and sickly they hardly reach the surface. The quickest way to regain youth, health and vitality is to start these energy centres spinning normally again«.

The above book goes on to explain that there are six »rites« or simple exercises one can do to stimulate these centres. These tools for longevity have been practised for eons of time by lamas at a monastery high in remote reaches in the Himalayas. Again, I recommend reading this most interesting book.

Creative Visualisation 15
Deprogramming and Reprogramming the Glands of the Body for Cellular Regeneration

This is a simple technique designed to switch the production of all hormones to be life-sustaining, not life-draining. As the mind has mastery over matter, the glands of the human body have been unable to support pure, regeneration of cellular structure due to the inherent belief in the need for death. *As long as we believe that death is natural, our bodies* must *and* will *support that belief regardless of their ability to do otherwise.*

A simple technique to reprogram the production of hormones within the body is as follows and can only be guaranteed to work when one has completely released »deathist« mentality.

- Sit in meditation/contemplation.
- Tune your energy fields with breath and light.
- Visualise a beam of light coming in from the highest source, passing through the twelfth chakra through which the I AM connects with your being, down through the other chakras and entering the top of your head through the crown.
- Let this beam of golden white light fill every cell in your brain.
- Instruct the light to fully anchor in and activate your pituitary gland, then the pineal gland.
- Instruct these glands to release old programming and beliefs, and from this moment only produce life-producing and life-sustaining hormones that promote and support physical immortality.
- Feel the light beam go into the throat area filling every cell with light.
- Instruct the thyroid gland in the throat chakra to do the same.
- Feel or visualise the light moving down through the body filling every cell.
- Instruct the thymus, the adrenals, the pancreas and the reproductive glands exactly as for the others.
- Thank all the glands for the wonderful service they have provided according to your previous instruction, but state that

you now embrace the state of physical immortality and demand them to support your new belief in perfect harmony according to your Divine Blueprint.

Chapter 27

Prana Nirvana

In order to understand how we can be sustained by only light, we need to understand what sustains us, i.e. prana – also known as the universal life force or »liquid light«.

Prana is a subtle element which pervades living tissue. Its biological counterpart is a fine essence which resides in the brain and nervous system, circulates in the organism as motor impulse and sensation and conducts all the organic functions of the body.

The term »prana« signifies both the cosmic life energy and its subtle biological conductor in the body. The two are inseparable. The extraction of prana to feed the brain normally is the task of a limited group of nerves, operating in a certain bodily area. When the kundalini is awakened, a radical alteration takes place and other more extensive nerve groups are called into play to supply a concentrated form of prana radiation to the brain from a vastly increased area of the body.

There are three energy channels (nadis) in the spine that can carry the kundalini energy and intersect through the chakras: the *pingala,* or solar nerve, regulates the flow of heat and starts on the right side of the *susumna* which flows inside the spinal cord. The *idakalai* is a cooling canal which starts on the left side of the spinal column. It represents the moon and is the correct channel to carry the kundalini energy. All three lie within the astral body.

The medulla oblongata is a brain centre at the base of the skull and is said to be a »minor« chakra as it is an induction centre of spiritual energy from the higher bodies. Holding the head erect in meditation allows the medulla oblongata to receive the flow of pranic energy freely and unhindered. The pranic energies flow into this centre through to the hypothalamus and, as it increases the light quotient in our being, this increase allows us to be more telepathically receptive.

The kundalini: Prior to the activation of the kundalini energy, I would recommend that the chakras be cleansed and fully activated with light and that the unified chakra meditation be done. I would also recommend that you instruct your I AM to switch on and connect the etheric and physical nervous systems so you are in complete alignment, although this should happen by doing the unified chakra meditation. *It is also most important that you instruct your I AM to oversee the activation of the kundalini energy to avoid potential »burn out«.* If we do not prepare our consciousness and align our physical vehicle, the awakening of the »sleeping serpent« (the kundalini) prematurely can create great damage to the body's electrical circuitry, and even death. More information on this is covered in Gopi Krishna's book on the kundalini. The awakening of the kundalini, depending on the individual, may occur quickly or slowly, as guided by your I AM.

To awaken the kundalini, simply program the following affirmation in meditation: »I call forth and fully activate my kundalini energy *as guided by* my monad and mighty I AM Presence«.

If we increase the intake of pranic life force by drawing on the cosmic life source, we can conquer death. Slow and rhythmic breathing absorbs more prana and allows it to be stored in the brain and nerve centres. Prana supplies electric force to the nerves, magnetises the iron in the system and produces the aura as a natural emanation.

Excerpt from »Babaji and the 18 Siddha – Kriya Yoga tradition«: »The secret to longevity lies in the technique of directing the breathing to subtle channels and centres. The secretion of nectar – amrita – comes from the cerebral region through the opening behind the uvula and the mystic gland in the hypothalamus. This elixir of life will strengthen the human system and make it invulnerable to decay, degeneration, diseases and death.«

In »Kundalini, the Evolutionary Energy in Man«, Gopi Krishna writes: »All systems of Yoga are based on the supposition that living bodies owe their existence to the agency of an extremely subtle immaterial substance, pervading the universe and designated as prana, which is the cause of all organic phenom-

241

ena, controlling the organisms by means of the nervous system and brain, manifesting itself as the vital energy. The prana, in modern terminology »vital energy«, assumes different aspects to discharge different functions in the body and circulates in the system in two separate streams, one with fervid and the other with frigid effect, clearly perceptible to yogis in the awakened condition«.

He goes on to say: »From my own experience, I can also confirm that there are certainly two main types of vital currents in the body, which have a cooling or heating affect on the system. Prana and apana exist side by side in the system in every tissue and every cell, the two flowing through the higher nerves and their tiny ramifications as two distinct currents, though their passage is never felt in the normal state of consciousness, the nerves being accustomed to the flow from the very commencement of life«.

Having understood prana as being the essence of life, we can then perhaps understand how an organism can be sustained by prana alone – some individuals have achieved this through manipulating their consciousness to higher vibrational frequencies that, in turn, change the molecular structure of their physical, emotional and mental bodies and free them from the necessity of taking substance in the form of food and drink. These beings are called breatharians. Others choose to exist purely on liquids.

Excerpt from »Seasons of the Spirit« by Hilarion: »It is incorrect to imagine that the energy that drives the physical body of man comes from the food he eats. This is one of the major misconceptions in the world today ... the energy of man's body must come from a far more subtle and refined source than that of carbohydrate molecules as is now believed. The life process in man does not exist at the mere chemical level, otherwise man would be nothing more than a beaker in which reactive chemicals were mixed, and with no more »life« intelligence or spirit than would be found in such a beaker. When the chemical reaction has run its course, the beaker would be quiet still, lifeless, empty and the same in the case of the human being.

No, the force that drives the human machine is not chemical but etheric. The ether is a form of all embracing substance more rarefied than the most subtle of man's – chemicals, and indeed is the «stuff« from which all the elements known to science are precipitated, just as water droplets can be precipitated from water vapour in the air. Mixed with the ether which fills all of man's three dimensional space (even between the protons and electrons of matter in what science considers to be »empty« space) is a substance which we shall call prana, using the Eastern word for life energy. Indeed the Eastern religions know of this miraculous substance and understand quiet well its role in supporting the »life« of man.

When a human body breaths air into the lungs, the prana within the etheric counterpart of this air is taken into the etheric counterpart of the body and is then transformed into the various energies that one uses in everyday life; mental energy, emotional energy and physical energy. The oxygen which is taken into the blood via the lungs of course plays a part in metabolism, but it is only a minor role compared to the importance of the intake of prana.«

Being Sustained by Light and Prana

A Personal Story

If it is possible to be objective, I would like to relay a process that I chose to undergo to be sustained by prana. I feel that this choice is a very personal one and must be undertaken according to the dictates of one's own heart. Many will not make this choice at this point in time but some may readily embrace the idea. Regardless of individual choice, know that it is possible to be sustained by light alone and to take no food substance. Knowing and then experiencing that we can be nourished and sustained by light is a fascinating and uplifting experience.

In early 1993 I was presented with an opportunity to undergo a specific process of realignment, some of the details of which I will share here. I must however describe it from two points of view: my understanding at the time and my understanding in retrospect.

At that time, apparently only half a dozen people had participated world wide. in such a process. As such, it was in its very embryonic and pioneering days. The information or »how to« was being received telepathically and there were no manuals or guide posts, only an »inner knowing« and confirmation of what felt »right« in the heart of each individual who chose that path.

When I was made aware of this process, I was open but detached. I thought it worthy of investigation and, after research, decided to proceed. The process itself, was quite simple. It entailed a period of preparation, the clearing of 51% of one's karmic debt and the healing of one's auric field.

After that, the process was a) to not eat or drink anything for seven days; b) to sip water or very diluted juices and rest for another seven days while the body healed and adjusts to the previous seven days; c) to rest for another seven days to allow for the integration of the energies of the Higher Self.

Now, what was the purpose of this 21 day process and what actually occurred? Firstly, the three bands of seven days is connected to the sacred geometries and we need to dedicate this time freely and without interruption. It was a sacred initiation, to be honoured and not rushed through lightly. This process has allowed me – and many others around the world – to be sustained by prana alone. Since completing the 21 day process, we have not had to eat solid food. We are completely sustained by the etheric realms. This is a fact. We are healthy, highly energised and have stabilised our weight.

As the months rolled by, I felt great. My energy levels were high and I displayed all the signs of good health, but my loved ones and relatives were not convinced. To allay their concerns, after five months of existing purely on light liquids and no vitamins, I underwent various tests and was not only given a clean bill of health, but found that I had never been so healthy in my entire adult life! Good news for the loved ones and complete confirmation for me.

The motivation of individuals who have done this process is as unique and varied as they are. For me, it seemed a natural step. I had been a purist regarding fuel choices for the physical vehicle for over 20 years. At age two, I rejected meat and by the time I was 15, I had taken control over all my dietary needs, fasted for purification and learned to listen to the needs of my body. I found it spoke a specific language that was easy to interpret. I studied health and protein sources and experimented. For me, light and live food became essential and my body responded.

Creating and then self-curing my cancer taught me about the effect which negative unresolved emotions stored in our body have on the physical body. It forced me to cleanse not only the physical body, but also the energy blocks within the emotional body and to realign and release cellular memory. Due to my lifestyle choice, meditation, diet and exercise routine, the tumour had remained small and its growth had been slow. Still, through stress, unresolved emotional issues and the learning I required, it was there and very real and took four intense months to dissolve and clear.

Consequently, as I began the 21 day process, my system was very clean. I had eaten lightly of soups and fruit in the prior weeks as I wanted the experience to be pleasant. Previous fasting taught that the release of toxins can trigger headaches, nausea, dizziness, muscle and joint aches, etc.

I was motivated by the desire for ascension, to realise my full potential while in this body, to be a pure vessel or instrument for Divine Will to manifest through. Again, this motivation was a natural progression for me after 20 or more years or regular daily meditation and metaphysical research. I had established via these practices, relatively clear inner guidance as to what was »right« for me, and this choice felt »right«. The insights and the learning gained since have been phenomenal.

So due to the preparation undergone, I flew through the first seven days with high levels of energy. I rested as guided and was put on an etheric drip of liquid light so that when I felt hungry, I simply asked the Ascended Ones overseeing this process, for a increase in the drip feed levels. This was always done as requested and the »hunger« always dissipated. Like others, I have keep a detailed journal of this time and since, but my desire is simply that through the brief telling of my own story, others will understand the power of light or prana to sustain us. In retrospect, I see that the 21 day process was a process of great cleaning (first seven days), healing and realignment (second seven days), and then filling with higher energies (third seven days) that could be likened to the purification and sterilisation of an old glass bottle to prepare it for re-use and refilling of another substance.

My research has shown me that this process that allowed for the descent of the Higher Self into the physical vehicle is comparable to the third initiation of the seven level initiation process as discussed by Dr. Stone in »The Complete Ascension Manual« and by the Theosophists and Alice Bailey. Inner guidance and research has suggested that – due to the differing vibrational frequencies of the physical body (personality), the Higher Self (soul) and the I AM Presence (monad) – until the four-body system is realigned, neither the soul or monad can express themselves fully in the physical vehicle on this plane.

The 21 day process »sped« up this realignment to allow the soul full emergence. Upon completion, the Higher Self maintains its new home via light energy – hence the cessation of the requirement for solid food substance.

However, the 21 day process involved mastering the physical body and, to a degree the emotional and mental bodies as well, as it takes both emotional and mental fortitude to even undergo such a process. Nonetheless, it is just a step on the »ascension ladder«.

I also soon discovered that eating is emotionally-based. A year later I experienced strong emotional stress due to the sudden death of a parent. My energy levels dropped and my »inner child« wished to seek solace in food. So began the journey of cellular release and reprogramming and breaking of old patterns.

As the emotional body also serves the mental body, this led to the intensification of my apprenticeship in mind mastery to create a reality that moved beyond even the conscious awareness of food. I learnt that I could program the body to maintain a desired weight and also to change its shape at will. I have learnt that my body reflects my emotional state and that my emotional body responds directly to my thought processes. I have also learnt that the emotional body is like a wilful child, and just because we have decided to keep the house clean from now on, that doesn't mean we don't have to clean out the emotional baggage from past thought processes that are held within cellular memory. Inner spring cleaning is imperative – only then can our being be clean and function at full capacity.

For me, this process opened another door that has refined my vibration to fully activate my intuition and sense of knowing. A by-product of this has been that channelling, self-healing, clair-voyance, bi-location and creating by thought alone now seem natural and relatively easy. I have learnt to honour and love all aspects of my being, to love and honour the choices of others, to communicate freely with various beings of light and connect strongly to my own I AM. My life is joyous and abundant and purposeful. I not only know how to, but do, create the reality I wish for in life and my life is exactly how I want it to be.

Having made this transition, I find my attitude towards being sustained by prana to be very matter of fact, yet to many the idea is impossible and the reality ludicrous. It is neither.

Full details on being sustained by prana, including exact details of the 21 day process, have been covered in my book » Living on Light - The Source of Nourishment for The New Millennium «   German publisher KOHA Verlag ISBN 3-929512-35-1.

Chapter 28

Telepathic Communication

It is both my experience and »knowing« that all higher abilities, including telepathy, occur naturally when we have raised our vibrational frequency and increased the light quotient in our cellular structure. The two go hand in hand, for the faster the rate of oscillation, the higher the light quotient.

It is reported that the Arcturians are the masters of light technology and also that Arcturus is one of the most spiritually and technologically advanced civilisations and is inhabited solely by Ascended Masters. Dr. Norma Milanovich and Dr. Stone have both had intensive communication and dealings with these beings of light. Dr. Stone suggests in his book »Beyond Ascension« that a quick way to build the light quotient in our bodies is to enlist the aid of the Arcturians and ask them to run higher light frequencies through the four-body system and increase our light quotient to maximum capacity. This can be done while you sleep, watch TV, work or do anything. Simply ask and it will be done.

I myself have been using the above technique with great success and have also been working quite closely with the being called Arcturius since mid-1993. His energy is intense but loving, his guidance clear and positive. Consequently, I have included the following information on the Arcturians here, and the following book is recommended reading for those interested in this civilisation and what it has to share with us.

Excerpt from »We the Arcturians« channelled through Dr. Milanovich: »A part of the process of mastery in this form of life is learning to clear the mind. ... A clear mind is essential in our mode of telepathic communication, for do we not need to learn to receive as well as to project? ... Listening is another form of clearing the mind and allowing it to receive information ... In order to be positive and receive, a soul must learn to increase its vibratory rate ... and there must be a sense of peace and satisfaction within before the frequency begins to rise. When this frequency begins to rise it begins to work miracles within. One only needs to bathe in the liquid light to feel the cleansing, purification and peace that it provides ...

All thoughts are electrical impulses surrounded by an electromagnetic field of energy. This field of energy has the ability to move at speeds the human mind cannot even begin to comprehend. In this movement, images are transferred that are directly related to visualisations, emotions and the coding systems of the universal language. It is a being's choice whether or not to send electromagnetic impulses to another place. The choice is determined by the amount of emotion and will power that a being is able to gather. In this choice and the consciousness of the mind, a being determines the degree of mastery over telepathic communication that he, she or it will obtain in one lifetime.

The force that propels and projects thoughts is based upon a tensor equation ... made up of two parts of electromagnetic energy and one part emotion. It is the brain and mind of an individual, coupled with choice and conviction, that determines the ability to send messages. Thoughts are part of universal consciousness, and the energy that moves them through one's consciousness is the intensity of conviction of needing to be one with this power ... All manifestations of creative energies result from combinations of light energy frequencies and sound vibrations. By combining them, one is able to channel the power to create from the universal consciousness and access its codes.«

The Arcturians state that the highest form of telepathy happens soul to soul and is only possible where a being is integrated and has the ability to focus in soul consciousness. It is also suggested that in order to truly comprehend telepathy one must understand the nature of force, of emanations and radiations of energy currents.

As previously covered, mankind has the conscious mind, the subconscious mind and the superconscious mind. Telepathic communication concerns itself with the superconscious state of being, the part of us that is not concerned with issues of survival like the »lower mind«, but is concerned with why we are here, what our true purpose and destiny is. The superconscious mind is the conduit for all communications from the higher realms. All communication comes through the Higher Self.

Telepathic communication is a natural ability of mankind that reveals itself to those who align their frequency to the higher resonance of their God essence or the pure energy force that sustains them. This is true of all »miraculous« abilities from clairaudience (telepathy) to healing by touch, to clairvoyance, bi-location etc. Please note that some individuals are psychically »gifted« with clairvoyance, clairaudience etc. but the purity of the message and/or vision will only be as pure as the channel. This is covered in detail in the chapter on channelling.

Telepathy is governed by the universal Law of Revelation – as you seek, so shall you know. Science records and measures electrical currents in the brain caused by mental and emotional disturbances. In metaphysics it is understood that energy follows thought and that thoughts are things to come. Telepathy allows us to tune to thoughts or guidance from our Inner Teacher, the I AM and/or from other beings from either the astral plane or above, depending on the transmissions and signals we emit, plus the clarity of our intention and will.

Brain dynamics for communication

1. Pituitary gland – the negative contact point and receiver of information.
2. Pineal gland – positive contact point and information transmitter.
3. Cerebral cortex.
4. Cerebrum – the tensor centre.
5. Thalamus.
6. Cerebellum.
7. Synapse gaps between the cerebral cortex and the cerebrum.

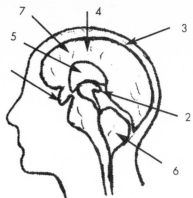

The functions of the human brain are vast and varied and are still being explored and understood by both medicine and science. In the following section I have briefly described the major areas of the brain and their role in telepathic communication.

The pituitary gland is the thought receiver and is the contact point within the physical brain that enables thoughts sent from elsewhere to come in and be placed in the resonating tensor centre for further interpretation.

The pineal gland has often been called the true master gland and is the thought transmitter. Positive action flows through the pineal doorway, negative action flows through the pituitary. Both act in unison to balance all mental faculties.

The cerebral cortex is where thinking, logic, deduction, evaluation, short term memory etc. takes place. It also controls the function of the five physical senses and extremity movement. It is the information gatherer for the various levels of consciousness. This area constantly interferes with telepathic communication and *must be stilled* in order to receive instruction through the superconscious (higher) mind. It is said to be 20% of the brain weight.

The cerebellum is like a half-way house to the unconscious and stores information until it is taken to the unconscious base-

251

ment. It also regulates vital bodily functions and habit patterns, co-ordinates muscle action, balance and posture and much more.

The thalamus is a mass of radiating, ganglionic nuclei with its grey matter divided by a strip of white matter forming a thalamus in the left hemisphere of the brain and one in the right. The electrical activity in the cortex is stimulated by the thalamus which sustains and regulates the normal resting rhythms of the cortex. The thalamus is a memory bank and is also said to be where dreams are formed. Its nerves are specially designed for forming mental images, and the thalamus is known as our »mental television« and is an electromagnetic area that responds to strong emotions i.e. fear, anger etc. It then is said to set up a blueprint of what is sent out to attract to you according to your transmission.

Nerve endings called **synapses** from the cerebrum come near to, but don't touch, the cortex. They communicate through electrical sparks. **Tensor** defines the potential for thought depth that exists in the synapse area.

The cerebrum is considered to be the »sleeping giant«, the huge area of the brain that is considered to be unused. It is our cosmic egg of infinite intelligence and wisdom – our personal guru and the centre of our electromagnetic resonating power. It is 80% of our brain weight. Imagine a car operating on one-fifth of its power. That is what we are doing when we are not consciously working with the cerebrum. Full human potential can only be realised through waking the remaining four-fifths.

Universal Mind is pulled into this centre through the resonating electromagnetic field surrounding the physical form. Thoughts then pass on to the cortex for translation, application and action. In the highest spiritual development there is co-ordinated action between the cerebrum and the cortex. This resonating centre acts independently of the human thinking process, but is where all spiritual awareness and inspiration comes from. It is ultra-consciousness, the medium for extra sensory phenomenon and the seat of all parapsychic abilities.

Resonance is moving energy, forging its pathway through living particles of light – through thought propulsion. Telepathy occurs by being mentally open to receive, and project, desire which – in turn – attracts the thoughts of the sender who responds to the desire and sends the thought energy to the open, receiving station. Thought resonance is binding energy.

Athena from the Ashtar Command says that, »the mind is a vacuum that attracts unto itself that which surrounds it in terms of electrical impulses. It then manipulates these impulses until they are born as thought. Through brain processes this then becomes idea, then action.« The quality of thinking is also reflected by the colour in the human aura which reveals a lot about an individual's state of being.

When the brain is still, thought transference begins. First, the sender connects through a beam of energy that hooks into the electromagnetic field of the receiver (the receiver prepares himself/herself through the five steps listed over the page). The thought idea is then filtered to the tensor centre of the brain and is converted into words. When well-practised distinct words are received, we have both a clear reception and a clear message. A receiver can clear his/her channels by aligning consciously with higher frequencies and energies through meditation, diet etc. as discussed in detail previously. The less electrical blockages there are, the clearer the communication.

In the book »Opening to Channel«, the guides Orin and DaBen explain: »Telepathy enables you to explore unseen worlds. All of you have more telepathic ability than you imagine ... Telepathy gives you the ability to travel to places that are not accessible through other means.

»Your eyes can only see the spectrum of the rainbow, and you often forget that there are many electromagnetic frequencies, such as infrared and ultraviolet frequencies that are just outside of the range you detect with your eyes. Some of you are developing the ability to sense subtle frequencies beyond the range of your normal senses. It is in these frequencies that you become aware of guides and of the realms where other living entities such as ourselves exist. Your increasing telepathic awareness gives you the ability to communicate with other life forms such as plants and crystals, and beings from other realms, as you fine tune your awareness.

»The belief in the ability to reach these unseen though nonetheless real dimensions is not yet commonplace, but there is increasing world wide. belief in the possibility of the existence of dimensions beyond the earth itself, as well as the belief in life beyond death.«

In the »Dynamics of Cosmic Telepathy« Tuella writes: »A Law of Affinity exists, with attracting and repelling actions which command the combination of chemicals to create a form of energy. It is an aggressive force, radiating in all directions, causing pressure on surrounding force space to create waves in that element. Thought is not sent out in one straight line, but in billions of lines in all directions, like a radiating spark of light extending in equal force in all directions. Mind is the medium with which thought is carried from one point to another.« She goes on to say that space is an attracting, repelling force of motion made up of tiny atoms (ethers) with indelible memory of existence and manifestation occurs when these particles are forced to unite through the Law of Affinity.

The development of my own telepathic capacity came about quite naturally. It could be said also a little unexpectedly, even though I had been receiving messages for some years from friends and relatives who had died. Shortly after under going the realignment and cleansing process that allowed my body to be sustained by only light (prana), I found myself being bombarded with various »voices« in my head. I knew that the process of channelling also came naturally as we align our frequencies to the higher octaves of light. Obviously the more one is aligned with the purer aspect of our God Self, the more things are possible.

However, there came a point where I wished to have communication when I wanted it, rather than just in set situations like group meditations and channelling evenings. I now understand that when you are tuned, all you have to do is »dial the number« so to speak, make the call, and you will be answered. It is that simple. However at the time, my logical mind decided to go into research mode and attend classes. So on this plane, I researched what I could and then sent out a »call on the ethers« for hands on tuition.

Having understood that we are energy systems that emit signals and transmissions of frequencies, I realised I could tune myself like a radio and connect with those of my choice. There are beings who actually have the job of monitoring thought transmissions across the galaxies. So as information on our physical plane was limited, I sought tuition from these beings. That is another story, but suffice it to say contact was made and tuition given.

This information correlates to that received by Tuella and other »channels«. However, I was instructed to concentrate on the raising of the frequencies of the four-body system and the maximum absorption of light. This, I was advised would automatically allow the free flow exchange of information as it cleared the air of static, but only those of like vibration could connect. Tuning ourselves to the frequencies of light means that we can tune into beings of light as light is their resonance.

It has been my experience that all communication in the higher planes is telepathic. Beyond telepathic communication, and/or an alternative to it, is the language of light. In the »Keys of Enoch«, it is explained briefly that the language of light is »instant communication with the Infinite Mind using ideographic and pictographic cybernetics ... it is the parent language of a Deity used in an overall plan or design to outline a procedure, to code knowledge into crystal etc. The language of light as a vehicle enables the Lords of Light to reach many planetary worlds and reality simultaneously and fuse the different languages into the same scenario abstract. This allows man to have communion with other planets of intelligence through super-holographic processes. The knowledge of this language comes from a core memory of information being shared by the higher spiritual levels of existence. It allows man to read the »records of the mysteries« in the higher heavens«.

I include this information here to show that there are levels within levels of knowledge and, while telepathy to some is a natural ability, to many others it is not part of their reality or understanding. Beyond the spoken language is telepathy – the language of direct communication from mind to mind via thought. Beyond telepathy is the language of light. Beyond that, I do not know. What I have found in my research is that our »normal« and accepted form of communication on Planet Earth – with its language and cultural barriers, ignorance and misinterpretation – is like kindergarten and can be vastly improved upon. The beauty of telepathy is that communication is pure as it does not need to pass through the mental »filters« of the lower mind with its limited perception based only on subjective reality.

The more we evolve spiritually, the more we remember and the more is revealed to us, for we are infinite beings of infinite wisdom. Some are now receiving via telepathic communication (channelling) instructions to anchor and activate things like metaphysical light envelopes within our computer memory banks. These contain key codes, sacred geometries and higher learning that we will evolve into.

I will not pretend that I understand the intricacies of life beyond this physical form, but I do know for certain that verbal communication upon this planet is the densest and most misleading that there is. The results of this state of affairs are evident. We need only to look at religious expression to understand that while in essence it is all the same, labels and interpretation via the lower mental body have led to much discord and war. I have found in both my personal experience and research that telepathy is expressed from higher mind to higher mind and does not come through the individual's perception filters until verbalised.

Telepathy is a form of communication that you absorb into yourself and does not need interpretation via thought. The only time one interprets telepathy into thought is when one wishes to consciously retain the body of the conversation or when one wishes to express that communication verbally. Telepathy is an energy exchange of higher mind and a *knowing*.

Personally, I have not spent much time developing telepathic skills for communicating with beings on the Earth plane, although this form of communication will be not just necessary but commonplace in future times. Many years ago under very inter-

esting circumstances, I had the opportunity to communicate telepathically for some hours with a dear friend with the odd verbal
interjection for confirmation. Somehow we'd slipped into a
frequency band where this all flowed freely, so I held no barriers
or disbelief regarding this type of communication – I just could
not achieve it then at will.

Five Steps to Opening up to Higher Communication

These techniques will still the cortex and allow us to open up
new synapses as awareness transforms the mental process. They
can be used for communication with our Inner Teacher, guides or
other light beings.

Step 1. Be still and know. Meditate. Tune yourself as previously
guided with breath and light. Be in silence and know that we
all have these abilities. *Doubt halts all progress.* Remember
feeling you can (positive thought) then feeling you can't (negative thought) neutralises the energy and nothing will happen.

Step 2. Invoke the light. Call down a cylinder of golden white
light, know that it comes from the purest energy source in all
the universes. Know that it is healing, transforming, and will
allow optimum alignment for purest communication. Breathe
this light in through the pores of the skin and let it fill every
cell of your being (as guided in previous visualisations).

Step 3. Visualise (and bring the higher mind into play) an equilateral triangle in your mind's eye. Fill it with blue light. This is
the universally accepted symbol or sign that you wish to begin
telepathic communication.

Visualise your chakras being fully open and activated and
absorbing into themselves the golden white light that
surrounds you in the cylinder. See your chakras become one
column of light extending up to the highest purest source,
allowing divine communication to flood into your being. See
the cylinder of light from the unified chakra column begin to

spin and radiate pure light into every organ, cell and all the energy fields of your bodies. (This will raise their frequencies to be more receptive). Ask for full activation and illumination of both the pituitary and pineal glands so that receipt and transmission of all information is clear and pure.

Step 4. ASK! Ask for communication. Call in who you would like to speak to – your Higher Self, I AM, guides etc. Always control this by stipulating that »only beings of light who work for my highest good are invited to communicate with me.« This, together with the above steps, eliminates the possibility of mischievous or negative energy forces connecting with you in answer to your call. The above allows you to control the contacts made by select invitation rather than having »open house«. Be prepared by having a list of questions you may want answers to.

Step 5. LISTEN! Learn to listen. If you don't still your mind through meditation or deep, connected breathing and the above, how can you expect to hear? At first it is like intuitive whispers or just a knowing, a »feeling« of clarity about an issue. With regular practice this will grow to a loud, clear voice that is indisputable. You know when the information received is for your highest good. You learn to trust it by the benefits that become obvious in your day to day life as you apply this »guidance«. Know it by its fruit! Our I AM and beings of light work with us solely for our divine unfoldment so that we may realise that we are in fact beings of light and the God essence expressed in physicality.

Remember, **do not doubt!** Test your guidance by how it feels within and exercise your own discernment. The more you go within and get to know yourself, the more easily you will be able to discern what is right for you according to your uniqueness. Eventually, with practice, you will be able to recognise who is communicating with you by their »energy fields« or vibration, before you even receive their name telepathically. Always ask the name of the being who wishes to seek counsel with you.

Chapter 29

Bi-location, Travel by Thought and Teleportation

Bi-location is the ability to be in two places at once. »Bi«
meaning »two«. Throughout the ages there have been various
stories of great masters who were often reported to be seen
concurrently – in different places at the same time. In modern
times devotees of Babaji and Sai Baba have also reported this
phenomena.

The ability to bi-locate comes naturally when our vibrational
frequencies are tuned closer to the speed of light. Many techniques are available, but I have found from personal experience
that vibration is the key, not technique. Consequently, we may
practise various techniques – like the ones recommended in this
chapter – but the shift will not occur if our frequency is not
aligned. I have also found that we all have *our own personal key,*
so what works for me may not necessarily work for someone else.
Practice and desire make perfect. Desire will attract to us the
appropriate way which will be revealed when we are ready, i.e.
tuned.

Having had regular contact with various beings of light both
telepathically and in the »dream state«, I began to feel as though
the »visual« relationship was one-sided. They seemed to tune in to
me at will and I wished to be able to visit and communicate when
I desired. Often I could »feel« their presence and sometimes
detect shimmering waves of light energy as thought transmissions
began. Consequently, I began to consciously develop those skills.
Others before me had suggested spinning the chakras alternately
to build up a certain momentum, then – by will, command and
desire – project out. So for some months I practised. I would call
a friend, say I was tuning in, go through the routine, send my
consciousness to them at their place of residence, try to see with
spiritual eyes what they were doing, wearing etc., then call back,

via telephone, to confirm. This met with varying degrees of success, but I soon became dejected as it all seemed like hard work.

At this point I was offered the choice – a common one in the path of every initiate – to serve Divine Will and allow no distraction, or to continue focussing on my own unfoldment and my own »games«. Both are valid and both lead to the same point. I chose service. A few months later, as a gift, my forgotten desire for bi-location was fulfilled.

For me it seemed as though the secret lay in where I was bi-locating to. It was easier to get in the car and visit a friend, but to go to the etheric retreats of the beings of light was another matter altogether! So the first step in bi-location was the *intensity of the desire*. The second was the *motivation behind the desire*. The third was *being tuned* to the right vibrational frequency.

As I have mentioned before, there are dimensions within dimensions, the majority of which cannot be connected with by our normal energy band of consciousness. We cannot pick up the transmission broadcast of channel nine television if our television is tuned to channel ten. We must consciously and physically switch channels.

Bi-location is a shift in our conscious awareness. Much of life on other planets, other universes and galaxies will remain hidden from the scientists of Earth until they shift their frequency, since the former all exist and operate on different energy bands. While there is much to learn and understand on the third and fourth dimensional energy band to keep us amused for eons of time, there is also much more on the fifth, sixth, seventh and so forth. Again, all choices are valid and we must explore according to our own inner guidance and inspiration.

So back to bi-location. For those beginning or interested in this training, it is well to understand that there are *varying degrees* of bi-location. All depend on the skill and ability of the bi-locator. There are those who can project a solid appearance of themselves that others see with physical eyes. They are literally in two places at once. Another possibility is, often due to the intensity of concentration involved with this method of projection, we may have other individuals look after and watch over our physical body which may be left in a meditative or sleep state. However, the energy projected is fully animated and appears solid, although it is said to have a »luminescent« quality. These two methods involve bi-location within this physical plane for various purposes – usually an embodied master appearing before a student. The book »The Nine Faces of Christ« by Eugene Whitworth describes this process in beautiful detail.

As the fourth dimension is the last requiring a physical body, beings of the fifth and above can take a body »at will« and often choose to appear to the initiate in the form of their last incarnation for easy recognition. Generally their vehicles are lightbodies. When I first began to bi-locate to these other realms, all who appeared before me materialised in a form resembling a physical body, clothed in robes etc. Now when I »visit« they remain as energy, as I *know* their individual vibration as they know mine. In order to tune in to these realms we need only to send our conscious awareness.

I have not fully explored bi-location on the physical plane, as mentioned above, and can give no guidance. I assume the methodology is similar, but greater command by mind over molecular structure would be required. While I have practised, and had limited conscious tuition in, dematerialisation of the molecular structure and actually »felt« my feet disappear, I have not advanced enough to give a workable formula or guidance at this point.

What I am aware of is that it is to do with the *implosion* of energy – the technique that I have practised has been to raise the vibrational frequency to the highest octaves of light. You have to shift your conscious awareness beyond the confines of the physical form and then, through the power of will and intention, gather up into that higher energy band the molecular structure of the physical form. You must allow yourself to dissolve and let go of any fear that is often common with any new experience of expansion.

The technique can be likened to a fisherman in a boat (your conscious awareness in the bi-located state) that casts a net out into the water (your will and intention) and allows it to gather all the fish (your molecular structure) before drawing the net plus fish up and into the boat again. Implosion is moving inside out through frequency bands where the boat is the highest band, the water surface another band and underneath the water a lower frequency band again.

This information and technique was confirmed to me by another channel who received the same information recently. Those interested in teleportation should enrol for these classes on the inner planes and gain tuition while the physical vehicle is in meditation or sleep.

The following then can be applied as the individual cares to apply it – making note that the information has been gained from the split of conscious awareness and consequent visitation to the etheric retreats of the Ascended Masters.

The first »barrier« I had to overcome was that I had imagined I would just »zap off« and have no awareness of the physical body and where I had left it. However, a split in conscious awareness is just that. It is like we have what I call the »watcher« – a part of ourselves that »stays behind« to keep watch over the physical form. When we relax in that knowledge, we find we can fade in and out of either realm at will.

Secondly, when we find ourselves where we projected, in the beginning it may take time to tune ourselves and hook in to that frequency band. Fading in and out can be common – like when you first tune into a TV channel and need to adjust the picture to get the clearest image. Being able to hold the vision and frequency may take practice.

Thirdly, be aware that all beings will present themselves to you in a form that has maximum recognition or appeal to your programming. So for example, if you have always held a vision of Mother Mary in long, blue flowing robes, then that is how she will manifest to you if it is your desire, and highest will, for you to meet.

Fourthly, if you find yourself asking whether what you are experiencing is not just a figment of your imagination, you may be told – as I was – that in these realms *all is manifested as a result of thought.* So as you desire it to be, *it will be.* Why not take a leap of faith? Let go of doubt. Allow the energies of these places to move through you and manifest in your physical body. Your energy fields are connected by the *antakarana* or rainbow bridge. This is the bridge from the physical to the spiritual realms that you have created through your meditations. This bridge allows for the transfer of energy from the higher to lower planes of frequency – for readjustment and realignment.

So basically the routine to follow may be practised remembering you may need your own unique key/s. My keys were purity of intention and strength of desire. Also note that, as I like to do a number of »routines« in one go, I have combined other affirmations for purification and reprogramming here. I suggest you play with it all, adding and eliminating according to your inner guidance and success.

Some of the following steps have been already covered in the ascension meditation and points five, eight and nine are not required for bi-location. What is required is to build up the light quotient and chakra momentum to project the consciousness from the confines of the physical body. I also found that unless I spun the chakras alternatively – anti-clockwise, then clockwise etc. – I could not build up enough velocity, spin and momentum and seemed to need to create a »double helix« woven strand type effect to achieve success. Again, it is necessary to practise and find the right formula for you.

In the past I bi-located by building up the light quotient within my four-body system together with the spin and velocity of the chakras, as described above. The exit point for me has been through the crown chakra, then up through the five chakras above, joining with the energy of the I AM and by the power of will and command tuning in to where I wished to be, then *being* there.

However, of late I have been programming prior to sleep to go the perfect place of the choice of my I AM for whatever light work may be required. As I have been consciously receiving tuition each evening, while the physical body slept, I felt this learning may be intensified and absorbed easier if I went for a tune-up first. One morning I decided to go for an alignment while I lay in bed in contemplation, so I simply willed myself to the ascension chamber my I AM chose. I was told this was the retreat in Luxor which I had not consciously visited before. I felt some energy swirl lightly within the physical body, but then the phone rang so I got up. (I was obviously not well-prepared for this impromptu experience, nor aware of how easy my night time »jaunts« had allowed the day time ones to become).

Distracted, I had a shower but felt completely faint as though I had undergone an enormous energy drain somehow. A quick tune-in and I was advised by Sananda that I was operating at »half capacity«, that the rest of my energy was still in Luxor and to go and lie down, complete what I had started or regroup my energies. I returned to bed, impressed at the ease of this bi-location, and sent my full focus to the happenings at Luxor. I am sure that with practice we can maintain physical activity while we send ourselves off to retreat for realignment or whatever. The process continued for some 20 minutes with some in-depth discussion with Sanat Kumara, then I felt to regroup. Interestingly, the moment I *thought it,* I was back in my body, followed instantaneously by swirls of energy that were also absorbed back into my body via the front top chakras.

So no technique is set and all are to be experimented with until we find our own formula that can be applied at will. Happy travels!

Creative Visualisation 16
Bi-location Techniques

- Desire stillness and communication. Program that all will unfold for your highest good and for the highest good of all with whom you may share.
- Be clear in your intention, motivation and desire.
- Get comfortable so you can be easily freed from the physical body and not return until ready. It is very important that you are somewhere you will not be disturbed.
- Bring down the cylinder of pure, golden white light.
- Activate the pituitary and pineal glands with a crystal and/or white light to receive and transmit, also ask your I AM to activate both glands.
- Affirm: »I release all old programming and instruct my pituitary, pineal, and all the glands in my body to be open, activated and operating to their fullest potential.«
- Feel these centres expand and visualise them explode in light, also visualise the thalamus and all major brain centres fill with, and be activated by, light to change their resonance.
- Breathe in light and allow it to fill your cells and change their vibrational frequency closer to the speed of light.
- Activate all the chakras, with liquid light pouring in from the crown centre. See the crown chakra expand and spin – then move down to the brow, throat, heart, solar plexus, sacral and base chakras.
- Do the following chakra affirmation with each: »I call upon Divine Wisdom, Divine Intelligence, the infinite power of God Most High to activate this chakra to resonate to its highest potential and flood my being with this wisdom NOW!«
- Instruct your I AM to bring your base chakra into perfect alignment with the perfection of the physical body. Repeat this procedure with the emotional body and the sacral chakra, and the mental body and solar plexus chakra. All chakras are to be huge balls of spinning light spinning in opposite directions – anti-clockwise, clockwise, anti-clockwise etc.

- Draw the light into every cell, every organ, visualising all being cleansed and aligned to the light right down to the feet, then feel the energy wind its way up around and through the body, spinning the chakras as they go.
- Feel the whole body resonating and vibrating as if being rocked.
- Feel the energy vortex rise up, up, up – intensely lighting up each chakra which is spinning to maximum capacity.
- Bring in your INTENTION to leave.
- Go up through the eighth, ninth, tenth, eleventh and twelfth chakras.
- Visualise being where you wish to be as you command: »I AM AT ———————NOW!«
- Do not doubt. Your body should stop rocking and/or reverberating. Settle back and watch. Be open. Allow the energy fields of any who »appear« before you to solidify. All communication will be via telepathy. You may see or feel or hear – according to your tuning.
- Keep alert. Keep your senses open to receive. *Be still and listen.* The »watcher« will be aware of the physical body. You will find a part of your awareness still anchored in the physical body. Be fluid and relax and let the »vision« flow.
- Call in the master of your choice, but accept who appears, and know that you have programmed all to unfold for your highest good.

Chapter 30

The Creation of the Lightbody and Increasing our Light Quotient

We are aware that while the planet is undergoing a shift to a higher frequency, all who reside within her energy fields will also experience this realignment because she is a living energy system. Consequently, I would like to cover two issues in this chapter.

Firstly, what many are experiencing naturally as the planet undergoes her transformation can be termed the »creation of the lightbody«. So the next few pages will outline the different stages we may experience as this occurs and how it is manifesting in our own energy fields – as bouts of flu, headaches etc.

Secondly, as many are enthusiastic about these changes, I would like to cover practical things that we can consciously do to build and increase the light quotient in our own bodies. Tuning ourselves to the higher octaves of light and changing our vibrational frequency has been explored extensively in previous chapters. I will briefly summarise them and then add a few additional techniques to accelerate this process.

The process of transition into light is a gradual one. We are not matter one day and pure light the next. Our energy fields have to be infused with, and realigned to, light gradually or else we would experience electrical »burn out«.

In the text »Revelations from an Archangel – Ascension to the Twelfth Dimension«, Archangel Ariel states that the entire crystalline structure of matter was activated to third level lightbody, for all planetary inhabitants, in April 1989. The creation of the lightbody is due to the planet's current transition process and is not an optional experience or process. Beings not wishing to be part of this process at this time will choose death by accident, natural disaster or disease. As mentioned previously, it is foretold that they will continue their cycle of evolution on another planet of frequency comparable to their own. There is no judgement involved. It is just the changing nature of energy.

According to Ariel, the lightbody is gradually created through the transmutation of our current physical body as it mutates and absorbs more light. Again this is interconnected with the realignment of our energy fields to higher frequencies and higher octaves of light, and the following information describes the actual physical process and common symptoms as this change occurs. We are all evolving and absorbing light at our own pace. Some are consciously working with these changes and so their transmutation is quicker. Some are unaware and are absorbing this light and change in direct relation to planetary change. However, one can classify this creation into levels:

1. **First level:** When body density drops. Common mutational symptoms are flu, headaches, diarrhoea, rashes, muscle and joint aches. Most flu epidemics are actually light epidemics! Brain chemistry changes. Right and left brain functions blend and the pituitary and pineal glands begin to change in size. The DNA structure and chemical components begin to change and pick up extra hydrogen atoms and chemicals that the cells need to take undifferentiated higher light and break it down into useable light encodements for DNA.

2. **Second level**: The etheric blueprint floods with light and releases karmic experiences. Individuals may feel disoriented as well as experiencing »bouts of flu«. »Why am I here?« is a question which many begin to ask themselves. Light in the etheric blueprint releases fourth dimensional structure and causes spins in the geometries of the emotional, mental and spiritual bodies. Change is rapid and many feel tired.

3. **Third level:** The physical senses become much stronger. Your bodies not only absorb light for their own transformation, but also acts as a transducer-decoder of higher light energies to the planet as a whole. The process of the cosmic in-breath is now irreversible – like an elastic band that has been stretched to maximum capacity, then been released and snaps back to its natural state.

4. **Fourth level**: Major changes take place in the brain and its chemistry. The symptoms are often headaches, blurry vision, loss of hearing and sometimes chest pains. Crystal regulators in the etheric body keep lines of light within the fifth dimensional blueprint from connecting again until you are ready. Chest pains are due to the expanding energies of the heart as it opens to deeper levels. Vision and hearing are being realigned to function differently. The mental body begins to wonder if it really is in charge and individuals get strong unexplainable and undeniable urges to follow Spirit without hesitation. Individuals may get flashes of telepathy, clairvoyance and nearly all begin to experience empathy. This is a time of feeling, honouring, accepting and validating the emotional body and learning to control it.

5. **Fifth level:** The mental body decides to tune to Spirit. Dreams change and may become more lucid. You get feelings of »déja vu«. Thought processes become non-linear. Beings oscillate between knowing and doubt. We understand the habitual nature of thinking and behaviour, and look at de-programming and re-programming to create the personality we wish to have, not the »I« we thought we were from our interaction with parents, peers and society etc. Change seems to be constant and we consciously begin to discern from our heart, rather than judge from »conditioned responses«.

6. **Sixth level**: We draw others to us for mutual support and stimulation of growth. We question what is »real«. We are critical

269

towards our mental processes. How we identify with others and ourselves changes rapidly. Re-evaluation may be uncomfortable, but we feel it must be done. We look at our relationships, jobs, home environment, living styles. It is a time of letting go, of moving on. We change our friends. Everything is in a state of flux, but we feel lighter, vaster, freer somehow. By this stage the light quotient in our being is 33%. We feel as though we are opening up our inner senses, and clairvoyance, clairaudience etc. seem normal and natural to us.

7. **Seventh level**: The heart chakra opens more. We are much clearer in the expression and experience of our emotions. We just *have to be ourselves!* We release blocks and old patterns. It is a time of great emotional clearing and great intensity as we seek to rid ourselves of emotional baggage. We feel more in tune with each moment, feeling very present and flowing with life. Often old relationships end or change rapidly as we dig deep and honour our feelings. There is simply no room for denial on any level. We begin to lose emotional attachment to others. Chest pains are more common as the heart continues to open its energy fields. (Doing the unified chakra meditation will assist in the heart opening).

Fear is released. The energy fields of all the bodies are realigned through the heart and, when the alignment is complete, fear drops away. Pressure on the forehead or back or the head is due to the opening of the pituitary and pineal glands as they absorb more light. When these glands are fully open, activated and functioning at the highest level, ageing and death cease. When the pineal gland is fully open, we experience multidimensionality. Yet the sensation of duality seems to increase as we leave it behind. Some days we feel connected and joyous, others we are in fear and caught up in survival issues.

Many wish to »ascend« and leave the planet as we sense the very real possibility of ascension through our deepening connection with Spirit. As we learn to follow our joy, we may then want to »save the planet« and have everyone follow their joy. ALL are stages of progression and reflect our changing perception.

Regarding diet, you feel the need to eat less and prefer light and live food. Many at this stage have ceased to eat meat, sugar and drink alcohol as they »feel« the effects of these substances on the vibrational fields of the body.

8. Eighth level: We see the master in all and purely wish to be of service. We leave the »saving and rescuing« mode behind in favour of the desire to serve Divine Will. The pineal and pituitary glands change shape. If headaches persist, ask the beings who are working with you to simply »tone it down« for they don't feel pain, or ask them to release endorphins – the brain's natural opiate. The brain is being activated – particularly the cerebrum. Cranial expansion is common. Triangular »seed crystals« in the brow and recorder crystals in the right side of the brain are activated along with the eighth, ninth and tenth chakras. We begin to be hooked into the languages of light.

The pituitary and pineal glands are opened fully and work together to create the »Arc of the Covenant«, a rainbow light that arcs over the top of the head to the third eye and is a decoding mechanism for higher dimensional language. You may find it hard to find words to express yourself as you may think in geometries and tones. If confused, do the unified chakra meditation and ask for messages to be decoded and translated.

Again, you become much more aware of the vastness and multidimensionality of your nature – aware that you can be anything that you want to be. You cease to operate from obligation and relationships become transpersonal. You share words from your heart and soul and others may feel disorientated when dealing with you as they no longer can »hook« into you. You operate from a deep level of serenity with heightened sensitivity and awareness, yet feel grounded and transformed. By this stage, it is possible to be sustained purely by light and prana. It is no longer necessary to take nourishment in the form of food or drink.

9. Ninth level: Decoding geometries and toning is easier. Spirit is using the languages of light which shift the sixth dimensional blueprint into a new template for your fifth dimensional lightbody. Your body may change shape as the energy fields shift. You feel interconnected to all beings everywhere and less connected to the opinions of others. You release the desire for – and the energy needed to sustain – the »game of separation and limitation« and feel truly free. The ninth level sees a mass descent of the lightbody into physical form. As with the third and sixth, this level sees a strong re-evaluation as we begin the final surrender to Spirit and we truly become a divine instrument. Here Spirit determines our income, our work, other beings in our lives, everything.

This is the dissolution of the ego-self and, while ecstatic, it can be most painful. Making the leap can be fearful, even though we have evolved through eons of time to reach this point. We may go back and forth, clinging to old comfort zones before letting go completely. There is no turning back and everything must be released. The ninth level is surrender, followed by ecstasy. We let go of the »I«. We realise that while free will is real, it is also an illusion as it only there to guide us and to empower us to be one with Spirit. Survival fears dissolve. Focus in on the now. At-one-ment.

Though fears may surface, they seem unreal and are easily put aside. We tend to disconnect from consensus reality and our choices and reality seem unreal to others. From the seventh, eighth and ninth levels onwards, the inner light noticeably radiates out and by now you feel unbelievably grounded, connected, centred, filled with purpose and desiring only to serve. For a while you may slip between the eighth and ninth, from feeling complete at-one-ment to being »a limited human being« again. This settles down by the end of the ninth level. You then continually feel connected and operate from your Christ level. Your intention and motivation is always for the highest, although others, due to their own inner triggers and issues, may not always choose to see that.

The ninth level is where we begin to hook up to our I AM. The last three levels unify all the energy fields. All the chakras are unified and you become totally connected to your I AM.

10. **Tenth level:** You are one with Source consciousness and know that everything is possible. DNA is no longer double-stranded but 12-stranded. Teleportation, manifestation etc. are instantaneous. The Merkabah (another name for our lightbody) has been built and allows you to pass through space, time and other dimensions complete in your totality. It has its own consciousness to be directed by you.

11. **Eleventh level:** All levels of the lightbody have been constructed and activated and are connected to your physical body via »spin points«. These light matrices lie along the physical acupuncture meridians and are lines of light intersecting in beautiful geometries: a new fifth dimensional circulatory system of light. Cellular regeneration has been accomplished. Time is no longer linear but simultaneous – past, present and future co-exist. There is no separation and you will fully manifest your vision of Heaven on Earth and express the ecstasy of Spirit.

In this frame of conscious awareness many now access and create new types of light-based technologies, new forms of community living, new systems of government and equitable food and resource distribution systems. All have received specialist training and skills to help create and manifest the New World – the »Golden Age«.

12. **Twelfth level:** The continuation of the creation and implementation of the New World systems. You hook up with other twelfth level initiates who bring into existence new governments, new financial and educational systems, better system of food and resource allocation etc. Everything will be redefined in the final stages of Earth's ascension so that all may exist in joy, equality and harmony. By this time the planet and her

inhabitants will have been »rewoven« into light to shine in their full glory as the final stages of this Divine Plan unfolds. The planet goes to light, shifts out of this dimension and is brought into a multi-star system where everyone is a lightbody and follows Spirit in total mastery. All parallel realities are rewoven and absorbed back to Spirit and all have aligned their will to the Divine.

Creative Visualisation 17
Increasing and/or Building your Light Quotient

- Tune yourself with breath and light techniques.
- Always imagine that you have a cylinder of light around you wherever you are, wherever you go. Breathe in this pranic, transforming energy with every breath as you **consciously** breathe throughout your day.
- Use white light energy in all meditations.
- Take only light, live fuel into the physical body.
- Do the ascension acceleration meditation daily for a while and see what happens.
- ASK for your I AM to hook you up to an etheric drip of liquid light and to regularly monitor and keep increasing this light quotient, while you meditate, while you sleep each night, while you watch TV (if you watch TV), while you work, any time your mind is focussed on something else.
- Ask the Arcturians – the masters of light technology – to oversee a program of building and increasing your light quotient each day to maximum capacity for you. Call in the Mahatma energies to accelerate and intensify the quality of your ingestion of light.
- Know that all energy that you focus on Spirit – from meditation, service, channelling – written or spoken – prayer and affirmation will aid in the creation of light within you, for what you focus on, grows.
- Light is the visual aspect of the God within – as you seek it, and align to it, and focus upon it, it will reveal itself to you more in every cell and every atom of your being.
- Obviously the purer our energy fields are, and the freer of »baggage,« the more light our beings can hold. This can be aided by realigning the energy fields of the emotional body through cleansing of cellular memory, by mind mastery and by being vigilant and aware of the power of thought.

Chapter 31

Universal Laws

Assuming there is a Supreme Power or a Supreme Being that created and controls this complex universe, then the following quote from the »Vision of Ramala« has great interest: »This Supreme Being manifests itself and maintains order and balance in its creation through what are sometimes known as the great natural laws of the cosmos. These natural laws are comparable to your Earthly scientific laws and define the relationship between all created things both on the physical plane and on the planes above and below the physical. They control and hold in perfect balance every divine manifestation of infinite spirit, every degree of spiritual consciousness, every molecule of matter.

»They control the lives of not only each and every human being, but of your Creator, the Solar Lord within whom you live, move and have your being, and also the great God within whom your Creator lives, moves and has its being. All levels and degrees of consciousness are bound by these great natural laws.

»The natural laws stand above the Solar Lords and all Gods. They govern the existence and the creativity, not only of many thousands of Solar Lords or Gods that exist within your visible universe, but also of those that dwell on other levels of creation.

»It is a wise person who recognises that science and religion are both seeking the same thing no matter whether it be called Truth, the Knowledge of the universe or God. The natural laws of the universe are the same as humanity's laws of science only expressed on a higher, more holistic level.«

The following is a quotation from Lord Sananda from the book »Oneness Remembered«: »The spiritual energy of the soul of each living unit of creation listens to the sounds of the universal flow of information which originates from the Source energies of God the Creator. This harmonic attunement brings forth within the lifestream of Earthmen, the comprehension of the principles known as universal cosmic law. These precepts have been given to and created also by man as he has lived out his life experience upon Terra, known as Earth environment.

»Today in your time, the accumulation of cosmic law resonates with the Holy Father and His giving of Love and life to each unit. The attunement to Self, then, in connection to the Will of Source Energy, known as Love by its very BEingness, creates a pathway of knowledge which one can follow to create in the Life expression Balance, Harmony, Peace, Love and Forevermore existence. The harmonic of this alignment has created the precepts known as cosmic law.

»Each Unit has free will choice to align with these laws or not. Your knowledge of cosmic laws lies within the encoded seed packets of crystalline energy within your soul entity who comprises the totality of you!«

It is said that there are 33 (numerologically 33 is the number of the universe) laws that govern the universal creations. Some of these are as follows:

1. Law of Oneness: Everything is interconnected and shares the same Source. Also known as the Law of Energy. Excerpt from the »Vision of Ramala« – »It is a wise soul who recognises that all humanity is indeed part of the one great whole, that every human being can be considered as an individual cell in the cosmic brain of your Creator. There is, truly, no separation except where humanity chooses to live it.

»So one of the great lessons of physical life is to rise above this apparent separation, to see that it is »apparent« and to learn that you are truly one with your Creator, not just in your physical, but also in your spiritual being.

»There is no separation in this physical world between you and your God. This world is your God. Your God is this world. You are living in and are an actual part of your God just as an aspect of your God is living in and is an actual part of you. So the greater is to be found within the smaller, which is contained within the greater«.

2. Law of Fulfilment: The following quotes and references are from the book, »Ye Are Gods« by Annalee Skarin: »There is a law irrevocably decreed in heaven, before the foundations of the earth, upon which all blessings are predicated; and if we obtain any blessings from God, it is by obedience to that law«.

This law is also known as the Law of Production or the Law of Creation. As you sow, so shall you reap. Plant the seed and bring in the harvest. Every thought has the power to create reality and as you judge, so shall you be judged.

This Law of Fulfilment deals with the power of thoughts and words where thoughts are seeds and, when coupled with emotion, produces a living vibration that will bring forth each after its kind. Desire is the heat that generates the seed and gives it power to manifest – the power of creation. The law is true and eternal, no matter what we desire, if we plant the seeds (thoughts) and keep out the weeds (doubt and fear) it will come forth.

»When we prepare our minds, without fears and without worries for greater things, greater things will be given. The power to govern our surroundings and to build perfectly is in our hands. It is the power of thought, which is the power of Godhood.«

3. Law of Cause and Effect: Also known as karma, this law assures a rebalance of energy in the cosmic energy pool, where for every action there must be an equal and opposite reaction. This law applies to the actions of all beings. Karma has often been seen as a judgement: that whatever you give out you'll get back, as if you will be punished. However it has simply to do with the exchange of energy: whatever energy is released (sent out) by a being, will attract like particles and rebound back. Energy expands and contracts, so if energy of a negative nature is emitted, then it will contract back to its transmission source in response to its original expansion, and bring negativity with it. Same is true of positive energy.

4. Law of Change and Transmutation: Every condition can be transmuted and everything is always changing. The only consistent thing in the universe is the indestructibility of energy and its changing form.

This is also known as the Law of Alchemy – every condition in life can be transmuted into glory and made divinely beautiful, no matter what that condition is. If we accept it, bless it, thank God for it or be »thankful in all things«, we can transmute even bitter and heart-breaking experiences and conditions of life into spiritual loveliness by this most perfect and exacting law. We can also receive the power to transmute our spiritual desires and dreams into tangible material manifestation.

This law never fails and includes the spiritual law of change and transmutation as well as material laws and elements. This alchemy is the power of God in action and is eternal and unchanging and brings exact results.

Annalee Skarin says »The Law of Spiritual Chemistry is the law transmuting all conditions, all vibrations, all darkness into beauty and music and light. One must learn to speak the language of the Angels, or speak with «new tongues«. He must learn to speak from the soul and never from the lips or even the mind. He who speaks from the lips chatters. He who speaks from an empty mind adds confusion to discord. He who speaks from a full mind feeds the minds of men. He who speaks from his heart wins confidence of mankind. But he who speaks from his soul heals the heartbreaks of the world and feeds the hungry, starving souls of man. He can dry the tears of anguish and pain. He can bring light for he will carry light. The language of the soul is »sacred« language and most beautiful ... It can only bring a benediction of glory, for it is the language of the eternal spheres and the language of Gods. It is the gift of the Spirit known as the «new tongues« ... The power of transmutation is the power to contact the centre of the soul through the heart. This method alone holds the power of fulfilment and perfection«.

5. Law of Balance: The integration of polarities. The term »polarity« means opposing forces with no competition between them. The forces collectively move towards a harmonised objective, resulting in growth. Duality is opposing forces of energy which have taken on a personality and have therefore become competitive, playing one against the other through judgement and competition, and thereby creating the ego as part of the incarnated personality. We live on a plane of duality and need to exercise the Law of Balance to create a polarity of male/female, positive/negative energies to achieve harmony and integration. The Law of Balance when integrated into our being is one of the first steps to enlightenment.

6. Law of Manifestation: Allows us to manifest our desires and needs when the intention is for the highest good of not just yourself but also others. Decide what you want, state it clearly, let it go and assume it is done. *Do not doubt*! Our ability to manifest our desires into physical reality is guaranteed when we are in synchronistic alignment with Divine Will, and have no internal sabotage patterns running from cellular memory.

7. Law of Synchronicity: Being in the perfect place at the perfect time. Perfect attunement and perfect alignment where everything flows magically and harmoniously. This law is also known as the **Law of Grace** which states that when beings are aligned perfectly, they will flow with the divine perfection of God as God manifests in their lives.

8. Law of Discernment: Also known as the **Law of Differentiation,** this law has to do with being totally in tune with what is the next step in our personal evolution. This concept has been discussed in detail on the chapter on discernment.

9. Law of Forgiveness: This refers to the paying of karmic debts, the rebalance of energy by those who have created the energy imbalance. It brings forgiveness of self and others as no healing can be achieved without forgiveness.

10. Law of Resonance: Like energies attract like particles due to their electromagnetic fields; so whatever we send out in thought, word or action, is amplified and returned to us.

11. Law of Perfection: Everything is perfect in its divine state.

12. Creative Law of Divine Affirmation: The power of thought and words which affirm that you are what you believe yourself or your reality to be. As you think, so shall you be.

13. Law of Compensation: The order under which one receives just remuneration. This law is universal and not subject to personal demands. It is associated with the Law of Cause and Effect and the Law of Creativity and is exercised in direct relation to an individual's choice of action.

14. Law of Assimilation: Allows no particles to be built into our bodies that we, as spirits, have not overcome and made subject to ourselves.

15. Law of Adaptation: The law of allowing and flowing easily with the only constant thing in the universe – the changing nature of energy as it expresses itself in many diverse forms. We must be flexible, as change brings growth. Opening up and allowing the purest energy to flow through our being unhindered will bring great joy and balance as we tune in to greater powers. Tuning our energy fields to accept only the purest of energies will maximise this experience.

16. Law of Causation: Works in harmony with the stars so that a being is born at a time when the positions of the bodies in the solar system will give the conditions necessary to experience his/her advancement in the school of life. This covers the science of astrology which influences our life according to the choice of birth sign and time of birth.

17. Law of Evolution and Rebirth: A slow process of development carried on with unwavering persistence through repeated embodiment in forms of increasing efficiency whereby all are, in time, brought to a height of spiritual splendour in recognition of Source and true identity. Also known as the Law of Periodicity.

18. Law of Analogy: »Know thyself.« It allows for a being to arrive at an understanding of the God Force within him/herself and within the universe by understanding all aspects of his/her own being.

19. Law of Duality: When a being is consciously connected to the Source or »enlightened« they are above this law and unaffected by it. Until that time, this law affects the polarity of energy.

20. Law of Mind: While Spirit is Absolute Reality, mind is the medium through which Spirit works, through which creation takes place into physical form on this plane. The Law of Mind states that as you believe, so it will be. This means that at this level, man's belief influences and creates his reality. »The Law of Mind is the summation of human belief.« Ann and Peter Meyer cover this law in detail in their book »Being a Christ« and it is also covered in detail in previous chapters.

21. Law of Respect: This law honours an individual's right to seek universal truth and Divine Wisdom in a manner that makes their heart sing provided that it also respectfully honours all life.

22. The Universal law: The Universal law is that knowledge, that awareness, that all living things, that all life has within it that vitality, that strength, to gather from itself all things necessary for its growth and its fruition.

23. The Law of Love: The Law of Love is that Law which places the welfare and the concern and the feeling for others above self. The Law of Love is that close affinity with all forces that mankind may associate with as positive.

24. The Law of Mercy: The Law of mercy is that law which allows one to forgive all error; to forgive equally those who err against you as you err against them. This is to be merciful. To be merciful is akin to the Law of Love, and if one obeys the Law of Mercy there can be no error in the world.

25. The Law of Gratitude: The Law of Gratitude is governed by the Law of Resonance. This law states that the more we express our gratitude for the things we enjoy in life, the more we will attract to ourselves things to be grateful for.

26. The Law of Patience: The law of Patience states that all things will have their time and their season. As all that unfolds in the Divine Blueprint does so in Divine Time, patience becomes a virtue where one understands that aligned focus will eventually bring all thoughts, words and actions to their proper fruition. In the Divine Will game, one becomes aware that what does not come to fruition immediately is simply not destined to do so at that point in time.

27. The Law of Example: The Law of Example states that the most powerful force of change will come from each individual »walking their talk«. It states that any person, concept or thing may serve as an example for others to follow. Those who have served as examples of love, service and the sharing of their better parts, have helped to bring about freedom, joy, beauty and peace upon this plane. Individuals who wish a for better world are encouraged to live their truth in each moment in each day in a way that honours all life.

28. The Law of Tolerance: The law of Tolerance is associated with the Law of Respect. It is a Law which inspires us to recognise the divinity in all. This recognition moves us beyond judgement and separation that comes from race, religion, culture, creed, age or gender bias.

Chapter 32

The Universal Brotherhoods

C.W. Leadbeater, one of the early influences of the Theosophical Society, in his book »The Masters and the Path« writes: »The consciousness of the Great White Brotherhood is an indescribably wonderful thing. It is like a great calm, shining ocean so strongly One that the least thrill of consciousness flashes from end to end of it instantaneously, and yet to each member it seems to be absolutely his own individual consciousness, though with a weight and a power and a wisdom behind it that no single human consciousness could ever have. This magnificent sea of »cosmic consciousness« of the brotherhood is something so great, so wonderful, that there is nothing else in the world like it: even those who belong to it by virtue of having passed the first great initiation can only catch glimpses of it, can remember only a little of it here and there. It can be felt fully only on the nirvanic plane, on which the brotherhood primarily exists, though it has its manifestation on the lower planes, even down to the physical world.«

It has been said that there are many brotherhoods of light of which the Great White Brotherhood is a part. »The Keys of Enoch« says that there are 70 brotherhoods or orders serving as a field of intelligence for the Father. This text states of the brotherhoods of light: »Advanced spiritual intelligence that can take on physical form and have the responsibility of governing stellar orders with respect to the local hierarchy/federation of the Deity ... the 70 brotherhoods which comprise the Great White Brotherhood that have the greater responsibility of administering the cosmic law ... »whole light beings« comprise the ranks of the spiritual brotherhoods preparing the physical and spiritual civilisations« and are in charge of renewing or reawakening creations.

The Spiritual Hierarchy can be likened to our government structure, but is far more complex. Again, there are many texts available that explore this hierarchy in great detail, including some wonderful work in the Theosophical Society. There are also a multitude of texts and channelled information regarding the Ascended Masters and the rays. From my research into both, it appears that there is conflicting information, perhaps also because various beings are assigned to a »job« or service and then may be »promoted« and so move on.

Of the Ascended Masters, Enoch says they are »Masters who have had several incarnations in the lower heavens teaching the cosmic law of the universe and who have ascended back into the presence of the Father from whence they receive new assignments to teach a variety of worlds because of their greater Love«.

To summarise points mentioned previously that to me, due to my personal experience and research, are now factual:

- Most of humanity has been »tuned« to a specific channel.
- Ignorance of other channels does not negate their existence.
- As we refine our frequencies we can tune into and be aware of other »channels« or dimensions of existence.
- Other beings and beings of light exist on other realms or dimensions that we can access by simply changing our frequency and, consequently, our channel. Not all who exist on other realms are beings of light or motivated by the highest good of all, e.g. disembodied spirits on the astral plane and also extraterrestrials who are technologically advanced with space craft and time travel but whose conscious awareness is still very third dimensional.
- All beings of light are by nature spiritually evolved and are called beings of light because of the degree of light they manifest in their form. Light is the visual aspect of our God essence.
- All beings of light are in conscious and committed service to First Cause.
- The service of the Great White Brotherhood is to aid Earth and her inhabitants in their reawakening and reunification with their God Self.
- Earth's evolutionary game is a speck in a corner of a quadrant in a universe which is a speck in the total galactic picture.

Continuing from the above, I would like to share a little of my experience and understanding from my dealings with these beings of light. I first had conscious contact with the Ascended Masters in 1992 when some audio and written channelled information came to my attention. For me, it was like being given the complete picture. Suddenly everything made sense, all my inner guidance, my years of private research and meditation – everything. It was literally as if someone had turned on the lights and I had reawakened. It took me beyond meditation just for inner peace and allowed me to reconnect with my destined purpose and also my personal role in the Greater Plan.

The Great White Brotherhood has been in contact with humanity for eons of time. I have been advised that Lord Maitreya and other Ascended Masters including the Sananda energy, »overshadowed« Jesus. St Germain was connected with the Rosicrucians. El Morya and Kuthumi worked directly with Madame Blavatsky, the founder of the Theosophical Society. Djwhal Khul worked with Alice Bailey. Throughout history and all religions, the brotherhoods have been interwoven. Dr. Stone in the »Complete Ascension Manual« and the »Keys of Enoch« covers these connections in great detail. In the last decade or two they have again made their presence more widely known through many reputable channels.

What I have found since entering the Order of the Brotherhood of Light, is that I have been assigned various masters for my tutelage and reawakening. Initially, my »personal« instructor was Lord Sananda. I also received instruction in specific areas from Mother Mary, Kwan Yin, Paul the Venetian, and others where appropriate – depending on my assigned task at the time. I regularly attend classes on the etheric realms, usually while the body sleeps and often in meditation. The intensity and regularity of this communication, plus the initial confirmation of information that was provided while I learnt to trust, has allowed my life to become truly joyous, abundant and completely purposeful in its expression on this plane of existence.

Due to the complex and in-depth range of material already available on the brotherhoods, I will not go into great elaboration here. However, I would like to cover some basic notes, from the »Keys of Enoch«, on the functions of various hierarchical structures.

- **The Council of Nine:** A tribunal of teachers governing our immediate super-galactic and galactic region, subject to change in evolving »new programs« of the Father's Kingdom.

- **The Council of Twelve:** Sons of Heaven working to supervise the creation and regeneration of the lower worlds. In the book »Mahatma – Books I and II«, Brian Grattan writes: »Pure love, wisdom, joy, peace, balance and every other quality of the light can only be attained through the One Great Presence, the Source Council of Twelve for this Cosmic Day, wherein each member represents one Cosmic Ray. It is this complete Council of Twelve, embodying the Twelve Rays, which enables this creation, this one Cosmic Day, to exist.« He also states that »The Twelve Rays that constitute this Cosmic Day are the self-luminous, intelligent substance of the I AM, Mahatma, which exists at all points (except for those third dimensional planets still limited to Seven Rays) and of which all of Creation is composed.«

- **The Council of Twenty-Four:** A council governing spiritual civilisation in the Son Universe and is not to be confused with the 24 Elders.

- **The Council of One Hundred and Forty-Four Thousand:** A tribunal of Ascended Masters administering the program of the »Ancient of Days«. The infinite mind working through the Creator God, the hierarchy of the »Higher Heavens« that governs the hierarchies of the mid-heavens and the lower-heavens, assessing the final »soul programs« of man and master alike.

- **The Council of Light:** The collective name for the above councils, which govern this galaxy and other regions of distant universes. These are not solar or planetary councils.

- **The Order/Brotherhood of Enoch:** Initiates the faithful into new worlds of consciousness by creating the spiritual-scientific scrolls of knowledge. The brotherhood builds the pyramid grids on the planets necessary to evolve the biomes of intelligence.
- **The Order/Brotherhood of Melchizedek :** Is in charge of the consciousness reprogramming that is necessary to link physical creation with the externalisation of the divine hierarchy
- **The Order of Michael/Brotherhood of Michael:** Guards the galaxies from biological/spiritual interference from the lesser forces of light except where necessary to test/train for soul advancement.

And so it goes on, systems of creation, all being born, programmed, reprogrammed, evolving, returning back to the Source. The in-breath and the out-breath ...

Chapter 33

A Bridge to the New World

I was originally intending to call this chapter, »A New World Order«, however I believe this to be the name of a political movement. This »New World«, of which I wish to share here, will be formed from a spiritual and not political basis. *However* when this spiritual alignment has been achieved, all other structures will also automatically be realigned – political, educational, economic and social.

In my meditations I have seen »visions« of this New World. The Bible talks about the new millennium which the Keys of Enoch describes as »a period of great happiness and perfect government. A linear concept of a thousand year period of peace in the orthodox theologies. In Enoch's teachings, the millennium is one of many openings through the veils of light, which man can enter to freely co-mingle with the higher intelligence and divinity of other worlds«. Enoch states that there will be multiple opportunities, during the millennium, which will permit beings to move through our consciousness time zone and into other regions of »spatial intelligence«.

In order to understand the vastness of creation, and how what is taking place on Earth is a »speck« of it all, I would like to insert here an understanding of the word »chiliocosm« as opposed to millennium. A millennium is a happening defined within limited space and time. A chiliocosm – according to Enoch – »represents the multiplicity of evolution and the greater connection between the many universes fused into the Father's plan«. It is the »interpretation of a thousand different levels of cosmic creation – all intertwined so that »purification and renewal« of creation can occur in all one thousand levels/cells simultaneously«.

Back to our quadrant of the universe! Our planet is evolving – reawakening – and all of Earth's inhabitants are undergoing great change in keeping with planetary changes. It is like we all have an inner radar that is magnetically drawing us back to a state of complete union with our I AM or Divine Spark. The Ascended Masters advise me that the earthquakes, floods, droughts and physical chaos on the planet are due to the stepping up of – and influx of – higher energies along the electromagnetic grid lines of the planet and the activation of major energy vortexes. This is allowing for the »overlaying« of the new grid systems upon and within the energy fields. Similarly, humanity is also being infused with more electromagnetic light energy through the meridian lines in the body. New grid structures are being overlaid and crystalline structures in the existing blueprints are also now being activated. All is designed to »throw out the old and bring in the new«.

In the book »Opening to Channel«, DaBen and Orin explain: »The energies hitting the earth right now will energise and activate whatever you are focussing on. For those of you who are sensitive and already focussing on your spiritual path, these new energies will make things work out better than ever before. Doors will open; your relationships will improve. You may find yourself looking inward, finding the answers that you've been searching for. You may go through some temporarily difficult times as you let go of the old and receive the new. Many of you have already gone through this period of adjustment. On the other side of it is a better life, filled with more abundance, love and success. Appreciate your lessons now as they come, and know that they are preparing you to handle a higher vibration.«

They continue: »You may see others in pain or difficulty. You may still read of disturbing world events. The challenge as you reach these higher realms is to remember that your balance will now be coming from a connection to the higher realms, rather than to other people. You will be able to provide balance and stability for others as you make this connection. It is important to help those who you see are having difficulty adjusting to the new vibrations, rather than getting caught up in their fears. As you open your channel, you will be the one holding the light, bringing positive encouragement and direction to others. It is a time of great opportunity. Some of mankind's greatest music, art, writing, and cultural expressions are yet to come, and will be produced under the influence of this higher vibration.«

It is said that this New World will be established by those who have connected and consciously merged with the divine nature of their being. As Archangel Ariel says: »many have been receiving very special training and developing skills and perception to assist the planet. You may be a specialist in intergalactic diplomacy, new family structures, new forms of government, or how to equitably allocate food and other resources on a global scale. Creating new types of community living, new rituals for an awakened spirituality, new light-based technologies, or new expressions through the arts may be what makes your heart sing.« As we realign our frequencies to higher vibrations we will have the ability to manifest this Heaven on Earth in accordance to the vision that has been pre-laid for humanity at this time in our evolvement.

New governments and councils working for the good of the whole of the planet will be formed; no longer will there be separation due to race or religion or culture or country, and all will be freely distributed for the good of the many and not just the few. I remember reading somewhere a few years ago that if all the wealth of the planet were redistributed evenly, everyone would be a millionaire. We do not suffer from lack of resources and abundance on this planet, just lack of conscious awareness to create equal distribution of such. While many starve from lack of physical nourishment, just as many starve from lack of spiritual fulfillment and lack of purpose.

For those who can comprehend simultaneous time, know that as the future already coexists now with the past and present, all that we wish to have occur, has occurred and is in existence. Again, by »tuning our antenna« – shifting our perception – we can pull into the present the vision of the future and so create how it is destined to be. This is quite a wonderful time-saving device but it relies on good clear, inner guidance from the Inner Teacher who exists multidimensionally and is the connecting link to the reality of simultaneous time.

Digressing slightly, I have researched with the assistance of Archangel Ariel, the matter of parallel realities that may interest some. Ariel says that each time we make a choice that is not in alignment with Spirit, Spirit's choice will occur but so will ours through the spin-off of a »parallel« reality to allow that choice to exist and to honour our free will. Our awareness follows our choice and our perception gives us our day to day reality. As we align consciously back to the will of the Divine, all these realities pull back together and so we now live with a constant merger of all those parallel realities until there is only the path of Spirit and the recognition of, expression of, and service to, Divine Will.

So planets and individuals ascend by literally being rewoven, where »now points« are the fabric of space and time and all are pulled up through the dimensions. This is like a large net that has been cast across the oceans of time. It is designed to maximise impact, maximise experience and is then winched back to its source of casting. The densest expression of our being is physical form that has always had free will to explore and create.

The Ascended Ones say that Earth inhabitants are much admired across the galaxies for their amazing powers of physical manifestation, for we have truly created the most interesting playground with many diverse learning experiences.

When we realise that we have the proven ability to create the reality we desire, the fun really starts. Mind mastery takes discipline, but as energy follows thought, we can then begin to simply create through thought alone. Coupled with a pure heart and deep integrity and alignment with Divine Will, all you desire to create will be made manifest as it is governed by the highest for humanity collectively, not just for a given individual. When we have aligned our free will to Divine Will, we automatically become part of the conscious creation of the Greater Plan. The Greater Plan is for the inhabitants of Planet Earth to experience, at this point in linear time, the Golden Age, the new millennium of peace where we recognise not just our own divinity but the divinity in all sentient beings.

It has been said that in the past, the consciousness of humanity has been too dense and we have been too unaware of our divine nature. Now that we have evolved, it is prophesied that we will soon be issued with the invitation to join the Intergalactic Federation of Worlds. This Federation has been in existence for eons of time, but could not make itself known to a planet of beings who have believed themselves to be the only intelligent species existing in the universe, and who at the same time have been completely governed by fear bred from their ignorance of their own multidimensional nature.

Research has shown that Earth has been an experimental station and most governments have recorded data on the comings and goings of extraterrestrials. I will not even begin to cover this information here; suffice it to say that anyone who wishes more information on this can seek it as it is now readily available.

So, universally it is recognised that we as a species are »growing up« and our graduation present will be our own, and the planet's, reawakening and consequent invitation to join the Federation.

At this point in linear time, we are invited to volunteer, to sign up and choose our desired »posts« in the New World. Again this is pre-laid, or preordained, selected by us prior to this incarnation. Again the guidance, training and invitation to take up our posts will be given by the Inner Teacher.

In line with the tenth insight of »The Celestine Prophecy« and the twelfth level lightbody activation, the Self Empowerment Academy launched M.A.P.S. – Movement of an Awakened Positive Society – in September 1996.

The concept of M.A.P.S. is fully covered in S.E.A.'s
«Cosmic Internet Academy -C.I.A.«
web site – **www.selfempowermentacademy.com.au**.

Creative Visualisation 18
New World Vision

- Sit and tune yourself using breath and light techniques.
- When feeling calm, centred and totally relaxed, allow your mind to wander, to imagine and fantasise about how you would like the world to be if there were no restrictions, no limitations, and the only guidelines were that ALL creatures were happy and joyous; that ALL creatures – human and animal and Mother Earth herself – were safe, not harmed in any way, nurtured, respected and cared for.
- Imagine and visualise our planet to be pollution-free.
- Visualise, clear, fresh, crystal blue waters teaming with myriad's of marine life.
- Visualise clear, blue skies filled with abundant bird life.
- Visualise thick, luscious rainforests and vegetation with all types of plant species .
- Visualise all creatures co-existing harmoniously without threat to their existence.
- Imagine that all are healthy, deeply content and at peace.
- Imagine that all have satisfying work, joy-filled relationships, harmonious living environments with enough food, shelter, clothing and entertainment for all.
- Imagine a world without poverty or hunger, without famine and war.
- Imagine then being part of the Intergalactic Federation of Worlds, of space travel where all can come and go across the universes freely and easily.
- Imagine being able to communicate telepathically, to heal by touch or thought alone, to create by thought without physical action, to be able to dematerialise and rematerialise at will.
- Just imagine. Imagination brings vision. Vision creates reality.
- Be clear about what you wish to create.
- Learn to create for the good of the whole so that all benefit.

»Heaven, nirvana or samadhi is an experience that we access
through a shift in our conscious awareness and perception.
We can do this through understanding and working with the
natural laws of energy.
Many now exist in Heaven on Earth, they are the builders,
the creators of this new »enlightened« world, this Golden
Age.
The Inner Teacher lights the path, has the blueprint,
and will teach us how to create and enjoy our place in this
paradise,
the prophesied millennium.«
Ñ Jasmuheen

»The personal self of every individual is endowed with the
Power of Choice as to what it wishes to think, to feel, to
create, and experience.
If one uses all the substance and energy of his being
constructively,
the Peace, Expansion, Joy, Opulence, and Glory
are the return unto Life for the Outpouring of Its Gifts.«

»To have in harmony drop away from the body or affairs,
the personality must let go of all thought, feeling, and words
about imperfection.«
Ñ St Germain, »The Magic Presence«

Summary – In Resonance

It's always interesting to go back in time and re-read a personal diary, or a book one may have written as our perspectives seem to change so rapidly as time unfolds and life reveals its mysteries to those who seek to know.

Since writing this book, we have completed the trilogy of the »Inspirations« channelings and begun a new trilogy called »Streams of Consciousness«. We have also expanded chapters 26 and 27 into a book on its own called »Pranic Nourishment« which has also been translated and is published now in Germany (by publisher KOHA Verlag). As »In Resonance« (retitled from »The Art of Resonance«) is also to be translated and published in German, I decided to re-read it, and where necessary, rewrite it to bring it up to date with my current understanding. So here we have the fifth edition, yet much to my surprise, I have neither added nor changed that much of the existing text.

Personally, my focus has shifted from being interested in my »ascension« to simply being tuned synchronistically and perfectly to the rhythm of the Divine Blueprint as it unfolds and manifests into the physical plane. My only desire is to radiate the Supreme Splendour of the Divine One Within, to BE in service and fulfill my pre-agreed piece of this blueprint joyously with ease and grace.

Over the last five years, my relationship with the Ascended Ones has deepened and strengthened as I have allowed myself to be inspired by their messages and then witnessed magical changes take place in my own day to day reality. Joy has become a natural state of being for me as have feelings of purpose and connectedness.

One of the original motivations in writing »In Resonance«, was to find the common understanding throughout various religions and then bring these understandings back to the simple idea that we are all just systems of energy. Having introduced this basic idea, we then explore further the idea of conscious tuning to awaken our telepathic abilities and so much more. Ideas to plant seeds for each individual to explore and nurture if inspired.

Consequently, the quotes used throughout »In Resonance« come from a wide variety of books, parts of which I have been inspired by in the creation of my own model of reality. As time has gone by for me, the idea of reality creation has now been integrated from an intellectual understanding to a cellular knowing and I have constantly experienced the many positive benefits of mind mastery and conscious re-programming.

· Simplistically, the message of »In Resonance« is to encourage us ... to honour our intelligence, knowing that as thinking systems of energy we are constantly creating, for form follows thought.
· To discover, and then listen to the voice of intuition – what I have come to term the Divine One within.
· To create a model of reality that allows us to live our life to our highest maximum potential in a manner that brings us limitless joy; a model that also honours all life forms.
· Regardless of what we call our God, or if we prefer to relate to this creative power as just energy, we are all people.
· It is time to bridge the worlds of science and religion, East and West, the physical and the etheric.
· It is time to focus upon the commonalties and yet honour the diversities of all cultures, creeds, races and religions.
· It is time to personally understand that the common unifying factor within us all is the Divine One within.
· If we focus upon it and invite it to express fully in our lives, then we will truly bridge the worlds and harmoniously and collectively realise our true human potential.

A Story of Creation

Excerpt from The Aquarian Gospel of Jesus the Christ by Levi

»Before the worlds were formed all things were one; just Spirit, Universal Breath. And Spirit breathed, and that which was not manifest became the fire and thought of Heaven, the Father-God, the Mother-God. And when the fire and thought of Heaven in union breathed, their Son, their only Son, was born. This Son is Love whom men have called the Christ. Men called the thought of Heaven the Holy Breath. And when the Triune God breathed forth, lo, seven spirits stood before the throne. These are the Elohim, creative spirits of the universe.

And those are they who, in their boundless power, created everything that is or was. These Spirits of the Triune God moved on the face of boundless space and seven ethers, and every ether has its form of life. These forms of life were but the thoughts of God, clothed in the substance of their ether planes. (Men call these ether planes the planes of protoplast, of earth, of plant, of beast, of man, of Angel and of Cherubim).

These planes with all their teaming thoughts of God, are never seen by eyes of man in flesh; they are composed of substance far too fine for fleshy eyes to see, and still they constitute the soul of things; and with the eyes of soul all creatures see those other planes, and all the forms of life.

Because all forms of life on every plane are thoughts of God, all creatures think, and every creature is possessed of will, and, in its measure, has the power to choose, and in their native planes all creatures are supplied with nourishment from the ether of their planes.

And so it was with every living thing until the will became a sluggish will, and then the ethers of the protoplast, the Earth, the plant, the beast, the man began to vibrate very slow. The ethers all became more dense, and the creatures and these planes were clothed in coarser garbs, the garbs of flesh, which man can see and thus this coarser manifest, which men call physical, appeared. And this is what is called the fall of man, but man fell not alone for protoplast, and Earth, and plant, and beast were all included in the fall. The Angels and the Cherubim fell not; their wills were ever strong, and so they held the ethers of their planes in harmony with God.

Now when the ethers reached the role of atmosphere, and all the creatures of these planes must get their food from atmosphere, the law conflict came; and then that which the finite man has called survival of the best became a law.«

Universal Laws and M.A.P.S.

This section is written for all who seek to know and demonstrate positive personal and planetary »refinement«. This is M.A.P.S. – Movement of an Awakened Positive Society – individuals who are open of mind, yet also discerning of heart.

M.A.P.S. is the tenth insight (of the Celestine Prophecy) being demonstrated and also the twelfth level of the lightbody being activated. M.A.P.S. is about Oneness, recognising the uniqueness of all, and focussing on commonalties rather than differences. Etherically and esoterically, the unfoldment of M.A.P.S. is being overshadowed by what is termed the »One Heart, One Mind« – O.H.O.M. – the masters in the paradigm of Oneness. They say that:

»We speak to you of Oneness for this conceptual idea will bring the unity, the balance, the full manifestation of a planet and humanity in the vibration of the ascended state of consciousness. This is enlightenment, this is nirvana, this is bliss for all human souls. Oneness is the most supreme vibration of refinement. It is who you all are – simply a finer expression of that which you now may be identifying with as yourself.

»The vibration of Oneness is so powerful in its capacity it can only be attracted to your field, or released from within you, to the degree that you are consciously tuned to its beat. Oneness is pure energy, pure Infinite Intelligence, the unified field, the backdrop and essence of creation.«

Each aspect of life as we experience and witness it, contains all the universal laws yet all these laws are fragments of the Law of Oneness which governs the unfoldment of a greater game – the Divine Plan.

The »New Age« is simply a movement focussed on bringing tools and information to tune and empower all drawn to its message. By activating the spiritual body to its highest potential – in a way that honours all – this automatically begins to tune the other bodies.

So, many of you have now activated the spiritual body and attained various degrees of attunement. The Inner One is now talking to you, and you are interpreting then integrating this within various levels of understanding.

Many have now realised that all is energy and that energy fields can be tuned. The question is – why and also to what beat? The Divine Inner One has the answers. You are prompted by an intuitive knowing that there is more, and universal laws make themselves known to you. You recognise them in action in your life. O.H.O.M. calls this the quickening then the awakening.

You seek to know, to dare, to be and to be silent. *BEing silent means to demonstrate by example.* In this time of noise you are intuitively guided to »walk your talk«.

With the awakening comes the gathering as all are drawn together via electromagnetic forces. Energy again. This is the *universal Law of Resonance.* Like attracting like. This law allows us to understand how we literally do create our own reality.

The quickening, the awakening and the gathering are simply microcosmic examples of the *universal Law of Oneness* contracting back in answer to a cycle of the in-breath and out-breath of the original force of creation.

The awakening requires us to utilise the *universal Law of Discernment.* This law allows us to tap into or tune to our own unique piece of the Divine Blueprint. It is about being totally in tune with the next perfect step in our own personal journey of evolution. Where we are powerfully connected without distraction or judgement of other realities. It is about recognising that there are many instruments in the »Divine Orchestra«, then knowing if you've agreed to be a violin or drum set this time around, then learning how to play harmoniously together with all the other instruments.

In the game of »Mastery of Reality Creation«, the beginning of physical reality is like a blank canvas. We have been unconsciously creating for many embodiments, paint layer over paint layer. As we awaken, we can see the depth, the complexity, the beauty of it all as we explore and remember the many aspects of our being.

We have learnt that the more we finely tune the physical vehicle, and the stronger it is, the higher the voltage – or frequency or light quotient – we can attract and emit.

Being a »refined being«, tuned to the beat of Oneness brings its own rewards. Joy, magic, synchronicity, purpose, bliss, fulfilment, great relationships sharing soul to soul, health, vitality ... the list seems endless. We move from survival to thriving, we activate the four-fifths of the brain housing higher consciousness, we are consciously aligned to Divine Will and aware of the Divine Plan as we joyously witness it unfold.

This is the *universal Law of Adaptation,* the law of allowing and flowing easily with the only constant thing in the multiverse which is the changing nature of energy as it expresses itself in its many different forms. Flexibility brings growth and change.

O.H.O.M. recommends that »humanity sits in the seat of discernment in their heart and honours the intelligence of all by gathering together to create mutual empowerment for the good of the collective whole.« This is the *social agenda* for M.A.P.S. It comes under the *universal Law of Balance.* The challenge for humanity currently is to create a pragmatic and demonstrable global unity and balance, by accessing and utilising the brilliance of all cultures, creeds, philosophies, races and religions.

Social refinement comes also from refinement of our existing educational systems. Individually and collectively, society desires positive global change. How quickly this change occurs is dependent on how tuned and connected each individual decides to be to the Law of Oneness. Working consciously for the good of the whole will mean activating specific agendas throughout the social structure. O.H.O.M. suggests that we become pro-active in the *refinement of existing structures* on the planet and not »reinvent the wheel«.

M.A.P.S. is about refining the existing educational systems to empower youth to discover their blueprint and life purpose and consequent joy from being in alignment with the game of Oneness.

M.A.P.S. is about pragmatically cleaning up the environment. Our *environmental agenda* now has the ability to eliminate 45% of the world's pollution caused by car exhaust emissions. This program also dovetails beautifully with our business agenda of *have fun, make money and do good.*

Socially those in M.A.P.S. have simply decided to make a difference. By tuning into our blueprint and finding out the contract we made to be in embodiment at this time, and then simply »getting on with the job«. Also choosing to be in our power and in our joy moment by moment, here and now by doing that which makes our heart sing.

Politically, we are *people politely pressuring politicians to perform for positive change.* O.H.O.M. shares that individuals in various degrees of awakening have now been positioned throughout all levels of society. I recently had the pleasure of meeting with a South American »mainstream« political ambassador for one of our Asian neighbours who is totally awake, working consciously with the Ascended Ones for Oneness within the political arena. He sat and joyously giggled through our whole meeting. What a delight to witness!

O.H.O.M. suggests that as we gather together, we find out each other's passion and support each other to only do what makes our heart sing. The singing heart is the true voice of the Inner Teacher who holds the Divine Blueprint in the Oneness game. Know it, do it, BE it, love it and share it!

After the quickening, the awakening and the gathering comes the bridging of worlds: awakened ones bridging the etheric with the physical realms, the East and West, the »haves« with the »have nots« and so forth. Each awakened one fulfilling his/her small but integral piece of a »bigger game«. Bridging hearts and minds, bodies and souls.

Bridging is also about consciously opening doorways to all levels of existence that need to be opened to bring the full collective awakening for the new millennium.

The Ascended Ones call M.A.P.S. a »sweet revolution«, a gentle refinement into the highest level of being. The Oxford

Dictionary defines revolution as »complete change, turning upside down, great reversal of conditions«. The old paradigms or energy patterns on our planet have been of »light and darkness«, »love and fear«. The new paradigm of Oneness is simply »light and love«.

Pragmatically demonstrating human potential, the first step is remembrance: remembering who we really are in all levels of creation. The second step is our application of this remembrance into our physical, day to day reality.

Other guidelines provided by O.H.O.M. to bring joy and purpose to physical reality are as follows:

- Focus on the *quality of the information* being shared, not external structures.
- Do not »reinvent the wheel.« *Utilise the gifts and talents of each other* to join together to create a powerful whole.
- Open to *co-operation* not competition as competition promotes separation; and co-operation brings Oneness.
- Check all guidance with the voice of joy within the heart's response.
- Take up the invitation by the Inner Teacher to attend classes on the inner realms via meditation and quiet contemplation and get to know who you really are.
- Be *limitless* in your thinking – quality thinking brings a quality life.
- Let your *imagination* flow – remembering that the imagination is a gift given by God to connect us to the realms of Spirit.
- Be clear in your vision and share freely of this vision to those who ask.
- This is a group initiation so all must volunteer themselves motivated solely by the joy in their heart and their recognition that you share a common vision.
- Pay attention to all who may volunteer to aid the physical manifestation of your vision, for all have a part to play, a gift to bring.
- Be aware of the power of language and use trigger words. Use positive language in the Oneness paradigm if you seek unity.

- Bring all your relationships into a state of completion so that you are free from karmic ties and can share simply for the sheer pleasure of being together.
- Walk your talk – be a living demonstration.
- Share information, time, and abundance freely. Tithe a percentage of your income.
- Remember you cannot copyright Universal Mind.
- Be fluid and flexible – expand into newness and BE in each moment.
- Choose to interpret everything in your life in a way that keeps you in your power and in your joy!
- Tune in, chill out, let it sprout!

The conceptual idea or vision of M.AP.S. has also been launched via the newsletter, »The ELRAANIS Voice«, in over 11 countries world wide. Details on M.A.P.S. can also be accessed via the Internet web site **www.selfempowermentacademy.com.au**. It is said that the Internet, or »information super highway« is currently the uncensored voice of the consciousness of the masses.

Background on JASMUHEEN
and her work as M.A.P.S. Ambassador

Although founder of the international M.A.P.S. AMBASSADRY
– The Movement of an Awakened Positive Society –
Jasmuheen is probably» best known globally for her work in
the field of LIVING ON LIGHT. Since 1993, Jasmuheen
has been part of a team that has pioneered and successfully
implemented a specific process to allow her physical body
to be »pranically fed«. As of mid-1993 she has taken her
physical nourishment purely from liquid light.

International lecturer and author, her fourth book, »Pranic
Nourishment« (also known as »Living on Light«) covers
the last four years of her research in this field in great
detail. This book has now been translated into the German,
Dutch, Italian language and will soon be published in
Spanish and French.

Jasmuheen is currently writing her final book in the light trilogy
titled – »Ambassadors of Light – Living on Light« which
looks at this ability as a practical and viable solution to the
current challenge of world hunger. It also covers the effects
that adopting this new form of nourishment would have on
global health care systems and much more.

The second book in this series titled »The 21 Day Process«, and
published also by KOHA Verlag, covers other people's
experiences with the process of living on light and includes
opening and closing chapters by Jasmuheen.

Jasmuheen is known as a »cosmic telepath« and is the author of
another five books including, »*In Resonance*« (also available in German and currently no. 4 on the best-seller list for
esoteric matter in Germany), the previously mentioned –
»*Pranic Nourishment*«, plus the channel and compiler of

the works »*Inspirations – Vol. 1 – with Lord Sananda & the Ascended Ones*« *volume 11 and also Volume 111.* Her latest trilogy of »received teachings« is called »*Streams of Consciousness*« »*Volume 1*« is complete and Volume II is due for release shortly. Jasmuheen has been channelling the beings of light, known to her as the Ascended Ones, since 1993 after many years of receiving telepathic messages from friends and relatives who had passed over. Her new book »*Our Camelot*« is due for release by the end of this year.

Jasmuheen is also the editor and publisher of the newsletter »The ELRAANIS Voice« This newsletter is the voice for M.A.P.S. and it focuses primarily on reporting on the creation, the discovery and the implementation of social, economic, political and educational brilliance – personally and globally.

As author and reputable channel, her articles are published regularly in many esoteric magazines globally.

Jasmuheen has practised meditation and researched metaphysics (the theoretical philosophy of human existence and knowing), Eastern philosophy and New Age thought for more than 25 years. She is trained in Reiki I and II and Magnified Healing, and is an experienced metaphysical counsellor/channel. She travels regularly facilitating workshops, with the Ascended Ones, throughout Europe.

As M.AP.S. Ambassador, Jasmuheen is also the founder of the Self Empowerment Academy (S.E.A.) – which holds the web site for the »COSMIC INTERNET ACADEMY« – (C.I.A.). This NEW updated site acts as a cosmic library and offers many »Cosmic Intelligence Alternatives« for the modern day challenges of our world. This web site is currently under reconstruction and will be operational by

the end of July 1998 – the current existing web site address
is **www.selfempowermentacademy.com.au**

Inspired by the Ascended Ones, she now works closely with
Arcturius, Kuthumi and St Germain to promote the
M.A.P.S. agenda. This is a »loose« term describing the
Movement of an Awakened Positive Society which focuses
on positive personal and planetary progression in the social,
educational, economic and political arenas. The ability to
live on light is the M.A.P.S. Ambassadry's solution to world
hunger.

Glossary of terms used:

Antakarana: A filament of light that is created life after life and is energised and strengthened through spiritual vibrations. This »rainbow bridge« is constructed upwards and is built through meditation, spiritual work and endeavour, motivated purely by our desire for higher knowing. This bridge allows us to bring the finer energies of the spiritual realms back to the physical plane. It is a bridge connecting our physical embodiment with our Higher Self through to our I AM and back to Source.

Arc of the Covenant: Is created when the pituitary and the pineal glands are opened fully and are working together to form a rainbow light that arcs over the top of the head to the third eye. It is also a decoding mechanism for highest dimensional language.

Axiational lines: Vibratory lines which connect levels of human electrochemical activity with astrobiological circuits that span the solar system and are connected with resonating star systems. The axiational lines connect the acupuncture mapping of the human biological system with superior astrobiological analogs.

Elohim: Creator Gods who control the calibrations of light necessary to evolve all the combinations of the »image and similitude through the eternal eye of the Divine Father«. It is said that the Elohim are mentioned 2,500 times in the Old Testament.

Helios – the Solar Logos: The being who ensouls the entire solar system, whose essence is anchored in our sun.

Light packet information: These are like metaphysical light envelopes that are programmed into our computer banks and four-body system and are said to be packets of information from the Higher University on Sirius.

Mahatma energies: The golden white light energies that are of the highest frequency and purest form available in the entire universes.

Melchizedek: Eternal Lord of Light – the Universal Logos in charge of organising the levels of heavenly worlds for transition into new creation. Together with Archangel Michael and Metatron, he is co-equal in the »rescue, regenesis and re-education of worlds«. Melchizedek is the being who ensouls the entire universe. The Order of Melchizedek is the core, essence and antecedent of all spiritual teachings on Planet Earth.

Merkabah: A divine light vehicle used by light beings for interdimensional travels. It can take many forms and is also our lightbody.

Metatron: The creator of the electron and creator of all outer light in the known universe.

Sacred geometries and fire letters: The fire letters (also known as flame geometries) code human consciousness into light and are specific letters of a sacred script, shaped in »fire script« so that the consciousness of the sacred letters of spiritual writings can actually penetrate the soul of the reader. It is said that the language of these letters can »pierce the three veils of conventional relativity and open the eyes of man to behold wondrous things of Divine Wisdom«.

Sacred languages: The languages recapitulating the multiple levels of knowledge connected with the full development of a planetary specie and its spiritual destiny.

Sanat Kumara: Our Planetary Logos, is like a president or king of the planet. Every being lives within his aura. This being is responsible for all life forms simultaneously on the planet. It is said that Sanat trained under Adonis on Venus.

The previous explanations of terms comes from the »Keys of

Enoch« plus the »Complete Ascension Manual« by Dr. Stone.

Bibliography and Recommended Reading

1. Alice Bailey – »A Treatise on White Magic«
2. Annalee Skarin – »Ye Are Gods«
3. Barbara Brennan – »Hands of Light«
4. Barbara Brewster – »Journey to Wholeness«
5. Brian Grattan – »Mahatma I and II«
6. Buddhadasa Bhikkhu – »Mindfulness with Breathing«
7. C.W. Leadbeater – »The Masters and the Path«
8. Charles Fillmore – »Dynamics for Living« and »Revealing Word«
9. Chet Snow – »Dreams of the Future«
10. Daryl Anka »Bashar – Blueprint for Change«
11. Dr. Bob Montgomery and Lynette Evans – »Stress and You«
12. Dr. Deepak Chopra – »Ageless Body, Timeless Mind«
13. Dr. Deepak Chopra – »Unconditional Life«
14. Dr. Deepak Chopra – »Quantum Healing«
15. Dr. Joshua David Stone – »The Complete Ascension Manual«, »Beyond Ascension« and »Soul Psychology«
16. Dr. Norma Milanovich – »We the Arcturians«
17. Edgar Cayce – »On Dreams« and »On Atlantis«
18. Eugene Whitworth – »Nine Faces of Christ«
19. Gopi Krishna – »Kundalini«
20. Grace Cooke – »The Jewel in the Lotus«
21. Hilarion – »Answers«, »More Answers«, »Other Kingdoms«, »Seasons of the Spirit« and »Symbols«
22. Joseph Cater – »Awesome Life Force«
23. Katrina Raphael – »Crystal Enlightenment Vol. I« and »Crystal Healing Vol. II«
24. Ken Carey – »The Starseed Transmissions« and »Vision«
25. J. J. Hurtak – Keys of Enoch – the Book of Knowledge
26. Laut and Leonard – »Rebirthing«
27. Leonard Orr – »Physical Immortality«
28. Levi – »The Aquarian Gospel Of Jesus the Christ«
29. Lyssa Royal and Keith Priest – »The Prysm of Lyra«
30. M. Govindan – »Babaji and the 18 Siddha Kria Yoga Tradition«

31. Mark and Elizabeth Prophet – »Jesus and Kuthumi – Corona Class Lessons«
32. Ramala Publications – »The Revelation of Ramala«, »The Vision of Ramala« and »The Wisdom of Ramala«
33. Sanaya Roman and Duane Packer – »Opening to Channel«
34. Shakti Gawain – »Reflections in the Light«
35. Solara – »The Star Borne«, »11:11« and »The Legend of Altazar«
36. Stephen Hawking – »A Brief History of Time«
37. The Holy Bible – King James Version
38. The Rosicrucian Cosmo Conception
39. The Teaching of Buddha
40. The »I AM Discourses« – St Germain and Godfre Ray King
41. Tony Stubbs – »An Ascension Handbook«
42. Virginia Essene – »New Cells, New Body, New Life«
43. Yogananda – »Autobiography of a Yogi« and »Healing Affirmations«

And many more! There is so much written material available today on most of what I have covered in this book. However, I recommend you wander into a bookstore and let your heart decide.

Living On Light
Jasmuheen

ISBN 3-929512-35-1 Pb 190 Pages

Since 1993, Jasmuheen has been physically nourished by the Universal Life Force of Prana. This book contains the details of her research and of her experiences of this profound process as it reveals a revolutionary form of nourishment for the new millennium. This way of beeing, formerly reserved for saints and sages, is now a possibility for everyone thanks to the information outlined here.

Tantra - Secret Love
Jasmuheen & Nhanda Devi & A. Brunnmeier & K. Halbig

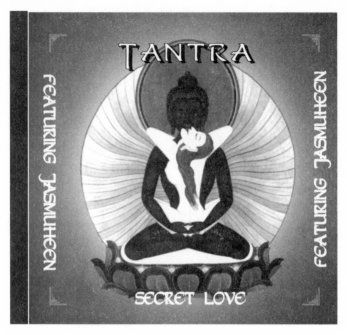

CD 60 min ISBN 3-929512-27-0

The spiritual background of this music is Jasmuheens mantra »One Heart - One Mind«. The first part is filled with love songs and tantric mantras helping you to open up your sexual energies. Part two contains soothing music allowing the listener to tap into their sensual energy.

AMBA - A LOVE CHANT
Felix Maria Woschek & Konrad Halbig

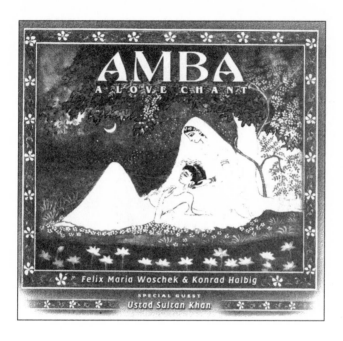

CD 60 min ISBN 3-929512-10-6

This music is particulary suitable for the healing support of therapeutic sessions. You are invited to listen and sing along. This will open your heart for the universal love.

Jasmuheen said: "As a writer I listen to a great range of esoteric and relaxion music for background ambience as I work. The one that always grabs my attention and gets me to pause, and then listen and enjoy is the wonderful AMBA."

Living On Light & Akashic Records Meditation

Jasmuheen

CD 60 min ISBN 3-929512-45-9

Living on Light Meditation for Empowerment. This meditation is to empower us in the inner realms of being to step into our queenly/kingly selves, to open up to inner giudance after beeing realigned energetically using the three-fold flame of love wisdom an power which belns together to form the Violet Transmuting Flame of Freedom.

Akashic Records Meditation activating the crown and brown chakras, the medulla oblongata, the pituitary and pineal glands to form the Inner Pyramid for active telepathy and Higher Communications. Then using the energy grids for linking into the Akashic Records to gain information for our life purpose and blueprint.

Sensous Spirituality & Selfhealing Meditation

Jasmuheen

Sensous Spirituality
&
Selfhealing Meditation

Vol.2

Jasmuheen

CD 60 min ISBN 3-929512-46-7

Sensous Spirituality Meditation for Blending Energies. Sexuality & Spirituality & Love. Meditation to harmonise our fields utilising the energies of the creative force of procreation, blended with the spiritual energies from the higher chakra centres plus adding the vibration of unconditional love through the heart centre. A wonderful and easy technique to harmoniously balance the signals we transmit.

Selfhealing Meditation utilising creative visualisation and light to activate the lightbody and retune and revitalise the skeletal system, the nervous system, the bloodstream, the organs and increase the energy flow through the meridians. A gentle daily healing meditation to strengthen the physical body set to relaxing classical music.

Modulation Set 1 - Personified Transients
Brian Vale

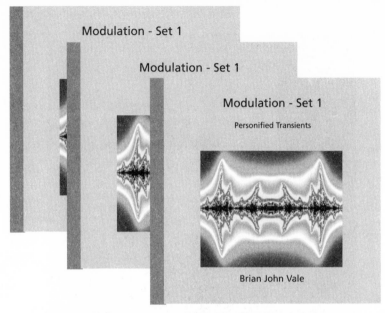

Modulation - Set 1

Modulation - Set 1

Modulation - Set 1

Personified Transients

Brian John Vale

3 CDs 180 min ISBN 3-929512-42-2

One of Jasmuheens tools for realignement came from the cosmic orchestra channel Brian Vale. Shortly after doing Brians program of specific frequency modulations she was able to access visions of the Cosmic Sacred geometric patterning. These programs are for the cosmic warrior and if it feels right then perhaps it may be a tool for you.

Modulation Set 2 - Master Vibrational Sequences
Brian Vale

9 MCs 7 hours ISBN 3-929512-34-3

Angelic Harmony

Jasmuheen

CD 60 min ISBN 3-929512-53-X

In this modern day busy world, Divine Alchemy allows us to personally interact with the angelic forces in a very practical way. Heavens Orchestra invite you to relax into the angels realms. Also a wonderful music for meditation background.